# AGAINST THE ODDS

# AGAINST THE ODDS

*The Life and Times of an Accidental Politician*

DAVID WARNER

mosaic PRESS

**Library and Archives Canada Cataloguing in Publication**

Title: Against the odds : the life and times of an accidental politician / David Warner.
Names: Warner, David (David William), author.
Identifiers: Canadiana 20240489985 | ISBN 9781771618281 (softcover)

Subjects: LCSH: Warner, David (David William) | LCSH: New Democratic Party of Ontario. | LCSH: Politicians—Ontario—Biography. | LCSH: Ontario—Politics and government—20th century. | LCGFT: Autobiographies.

Classification: LCC FC3076.2 .W37 2024 | DDC 971.3/04092—dc23

Published by Mosaic Press, Oakville, Ontario, Canada, 2024.

MOSAIC PRESS, Publishers
www.Mosaic-Press.com

Cover Design: Amy Land
Cover Photo: Rick Eglinton



Printed and bound in Canada.

ONTARIO CREATES

Funded by the Government of Canada
Financé par le gouvernement du Canada

Canada

**MOSAIC PRESS**
1252 Speers Road, Units 1 & 2, Oakville, Ontario, L6L 2X4 (905)-825-2130
info@mosaic-press.com • www.mosaic-press.com

# Table of Contents

## PART THREE

*My Term as Speaker of the Ontario Legislature*



## PART FOUR

*The Non-Elected Years*

## PART FIVE

*My Life After Politics — Political Skills Connect with Civil Society*



## PART SIX

*Political Travelling*



## PART SEVEN

*Tales from the Trails*

## PART EIGHT

*The Joy of Teaching*

## PART NINE

*A Quest for Justice*

## PART TEN

*My Journey Continues*

# Dedication

I am dedicating this book to Canada's former Ambassador to the United Nations, Stephen Lewis. Stephen embodies the essence of my conviction that former politicians have a moral imperative to use their skills and experience to help create a better civil society. He used his remarkable oratorical skills and his years of political experience to find mutual agreement where no agreement seemed possible between two opposing views. Stephen Lewis projected a deeply held passionate belief in a peaceful global community, something which was evident every time he rose to speak at the United Nations.

There could be no more dramatic example of a politician using their skills to the betterment of society than when Stephen Lewis worked as United Nations Special Envoy for HIV/AIDS in Africa. In his role, Stephen drew attention to the HIV/AIDS crisis and convinced leaders and the public that they have a responsibility to respond. When he retired Stephen established the Stephen Lewis Foundation, a non-profit organization that helps people affected and infected by HIV/AIDS in Africa.

I had the privilege of serving in the NDP Caucus when Stephen was Leader. He was an inspiring mentor and remains a valued friend. My journey has been influenced by his sincere heartwarming kindness, all embracing humanity and his passionate leadership on social justice issues. I have a successful story to tell because of Stephen Lewis.

# Foreword

David Warner is one of the most decent and hardworking people I have ever known. We first met when I was campaigning for the leadership of the Ontario New Democratic Party in 1981.

At that point he had already been elected and defeated in his constituency in Scarborough Ellesmere (riding later became Scarborough Centre), and expressed nothing but goodwill and determination about the next election. He was never bitter to have been defeated. He was always proud to have served, and optimistic about serving again, which he did.

He was a terrific caucus colleague, positive, upbeat, looking at possibilities and the upside. It was this indefatigable optimism that led to his success. Public life is full of challenges, and many bumps in the road, but the reason David remains a beloved figure in Ontario's public life is because of the sense of decency that inspired him.

David was elected Speaker of the Legislative Assembly in 1990, and it was then that his sense of fairness, service and political experience was put to great purpose. As leader of the government, I was not always happy with his rulings, but that is as it should be.

He took great interest in parliamentary procedure and relations with provincial assemblies across the country and throughout the Commonwealth. He loved welcoming visitors to the Assembly and took a deep interest in the history and architecture of the nineteenth century building known as the "pink palace."

Throughout his political life David had the warm support of Pat and his children, Sherri and Barbara. They knew firsthand the ups and downs, the victories and defeats of political life, and as David describes in this account were there for him every step of the journey.

Political defeats took him back to the classroom, a place he loved, and retirement did not mean at all a retreat. David almost single-handedly revived the alumni association of the Legislature, of which I am a proud member.

David has always believed in the fellowship of politics as a calling. Arlene and I have long shared in a deep admiration of the Warner family.

In this book, David describes a public and political life of which he can be very proud. He was a happy warrior in every sense, and we are all better for it.

David loved the ride, now you can enjoy the read.

Bob Rae
Premier of Ontario, 1990–95
Canada's Ambassador to the U.N. 2020–present
Ontario and New York

# Preface

"Do what you can son to make this a better world," was the moral imperative given to me by my parents. In fulfilling that mandate comes my story which counters public cynicism about politicians. My story is a timely one of being an accidental politician who used his acquired political skills to connect with local, national and international organizations who are focused on strengthening civil society.

Having the ability to listen, be patient, find compromise, make rational decisions, and possess a thoughtful visionary approach are the very skills needed to help strengthen civil society. Once you are no longer elected there is a moral imperative to use those skills and your experience to help strengthen civil society.

The atmosphere in Canada's Legislatures and House of Commons is toxic. Members have become blinded by political partisanship. In sharp contrast is my experience of hands across the aisle instead of fists in the air; collaboration instead of confrontation.

Misinformation and sometimes outright lies have badly obscured the reality that politicians, working with citizens, play a vital role in creating the substantive elements of civil society. My story is based in that reality; before, during and after being elected.

As Speaker of the Ontario Legislature I took on various initiatives which I explain in detail. Some of these initiatives have become integral to legislative and diplomatic life in Ontario. The Ontario/Quebec Parliamentary Association, as well as the Midwest-Canada Relations Committee meet on a regular basis to discuss matters of mutual interest. Indigenous art is an intrinsic element of the Legislative Building, serving as part of the reconciliation process with Indigenous communities.

My narrative is woven with humourous tales from the political trails. Balancing humour with the agony of defeat is my experience. A cautionary tale for anyone considering entering the political arena.

Balancing political life, family and community is a serious challenge that I address in the book. I share how I manage this delicate juggling act, offering valuable lessons for our society if we want to attract good people to the demanding task of being an elected official.

# Introduction

*"Be kind, for everyone you meet is fighting a harder battle."*

— Plato

"If you think everything is so bad with the Tories why don't you do something about it!" blurted a frustrated teaching colleague of mine. Every day since school started in September 1969, we engaged in political debates. Doug, an ardent conservative, had reached the end of his tether with me.

My response was "I just might. I'll think about it." Think about it I did and a few days later I informed Doug that I would run for public office. I took his question as a challenge. Could I make a difference? Accepting it was the start of a journey which would culminate in being elected by my peers to the position of Speaker of the Ontario Legislature.

I wasn't aware of it at the time, but I'd been bitten by a bug.

There is a bug, called "Hemptera Politicus," whose bite has a life-long effect. It is a type of blood disorder. It took a while before I realized that I'd been bitten. So, even today, long retired from electoral politics, I continue to follow, discuss, debate the political issues of the day. I simply can't help myself.

What was it about me that prompted "Hemptera Politicus" to take hold?

## … Maybe it was genetic

My parents never belonged to a political Party. At least, that's what I surmised. As a general rule, dinner time was an opportunity to talk about events, local and global. I can not recall a single instance when my mom or dad would mention voting for, or against any Party. Issues were important. Issues were discussed. While my parents held principled positions, their opinions were never forced on their children.

I remember my dad breaking his political silence only once, during the 1957 Federal General Election. Frank McGee, a Conservative, was seeking re-election and he came to our door. After the honourable member had moved on to the next house, my dad declared he was voting for MP McGee.

Decades later, I learn that both my parents were lifelong CCF (Commonwealth Cooperative Federation) supporters. Dad had voted for Frank McGee because Mr. McGee had championed the abolition of capital punishment, at a time when public opinion was approximately 80% in favour of "hang 'em all."

In 1967 my dad, age 55, died suddenly of a brain aneurysm. It was a devastating blow to me and of course my mom, brother and sister. At age 24, I was too young to fully appreciate the life lessons imparted by my dad. Had he lived to be the same age as my mother, who passed away in 2013 at the ripe old age of 104, he would have witnessed the outcome of those life lessons.

## … Maybe it was early life lessons

*Lesson One*: Gender Equality

At 14 years old, I was your typical smart-aleck teen. One summer day, my dad said his usual cheery hello to me on his way in as I sat on the porch listening to rock 'n' roll on the radio. He wasn't in the house very long before coming back outside to chat.

"Your mother tells me that you refused to do certain chores today because you said it was women's work. In this house there's no such thing as women's jobs or men's jobs. There are simply jobs. So, when your mother asks you to do something, you do it."

Much later I realized that my dad was ahead of his time for an era modelled after the TV shows, such as *Father Knows Best* and *Leave It To Beaver*.

*Lesson Two*: Workers' Rights

I was a teen when I landed my first part-time job as a parcel boy, working Saturdays at a local grocery store. After arriving home one day, dad asked me how it went. I replied, "Not great. There really wasn't anything for me to do, so I sat in the lunchroom."

"So, you got paid just to sit around?" asked dad.

"No. I didn't get paid."

My dad was furious. He grabbed me and we headed for the grocery store. Dad and I met with the manager. "When you ask my boy to come in to work, then you have a responsibility to pay him, whether there is something for him to do or not."

*Lesson Three:* Universal Health Care

Sadly, this lesson didn't happen until I was first elected in 1975. My mom produced an old news clipping which was kept in the family bible. It was the notice of sale, of my dad's parents house in the east end of Toronto. My mom told me the story of the news clipping and why it was kept in our large, ornate family bible.

My grandmother who passed away just before I was born in 1941 had been ill for 10 years. Medicare didn't exist at the time and the doctor's bills and the hospital bills kept mounting to the point where the house had to be sold in order to cover the debt. My mom and dad had stored that clipping in the Bible as a reminder of the importance of Medicare. I made sure I took this reminder with me to Queen's Park.

In 1976, I participated in a health care debate in the House. A Conservative Member made an assertion that it was the responsibility of the individual to take care of themselves. If they got sick it was their own fault. The state should not be required to provide care free of charge. The views from the Member were not uncommon at the time, but I was incensed.

I left my seat in the House, and dashed off to my office. I retrieved the clipping of the sale of my family home. The first chance I got to join back into the debate, I let loose with an emotional rant about how my dad and his parents lost our home, that no one should have to sacrifice their home to pay medical bills. It was a heated, emotional debate. While nothing substantive was achieved, I felt I had signalled to the Conservatives that I was a fierce fighter for universal medicare.

I did not plan on a political life. I grew up in a middle class family, the eldest of three children; brother Paul four years younger and sister Marilyn nine years younger. Our parents raised the three of us to always be concerned about what was fair and to help others. I might never have ended up in the political arena if it hadn't been for my stubbornness to not back down from the challenge which arose in my daily debate with Doug, my teaching colleague.

It didn't take long however, for me to realize that politics is about doing public good, being a builder, and helping to create a better society. I've tried to maintain that focus with my family and my community involvement. It's been an exciting and richly rewarding experience that started in 1966 with door knocking in a wealthy neighbourhood in Etobicoke.

# PART ONE

# Becoming a Politician

# 1

# Political Learning Curve (1954 - 1961)

*"It is in your hands to create a better world for all who live in it."*

— Nelson Mandela

## A french-fry rebellion

It started out as an ordinary school day. The morning classes, if not exciting, were uneventful and led to my favourite time of the day, lunch! I headed to the cafeteria to enjoy my bag lunch. I never bought anything in the cafeteria, but this was where I would find my friends. I walked into an uproar. There was a large number of very upset teenagers.

The school cafeteria had not only raised the price of french fries by five cents, but reduced the quantity by putting the fries in a paper cone instead of on a plate. Outrageous! I was incensed by this injustice. Truthfully, I don't know where I got the nerve as a grade ten student to organize a boycott of the cafeteria, but I did. With the help of my friends a message was quickly circulated, "Tomorrow, no one is to purchase anything in the cafeteria."

Sure enough. The next day the cash registers did not ring. Not one student bought a thing. Even the school's athletic hero, Gary Jarrett, who had mistakenly brought a bag of apples to school instead of his lunch, was booed when he wandered toward the food counter. The students were serious about the boycott of the food service. Gary simply turned around. As soon as he sat down several students then shared their lunch with Gary.

"Well Warner, what do you know about the commotion in the cafeteria today?" asked the Principal, Mr. Patterson. I was surprised that Mr. Patterson had figured out so quickly that I was involved in the "french-fry rebellion." The staff were a bit sharper than I had given them credit for. I told him why the students were upset. The result of this one day boycott was that the price of french fries were back to their previous price and the paper cups were gone. Although I didn't realize it at the time, this was my initiation into the world of politics.

## Blame it on rock 'n' roll

In my teenage life Elvis Presley was King! Rock 'n' Roll reigned! My life centred around Buddy Holly, The Diamonds, Little Richard and so many more. I subscribed to the Columbia record club with a new LP (long play) record every month. Wolf Man Jack captured my radio ear every night. However, there was something missing. The Friday night school dances had stopped. Not sure why, but this teen treasured event was no longer available at Agincourt Collegiate. It seemed that even the Students' Council couldn't restart the turntables.

My buddies had a bright idea, that if I was on the Students' Council I could help restore the Friday night dance. The cafeteria boycott had raised my profile, but I needed something more. Being on the Students Council would provide the influence needed to bring back the dances. The members of the Students' Council were usually either academically or athletically successful. I was neither. To date the Council Secretary had always been a female. I would be the first male elected to this important position. I was confident I could handle whatever the job entailed. I was enrolled in a Commercial

Option, which included typing. I was excited about the prospect of being on the Council, not the least bit concerned about the decision making aspect involved. At the time, the end goal was to reinstate the Friday night dances!

I put together a team. We created "Vote For Dave" posters. Classes changed every 45 minutes during the day, providing opportunities to meet and greet in the hallways. "Hi! I'm Dave Warner. A vote for me is a vote for Friday Dances." The key to winning was getting the support of the senior students. I don't know if it was my sincere, enthusiastic approach or being up front about why I wanted to be on the Council, but after a while the rumours were that I had good support from grades 12 and 13. The last day of the campaign featured all-candidates' speeches in the gymnatorium. In my speech, I informed everyone that one great reason to support me was because I was in the typing class, therefore easily able to provide accurate minutes of the meetings quickly. I finished my speech with an upbeat, joyous slogan "Be Brave. Vote For Dave!" When the results of the election were announced, I had achieved my first election victory.

The Friday night dances were back into our high school lives. I was the disc jockey. I organized a group to solicit prizes from local businesses for the spot dances. CKEY, the go-to radio station for rock 'n' roll, provided a box full of 45's vinyl records each week, free of charge. Just one caveat. Play one or two newly released records and gauge their popularity.

I prepared a program for the turntable, carefully selecting which records would kick off the dance. I sorted records with a ratio of three fast to one slow to start the evening. The ratio would eventually be reversed by the end of the evening. "Save the last dance for me" was a popular way to conclude. There were volunteers to sell and collect tickets at the door. There were some excellent prizes ready to be awarded. A local restaurant had donated a dinner for two. Now, all we needed was a crowd. Week one garnered a hundred or so students. Not too bad! Those who attended must have had a good time, because from the next week onward we had a full house at every dance for three years!

I certainly didn't realize it at the time that this was a building block in what would eventually become a successful political career.

## A political awakening at Carleton University 1960

I arrived at Carleton a young, eager and naive student. My enjoyable high school years were in a world of white. Mostly middle-class kids. Some, like me, were from the suburbs. Others were from the Village of Agincourt. A few were from the nearby farms. Carleton, being situated in our nation's capital, attracted students from across Canada and from various parts of the globe. Quite a different mix of students from my experience at Agincourt Collegiate.

There were three political lessons which made an indelible mark.

*Lesson One:* The Oppression of Blacks

Student Residences were opened in time for year two of my life at Carleton. I was one of a small group, who gathered one evening in one of the rooms to socialize and chat about whatever popped up. What started as a rambling, hodgepodge of a discussion morphed into a riveting tale of brutality and oppression, told by a Black student from South Africa. I did not know anything about apartheid. I was shocked and stunned as the student told us about Pass Laws, police brutality, "Whites Only" beaches, and the difficult life in the townships. Wandering back to my room well past two am, I realized that I had led a sheltered life. How different is my life because I am white.

Canada, many years later, partnered with other countries pressuring the South African government to end apartheid. One tactic was to boycott South African products. The government of Ontario did its part by banning the sale of South African wine. When Premier Peterson, in 1985, announced the ban I had a flashback to that late evening discussion in a student residence room. An evening which had a profound effect on my life.

*Lesson Two:* Politics As An Art Form

What an exciting political event. During my second year at Carleton, Real Caouette, Quebec Leader of the Social Credit Party of Canada, visited the campus. In 1961 Mr. Caoutte had lost his bid to be the Social Credit National Leader. There was a federal election looming at the time of Mr. Caoutte's visit to Carleton. A significant number of Carleton students came from Quebec where the political battle was between the Liberals and Social Credit. The result was an atmosphere which was absolutely electric. There was undercurrent of anger, with many students wanting to confront Mr. Caoette. Introduced on stage, he was booed, then remarkably, within a short time the booing ceased, replaced by peals of laughter and eventually thunderous applause. Mr. Caouette, former car salesman, was totally unmoved by the earlier negative welcome. He delightful sense of humour calmed the clambering throng, then shifting gears his speech became emotional, at times fiery. There was energy, enthusiasm, passion. The most impressive part for me was an element which I would use when I entered the political arena. Humour to diffuse a tense political situation.

*Lesson Three:* The Power of the State

My good buddy Vic Draper, later my brother-in-law, and I shared a room. There was an adjoining room occupied by a Masters student, Max McGregor. Max became a valued friend. On one quiet day, Vic and I were both working away on our academic assignments when Max popped into our room, visibly upset. The tale which unfolded was unnerving, and a motivator.

Max was studying Russian history. In order to obtain important information needed for an academic assignment he visited the Russian Embassy, where he was able to borrow a few books. Max had no sooner returned to residence when he got a call from the RCMP. They wanted to know why he had visited the Russian Embassy. My first question was "How did the Mounties know that Max had been to the Russian Embassy?" Max explained that the RCMP had a house directly across the street from the Embassy. They would record and identify everyone who visited.

Max went on to relate that he told the Mounties the purpose of his visit. The officer then suggested to Max that once the books were returned to not revisit the Embassy. Max was furious. Vic and I were speechless. How could this happen in a democracy, where the police could tell you not to visit an Embassy!

After our anger subsided sufficiently to contemplate a response to this attack on our rights, I put forward a plan. Either Vic or I would visit the Russian Embassy to borrow some books. We would set up a tape recorder beside the phone in our room. When the RCMP call us, we would record the conversation, and take the tape to a local radio station. Expose this abuse of police power to the Canadian public.

Max calmly asked Vic and I if we were still thinking about being teachers after graduation. We said yes. Max then itemized what would very likely happen. "The police will identify you. You will be probably be listed as a Communist sympathizer. So, when you apply for a teaching job, a background check will suggest you are a security risk. This won't be a school board in Canada willing to hire you."

Wow! This was more serious than we thought. Vic and I had to consider the consequences of our quest for justice. The prospect of being branded a communist and not being able to follow our dream of being teachers was sobering. Practicality won out. We dropped our amazing plan.

The years following that experience have provided a perspective. The 'Cold War', especially in the 1960's and '70's created paranoia about communism, which led to overreach by the police and other government authorities. My experience at Carleton was a valuable lesson. Law and order is important, but be careful how you deal with those who enforce those laws. As a counter point, Canadians have rights and freedoms which can only be dreamed of in many other countries. Throughout my political life I have always tried to balance the security of society with the rights of the individual. It is indeed a constant balancing act.

# 2

# Political Baptism (1966 - 1974)

*"There are rewards in public life, not monetary, but there is a tremendous satisfaction in being able to say I tried, I stood."*

— John G. Diefenbaker

## Try the servants' entrance

Pat and I were married June 26, 1965. We found an apartment in Etobicoke, a suburban area of Toronto; an apartment located approximately half way between the schools where we were teaching. Pat taught at the Ontario School For The Deaf in Milton and I at McCowan Road Public School in Scarborough. We were two very happy newly weds enjoying this new life together while getting to know our surroundings. If you were born and raised in Toronto you knew the world was divided by Yonge Street, 'east is east, west is west, and never the twain shall meet'. We were from the east, now living in the west. That fall there was a federal election. On one of my exploratory wandering I came across the local NDP campaign headquarters.

"Why not volunteer?" I walked into the campaign office, introduced myself and explained that I supported the NDP, that I had never canvassed, but was willing to learn. I really didn't know what to expect, but I was excited to be helping out. Whether by design or a mistake, what unfolded toughened my resolve and whetted my appetite for greater political involvement.

I was given some election literature, a few instructions on what to say at the door and told to mark down on a form those who would support the NDP candidate, those against and those undecided. I was then sent off to an area comprised almost entirely of opulent, palatial houses on beautiful tree-lined streets. There were very expensive looking automobiles sitting in the driveways. Quite intimidating to look at. Ringing the doorbells turned out to be even more intimidating. Sometimes the servant answering the door would wordlessly slide away from the door to summon the owner. The owner would take one look at me, then ..... (a) not say anything, just close the door, or (b) say something such as "Communist, get out of here", or (c) something a bit more frightening, such as "if you don't clear out of here right now, I will sic the dog on you!".

It didn't take too long before I realized that I had to either give up or find a different approach. I decided to try the servants' entrance at the back of the house. Got a much better reception from the hired help!

I never found out why I, a rookie canvasser, was sent there. If it was by design, it was a clever move. The experience provided the incentive to work harder in support of social equality. I also realized that if I was going to support the ideals, philosophy and policies of the New Democrats then I should take out a membership. Which I did.

During the 1965 federal election Pat and I had the opportunity to attend one of the most remarkable events we have ever experienced. Maple Leaf Gardens, home of the Toronto Maple Leafs was the venue. It would be just two years later that the Leafs would win their last Stanley Cup, at least until now (2024). The large crowd, joyously waving local candidates' election signs, were absolutely jubilant in anticipation of the arrival of the federal leader,

Tommy Douglas. The roar of the crowd was deafening. Yet, one hand motion by Tommy and instantly there was complete silence. This diminutive former Premier of Saskatchewan, who had won the 1922 Lightweight Boxing Championship of Manitoba, the father of medicare, delivered serious messages cloaked in humour. He could make you laugh. He could make you cry. Most of all, he could make you more determined than ever to make a difference in the quest for social justice.

It seems there is always an election right around the corner; federal, provincial or municipal, therefore multiple opportunities to learn the art of door-to-door canvassing. The next opportunity for me following the 1965 federal election was the 1967 Provincial election. I think the local Riding Association was short of volunteers because I was asked to be part of the campaign organizing team. I was flattered and excited. This was my first opportunity to be on the inside, learning how to run an election campaign. The planning sessions provided enough details to make my head spin! The most salient message was that effective, efficient campaign organizing is complicated and demanding, but absolutely essential if you want to have a chance to win. I was eager to hone my canvassing skills as I already knew how to get votes in the wealthy areas.

## Political roots are planted in Scarborough 1971

My dad passed away suddenly on March 23, 1967, of a brain aneurysm. It came as a severe shock to our family. My younger brother Paul was living on his own while Marilyn, still a teenager, was living at home and attending high school. To this day the visitation, service and burial remain a blur. One day our dad was an energetic, hard working salesman, loving and kind father, and the next day he was gone. I know that harbouring regrets is not useful, however the one regret I have is that I never told my dad how valuable were the life lessons I gleaned from him. At age 26 I wasn't sufficiently astute to realize that he was my role model.

The following year Pat and I purchased a house in Agincourt. Our romance started when we were senior students at Agincourt Collegiate. Both of us pursued further education; Pat attending Teachers' College in Toronto followed by a year specializing in deaf education at the Ontario School for the Deaf, Belleville, while I went to Carleton University in Ottawa. The long distance romance was not ideal, but we made it work. Now we were going to live close to the school where it all started. As I write this memoir we remain in the house we purchased in 1968.

There was a provincial general election in 1971. Our local Scarborough North NDP candidate was a jovial, dynamic fellow, John Brewin, son of a veteran MP, Andrew Brewin. John had lost the 1967 election by just 1,500 votes, a slim margin in a populous riding. This was a robust campaign, full of energy, lots of volunteers and a significant budget.

Being involved in this campaign turned out to be extremely valuable in my political campaigning education. The lessons I learned here I later used in my own campaigns. Lesson one was about canvassing. The standard approach was to canvass door-to-door at least three times, noting who was for, against, or undecided. Ideally there were enough volunteers so that each poll had a canvasser. This campaign appeared to have reached that threshold. I was given a poll which had voted for the sitting Conservative MPP, and Cabinet Minister, Tom Wells. I took it upon myself to canvass my assigned poll not three, but five times. If there was no one home when I called, I made a note, then later at home would check the phone book and give the people a call.

By election night I could account for the voting intention of every one of the approximately 170 houses. I presented my credentials to the Returning Officer at the polling station and stayed for the counting of the ballots. I was ecstatic when the count revealed that John Brewin won, by a large margin, a poll which previously he had lost by a large margin. I quickly made my way to the Canadiana Hotel where everyone was gathered in a large banquet hall for the results. I found John standing with his campaign manager, staring at the boards on which were recorded the election results, poll by poll. Without even glancing at the board, I excitedly blurted out "We won!" I made the assumption that since my poll had gone from a large minus to a sizable plus, we must have won the riding. When there was no response from John, I followed his subdued gaze. The results on the board, while not complete, revealed that John Brewin had lost the election — by a huge margin! I was stunned, shocked. How could this be!

John Brewin had lost by about 12,000 votes. I was disappointed and puzzled. In the days which followed the election of a majority Progressive Conservative government the John Brewin campaign team held a postmortem discussion. I listened carefully, adding a couple of my own observations. The lessons I learned were the following:

1. **Solid, thorough canvassing, door-to-door, houses and apartments, can produce a win.** The challenge is to have one excellent canvasser for each poll.
2. **Money is not the determining factor.** You need a sufficient amount of money to run a serious campaign, but simply spending a lot of money does not produce a winning election. In every one of my nine campaigns we always had the lowest budget of the three major parties.
3. **Some things are simply out of your hands.** The public image of the Party Leaders, as well as the issues they choose to highlight make a huge difference. Of course media coverage, favourable or negative, can have an impact.
4. **A critical issue can be a huge help or the cause of your downfall.** In the 1971 election, extended funding for Roman Catholic schools was a ballot box issue. At the time there was public funding up to, and including grade ten. The Liberals and New Democrats pledged, if elected, to extend public funding to grades 11, 12 and 13. The

Conservatives opted for the status quo, a position which turned out to be popular with a majority of the voters.

5. **Having a personable, hard working candidate is great for the morale of the volunteers, but doesn't necessarily make a difference in the vote total.**

What I learned from the 1971 John Brewin campaign, especially my own door-to-door experience, fuelled my desire for my own successful election. I felt ready to enter the political arena as a candidate. I didn't have long to wait.

## 1972 Federal Election Capital punishment and abortion ignite the nightly debates

"Trudeaumania" swept the country in 1968. Prime Minister Pierre Trudeau had rock-star status, not only in Canada, but internationally. He had, however, initiated some changes which sparked controversy. Canada officially became a bilingual nation in 1969. Many English-speaking Canadians embraced the bilingual ideal, but others opposed it, accusing authorities of "forcing them to read French on their cereal boxes." That same year the government legalized some abortions; those where a committee of doctors certified that continuing the pregnancy would likely endanger the woman's life or health. There wasn't a more emotional or divisive issue than abortion; within religions, families and political parties. NDP Conventions for a number of years featured emotional debates on the highly sensitive issue. The New Democrats adopted a policy that it is a woman's right to choose whether to have an abortion or not. I was impressed by the loyalty of those party members whose religious belief was anti-abortion but who took the position that the overall philosophy of the NDP superseded the policy on abortion.

Another controversial issue was added to the backdrop for the 1972 election. In 1969 we were in the middle of a five-year moratorium on the use of the death penalty, except for the murder of police and corrections officers. Despite the public being overwhelmingly in favour of the death penalty, the government appeared ready to put a stop to the practice.

The 1972 federal election was my opportunity to fulfill the pledge made to Doug Puddicombe that I would run for public office. This wonderful opportunity meant teaching during the day and campaigning in the evening. Thankfully, I wasn't a classroom teacher with the attendant responsibilities of marking tests, and assignments in the evenings, as well as having extra-curricular duties after school, such as coaching soccer. Early in 1972 I had been promoted to Audio-visual Teacher Consultant, a position which meant working with teachers in 75 schools helping them make the best use of the AV equipment available. I had an opportunity to use my knowledge and be creative. And, it was a "9 to 5" job, so my evenings were open to work on my political campaign. Pat was at home with our 8 month old daughter. Since I was the sole wage earner in the house, asking for a leave of absence without pay was out of the question.

Being unopposed for candidate nomination can mean the prospective candidate is well known and popular. In my case, it was that no one else was willing to be a sacrificial lamb. The huge sprawling urban riding of York Scarborough had more than 125,000 eligible voters. The sitting Liberal MP and Cabinet Minister, Bob Stanbury, was seeking his third term in office. He was a formidable political foe, yet, as I discovered, a warm, friendly guy.

New Democrats were always known as being obsessed with policy. Every policy convention produced reams of pages added to the policy book, none to be discarded. So, off to my first all-Candidates meeting I went, with one very large policy binder tucked under my arm. Every question must have an answer somewhere in this binder I reasoned. At the end of my first foray into verbal political battle, Peter Hitchen, my campaign manager, stated simply and emphatically, "Get rid of the binder!"

Fortunately for me, this initial all-candidates' meeting was in the basement all-purpose room of an apartment building, with about 40 people in attendance.

The Conservative candidate was Winnett Boyd, a brilliant and accomplished mechanical engineer. Among his numerous achievements was designing the nuclear reactor at Chalk River, Ontario. He had a pleasant personality and quite clearly an abiding interest in politics, having written several books of a political nature. However, exciting speech making was not one of his attributes.

I peeked out from behind the stage curtain to see how big an audience this election event had attracted. The high school auditorium was full, standing room only. I estimated about 1,000 people. The three candidates were called on to the stage, introduced, then the house lights dimmed, spot light turned on. Stepping forward to face a huge audience which I couldn't see was daunting. The drama lessons I had taken at age 13 kicked in; "deliver the speech to the back row while picturing everyone wearing pyjamas." Fortunately for me, I did not have to go first. I had an opportunity to watch Bob Stanbury smoothly deliver a speech which was both inspiring and humourous.

"I am astounded that the Liberal government continues to support corporate welfare," I declared, referring to the huge subsidies which a long list of corporations had received over the past few years. Energetically I continued on, without referring to notes and injecting humour from time to time, explaining that the NDP would eliminate grants and subsidies for corporations, and use the money to build housing and transportation infrastructure, and fund municipal services to create jobs. At the end of my speech I received polite applause. The good news was that no one threw heavy objects. Success!

The following five weeks of nightly all-candidates' meetings, with a few days of two meetings in one night, were spent in front of audiences ranging in size from 600 to 1,500. I quipped to Bob Stanbury one evening, "I get to see you more often than my wife."

Bob smiled and replied with, "Welcome to the world of politics." Although I didn't know it at the time, the experience of lively debate 35 times in 30 days, would provide excellent training for my career at Queen's Park.

David Lewis was the Leader of the federal New Democrats. His fascinating story was inspiring. Born in 1909, David Losz (Lewis later) was politically active from an early age. War in the Polish/ Russian border area made life dangerous so in 1921, David Lewis emigrated to Canada, arriving by ship in Halifax, then taking the train to Montreal where he stayed with a relative. He quickly learned to speak English and distinguished himself academically in high school, then university. Being accepted as a Rhodes Scholar got him to Oxford University, England. There his political activism continued. In 1935, as David Lewis graduated in law, he had the opportunity to be with a prestigious labour law firm and a seat in Parliament. In fact he was being groomed to be Labour Party Prime Minister. He turned down the offer, returning to Canada to marry his high school sweetheart, Sophie Carson, and become National Secretary of the CCF (Cooperative Commonwealth Federation), forerunner of the New Democratic Party. He became a key player in the creation of the NDP in 1961. The following year David Lewis was elected for the first time as a Member of Parliament for York South, a seat he held until losing in 1974. In 1971 Tommy Douglas retired as federal Leader of the New Democratic Party. In the ensuing leadership convention David Lewis was elected Leader.

The passion for equality and social justice was forged in those early political years in the Russian Empire. Combine that passion with a razor sharp mind and debating skills honed at Oxford it was no wonder that I and countless others were inspired to work tirelessly for this remarkable leader.

The centrepiece of the NDP's 1972 campaign was an attack on corporate incentives and taxation, dubbed by our Leader as the Liberals catering to "corporate welfare bums". The slogan garnered lots of attention, but did not create a tidal wave of support. In fact, the NDP lost six seats. The result of the election was a Liberal minority government. I received more than 16,000 votes in York Scarborough which was more than 100 M.P.s each received. Every candidate had to deposit $1,000. with Elections Canada in order to be registered. If you got at least 50% of the winner's total you got your deposit back. I lost my deposit. There was a small media story focusing on the anomaly of attracting more votes than approximately one-third of the Members in the House of Commons yet losing my deposit. A short while after the article appeared I received a letter from an American high school student who didn't understand why I should lose the deposit. I responded that I didn't understand this strange system either! Oddly enough the deposit requirement remained in place until 2017.

Losing was not a whole lot of fun, but out of the loss came an unexpected new path, one which would turn out to be important in my journey towards doing public good.

## 1974 Federal Election A personal springboard

Minority government came to a crashing halt when the New Democrats, along with the Conservatives voted against the budget. The election campaign was underway in May. As with the previous election, I couldn't afford to take time off from teaching. I was still an Audio Visual Teacher Consultant with the Scarborough Board of Education, so as in the '72 election, I worked "9 to 5," with the evenings available to focus on election campaign basics, such as designing literature, getting election signs printed and planning fund raising. Our second daughter, Barbara, was born August 1973, so Pat was at home with two infants.

First, I needed to find a campaign manager, then a campaign office. It was a stroke of good luck when we spotted a vacant store in our local plaza, a plaza which included our favourite restaurant, and was just a short walk from our house. Good luck was followed by bad luck. I had asked a veteran political campaigner, Dave Robertson, to manage my campaign. When Lever Brothers, a manufacturer of soap, found out that Robertson would be managing an NDP campaign, they imposed compulsory overtime on him. I was now my own campaign manager.

Bob Stanbury, still a cabinet minister, was seeking his fourth term in office. The Conservative candidate this time was Ron Collister, CBC TV news anchor, who later would be awarded the Order of Canada. He was friendly, easy to chat with, likeable. There was the same lively interest in all-candidates' meetings as in the '72 campaign, but the issues were different. Nationally, the twin issues of inflation and the Liberal government's remedy of wage and price controls dominated the debates. Locally, the York-Scarborough meetings had two other issues which ignited each evening's packed auditoriums; a change in who could vote and the amalgamation of the branches of the Armed Services.

Prime Minister Trudeau announced that in all elections subsequent to this one only Canadian citizens would be eligible to vote. British subjects would no longer have the right to vote. A person needed three years residency in order to qualify for citizenship, so therefore it was status quo for the 1974 election. It seemed pretty straightforward to me. If you weren't a Canadian citizen you could vote in this election and you would have time to obtain your citizenship prior to the next election.

Bob Stanbury had never missed an all-candidates' meeting, except one particular night when he was summoned to an emergency cabinet meeting. His replacement was a Liberal Senator. I have forgotten his name, but not how he almost caused a riot. Someone asked why British subjects who had helped build this country were now being denied a vote. The Senator stated clearly and unequivocally that such was not the case. The government, he said, had no intention of taking away the vote of British subjects. The crowd of about a thousand was angry and started moving toward the stage. Quick as a jack rabbit, I jumped from my seat on the stage and grabbed the microphone from the somewhat tipsy Senator. "What the Senator was trying to say is that if you are a British subject you can vote in this election. The change is for the next election, after British subjects have had time to get their citizenship." The crowd ceased their charge of the stage. They still weren't happy, but some measure of calm had been achieved.

## Mistaken identity

I was canvassing door-to-door in a town house complex which had a central hallway. The response to my knocking on one of the doors was swift. The door opened immediately and a man cheerily said, "Come on in. We've been expecting you. Welcome. Glass of wine?" I was momentarily without words, which prompted a question from the host, "You are Ron Collister?" My answer created total silence. The group of about 20 people stood still as statues, wine glasses in hand. The silence was broken by a knock on the door. I knew exactly what to do. I quickly opened the door. "Hello Ron. Come on in. We've been waiting for you. Glass of wine?" Ron was speechless. As Ron entered, I turned to the still silent group. "Ladies and Gentlemen, Ron Collister." I left to the sound of raucous laughter.

## Election Day leads to a new chapter in my life

Election Day, July 8, produced for me the same third place finish as the '72 election. With no money for a place to celebrate, our intrepid band of volunteers gathered at our house, out on the deck, a television perched on a table so we could watch the results come in. What bothered me greatly wasn't my loss, but that of David Lewis, our Leader. He was truly a remarkable person. Later I organized a dinner to pay tribute to David Lewis, at the then Canadiana Hotel in Scarborough. A celebratory atmosphere prevailed at the sold-out event as several hundred people thanked David Lewis for his stalwart leadership. I had the privilege of spending some time with

David and his wife Sophie. There was no pretense about either of them. They were genuinely warm and gracious.

My involvement in the 1971 provincial election and being a candidate in '72 and '74 federal elections had affected me. I had definitely been bitten by the "Hemptera Politicus" bug. The door-to-door canvassing was exhilarating, but so too was planning and developing campaign literature, working out an election strategy with a team, planning a sign blitz, finding volunteers. The only not so much fun part was raising money. I have never liked asking people for money, unless it was for charity. As it turned out I didn't need to wait too long before deciding which path to tread. Early in 1975, redistribution provincially had created a new riding, Scarborough Ellesmere, a riding which would need a candidate for the anticipated election later that year. This was an opportunity too good to turn down!

# PART TWO

# My First Three Terms as MPP

# 3

# 1975 Provincial Election

By the summer of 1975, I had taught in three schools; McCowan Road, John McRae, Joseph Brant, as well as a stint at the Board Office. The result was that I had acquired quite a few teaching colleagues. Those colleagues along with thousands of others were ready to express an anger which had been building for some time. Low salaries, and not having the right to strike was at the heart of the discontent. Teaching was known as the noble "profession," therefore remuneration should not be of concern and it would certainly not be appropriate to have the right to strike. That sentiment wore thin as salaries remained low and negotiating for higher salaries was going nowhere.

On December 18, 1973 all the teachers in Ontario walked out of their classrooms, shutting down almost every school in the province. I joined a crowd of 30,000 teachers at Maple Leaf Gardens; 22,000 accommodated inside, the rest outside listening via loudspeakers to rousing speeches, then a march to Queen's Park for more rousing speeches, creating quite a din for the MPPs inside. The walkout eventually proved to be a successful tactic.

Governments prefer a calm atmosphere, especially headed into an election. The last time the House would sit prior to the anticipated general election was spring, 1975. The Davis government likely thought that by passing The *School Boards and Teachers Collective Negotiations Act*, 1975, which provided teachers with the right to strike, they would create the calm atmosphere they were seeking; that the teachers would no longer be angry. Instead of calmness, a significant number of teachers were politicized, getting involved in the election as they had never done before. I was one of the beneficiaries, with a significant number of teachers volunteering to help in my election campaign. Teachers, being used to organizing their classroom, keeping track of marks etc., make excellent election workers, either door-to-door or on the phone. One teacher and his spouse, both with artistic backgrounds, provided the most attractive store front windows of a campaign office I have ever seen.

I saw the newly created provincial riding of Scarborough Ellesmere as a victory within easy grasp. I asked the riding executive to set an early nomination date so that whoever the candidate was would have lots of time to campaign. Since a significant portion of the new riding was from Stephen Lewis' Scarborough West Riding, with its long history of NDP support, I was sure this amazing opportunity would attract quite a few people wanting to carry the NDP banner. I put my name forward to be the candidate and was unopposed. Could it be that few people shared my optimism about a victory?

It had been four years since the last election. There was no legally set date for a general election at the time so lots of guessing as to when this anticipated election would happen. The '71 voting day had been October 21, so the common wisdom was the fall of '75. An actual date didn't matter to me. What could be more fun than knocking on doors all summer. The good people of Scarborough Ellesmere, if they were not away on vacation, were relaxed, enjoying the warm weather.

My door-to-door; walk, knock and talk, was great exercise, and enjoyable. The casual conversations, the occasional raising of political issues convinced me that this attempt at electoral victory would be successful. In fact, part way through the summer, I boldly called Stephen Lewis to inform him that I would win the election. Not sure where I got the nerve. To his credit, as a wise, patient leader, Stephen accepted this valuable information without comment. He wished me well in my endeavour.

The Conservative candidate was Brian Harrison, a Scarborough Council Controller. As the campaign unfolded rumour had it that Brian spent most of his time sipping coffee in his campaign office. Well after the election I learned that the Conservatives pre-election polling predicted a 4,000 vote margin of victory for Brian Harrison. No wonder Brian was so relaxed. The election reality was my victory by a margin of 1,200 votes.

Unlike the two federal elections I had experienced, there were very few all-candidates meetings. That didn't mean there weren't important issues. Tenants had very little protection from unscrupulous landlords. A tenant complaining about needed repairs to the apartment or the building could result in eviction. There was no protection against arbitrary rent increases. Numerous stories of tenant injustice began to emerge. One example: There could be a clause in the lease stipulating that the tenant can not be away from the apartment for longer than two weeks. A tenant, returning after a three week vacation, could find new tenants in their apartment.

In Toronto at the time there were more than one million tenants. The Toronto Star, likely trying to sell newspapers in apartment buildings, began to feature stories of the effects of sky-rocketing rents as well as the injustices faced by tenants. About 30 percent of Scarborough Ellesmere was rental accommodation. We began a serious focus on apartments.

The 1972 and '74 losing federal campaigns turned out to be a source of volunteers. New Democrat members and supporters who lived in the federal riding, but outside the boundaries of the new Scarborough Ellesmere came to help with what looked like a possible victory. Fellow teachers, many of whom were not usually NDP supporters, came to help. A more enthusiastic and dedicated group would be hard to find! We had enough money to print a few hundred signs and two pieces of literature which would be distributed across the riding, all well organized by my 20 year old campaign manager, David Lee. He had helped in the two federal elections, but this was his first campaign as manager.

A televised Leaders Debate toward the end of the campaign had a positive effect on our local campaign. The spirited verbal jousting of the three Provincial Leaders; Premier Bill Davis, New Democrat Stephen Lewis and Liberal Bob Nixon, with Stephen having a dramatic presence, helped to create added enthusiasm for our supporters.

The closer we got to election day, our group of volunteers seemed to grow in leaps and bounds. There was an upbeat atmosphere in the campaign office as our election workers reported wonderful stories of support from their canvassing.

Election Day, September 18, was a wet one! Pat and I hurried and scurried through one last townhouse complex, urging those who hadn't voted to get to the poling station. Soaking wet, we returned to the campaign office to await the returns.

The large crowd gathered at a local union hall included Pat's aunt Mary and uncle Ron, who had just arrived from England. Certainly an interesting way to start one's first trip to Canada. Pat's dad, a life-long Liberal supporter, tended bar. Later, when we had to tally all our expenses and revenues for Elections Ontario, it was clear that we lost money on the bar. With such a happy, thirsty group how was that possible? "Your father-in-law was so happy for you that he was pouring doubles!" explained a volunteer who was helping with the bar.

I was now a Member of Her Majesty's Loyal Opposition, the NDP having doubled its seats from the previous parliament and finishing one seat ahead of the Liberals. It would be a minority government. I could scarcely believe it.

It was two am by the time Pat and I got home. Exhausted, but deliriously happy, the two of us were ready for some sleep, but not before Pat posed a practical question, "What is the salary?"

"I think there is a salary," was my reply. Pat, was full-time at home, minding two small children. Me having an income was a very good idea! I promised to call Queen's Park first thing in the morning. I did so and could happily report that indeed there was a salary.

Now that I was assured an income, the next step was to apply for a leave of absence from teaching, just in case I became un-elected at some point. I was aware that a Scarborough teacher, Bob Wong, in an earlier election, had applied for a leave of absence to be an NDP candidate. He was denied the leave and admonished, "You need to choose one or the other. You can not be a teacher and a politician." Bob challenged the administration over their ruling. Although he lost the battle, he had ignited a discussion, the end result of which was my application for a leave while elected was approved.

The staff at Joseph Brant Senior Public School, where I had taught for only one year and two weeks, threw a congratulations and farewell party. One of the gifts was a World War I wooden munitions box. The suggestion was that given my height of five foot five it would be helpful to have something upon which I could stand and of course since I was going to battle on behalf social justice issues, a munitions box. I gratefully accepted this unique gift, took it to Queen's Park and on an occasion when I was slated to make a speech on just such an issue, stood on it.

Imagine my surprise when I arrived at Queen's Park for the inaugural gathering of those who had been elected September 18, to meet Doug Puddicombe. I hadn't seen Doug in several years. We both left McCowan Road in 1969, me to McCrae, the new Senior School and he to be a Principal in Woodstock, Ontario. I wanted to know what he was doing at this gathering of newly elected MPPs. Doug informed me that he had been the campaign manager for Dr. Harry Parrott, Minister of Colleges and Universities. "Well Doug, our paths cross again. I am the NDP critic for Colleges and Universities."

# 4

# The Pink Palace

## September 1975

I was in awe. I stood in front of the Ontario Legislature, a majestic, pink sandstone, Richardsonian Romanesque style building, thinking about how on a cold, snowy December day 1973 I had been part of the more than 30,000 teachers protesting for the right to strike. That day I was on the outside of the Pink Palace. Starting today, I would be on the inside, with the privilege of having a seat in the Chamber.

As with so many other newcomers, the first challenge was to find the washrooms. I wandered the halls, enthralled with the gracious architecture and the magnificent art collection, eventually locating the washroom. I was anxious to see the Chamber, the place where I envisioned participating in lively debate. First, however, there was a caucus meeting where I would meet my new colleagues.

I looked around the Caucus Room. There were two people I recognized, our Leader Stephen Lewis, and Donald MacDonald, our former Leader. Donald had been the keynote speaker at my first nomination meeting in 1972. His incredibly upbeat, optimistic approach inspired me. Donald C. MacDonald was my mentor. My new found friends were from all over Ontario. We quickly got to know each other. It was fascinating to talk with the veterans. Their speeches about the myriad of issues they had been pursuing was impressive. One piece of advice from veteran MPP Fred Young (Yorkview, Toronto) stuck with me. "Ignore one phone call, that's worth 10 lost votes. Ignore one hand written letter, that's worth 100 lost votes." I was determined to return every phone call and personally answer every letter.

I did not have to think twice about who I wanted as my Executive Assistant. Lorna Prokaska was the Executive Director of Agincourt Community Services when I was Chair. We had worked exceedingly well together. I asked Lorna if she would be my E.A. at Queen's Park. "I can't type.", says she. My response was "I am not hiring you for your typing skills. It is your political brain which is so important." Lorna's advice over the years was absolutely superb. As for her typing skills, years later I learned that Lorna was taking unfinished letters home to complete after hours. Lorna retired about the time I became Speaker, however the two of us kept in touch on a regular basis. When Lorna, due to declining physical health moved to a long term care facility, Pat and I would wheel Lorna to a nearby pub for lunch and a chance to catch up on each others' lives.

I was assigned a small windowless one office with a dividing partition. On the other side of that partition was Mel Swart, MPP Welland. He had an equally small, windowless cubicle. Very quickly we became trusted colleagues and good friends. Mel and I were both elected in 1975, for the first time. Mel, however kept getting elected. Five successive times, then retired in 1988. Add in 14 years of municipal politics, Mel totalled about 28 years of elected public service. Mel was inspiring, as reflected in this tribute: "Mel Swart, a larger than life politician who will forever be remembered as a social crusader, a land conservationist long before society gave farmland protection a fleeting thought, and fearless advocate for working men and women and their families, has died."[1]

Mel was assigned the role of Critic for Consumer and Commercial Relations. No better choice could have been made. Mel Swart was an ardent crusader for public auto insurance; campaigning tirelessly across the province, gaining an impressive public profile. While he garnered significant public support creating the expectation that a New Democrat government would adopt a government run plan similar to what had been in Saskatchewan for decades, the reality was rejection by the Bob Rae government. The decision to jettison public auto insurance was hugely disappointing to the membership of the NDP and a devastating blow to Mel Swart.

Mel Swart had a theatrical way of highlighting the issue of cross-border shopping. The first thing I noticed when I walked into his office were the shelving. The appearance was that of a mini-grocery store. There were a wide variety of products, all of them made in Canada, and below each one a price tag; purchase price in Canada and purchase price in Buffalo N.Y. Every Canadian made product was cheaper in the US. Mel consistently badgered the Ontario government that this unfair situation was costing Canadian retailers profits and ultimately jobs. Periodically it was 'show and tell' time in Question Period. Mel would energetically wave around a particular item while providing a cross-border cost analysis. One day, Mel, who sat directly in front of me was taking on the Minister of Consumer Affairs in Question Period. Suddenly a roll of toilet paper was being waved in front of my face. The laughter drowned out whatever response there might have been from the Minister. The day that the Speaker ruled no more props allowed during Question Period, Mel was one of the most disappointed Members in the House. Mel Swart was a wonderful colleague and a good friend. He set the bar high when it came to public service.

---

1 Paul Forsyth Niagara *This Week* - St. Catharines, Friday, March 2, 2007

The Ontario Commission on the Legislature, better known as The Camp Commission, had a profound effect on how things were done at Queen's Park. MPP salaries were increased, a pension introduced and Members would have constituency offices. I needed to hire an assistant for my local office. It soon became apparent that a local office meant constituents had easier access to their MPP. Scarborough Ellesmere had a population of about 80,000. No shortage of issues, concerns, personal difficulties to tackle. Members on both sides of the aisle faced the same challenges.

## Lofty political notion — Question Period

Lively political debates each evening through the entire campaign period of both the 1972 and '74 federal elections were remarkable experiences for me. It was on the job training in front of audiences of 600 to 1,500 people. My debating mentor was Hon. Bob Standbury. He had a convincing way of presenting his Party's platform and warding off criticism with a mixture of logic and humour. I was able to quickly emulate my mentor. It was indeed an exhilarating experience. I convinced myself that as an MPP I could use those same skills to convince those across the aisle to see the error of their ways.

I looked forward to Question Period as an opportunity, using well-researched, clearly articulated questions, to put the government on the spot. Logic, reasoning, sincerity and sound public policy would rule the day. I could influence those in power to change their policies.

## Reality check

I soon found out that the daily Question Period is not Question and Answer Period. No question is asked without knowing the answer beforehand and there are only replies, not answers. At first I found it frustrating to champion a serious issue only to receive a 'non-answer'. I soon learned that the reply was not so important. What was important was catching the attention of the Press Gallery. An effective strategy was crucial. And timing. I could prepare a press release in advance of Question Period, but .... one — I couldn't guarantee that even being on the list for Question Period would mean being able to ask my question. Question Period had a life of its own. There were times when a critical issue occupied almost the entire 60 minutes; two — I could anticipate the reply but not know for sure what the Minister would say. One approach which was successful was pursuing an issue on my own and getting media coverage. Then it was easier to get on the list for Question Period. Issuing a press release afterwards could keep the issue alive. An excellent example was the issue of the need to expand the Emergency Ward of Scarborough General Hospital where I took notes during my all-night shift in the Ward, then got a press release out in time for the morning paper. The story was known before I was on my feet in Question Period. It was easier then to engage the Press Gallery.

It was exciting to be a part of the "cut and thrust" of an electrifying 60 minutes. I always looked forward to being able to ask tough questions related to my Critic portfolio or my riding. I also found that I could heckle effectively; often mischievous but never malicious. It turned out to be a good way to connect with members in the other Parties, which in turn revealed that political partisanship was often more for show than anything else.

## Lofty political notion — local political discussions

Debating policy at Queen's Park was important, but so too was connecting with voters in my Riding. As one veteran Member stated, "No one at Queen's Park votes for you." I wanted my constituents to have the opportunity to discuss the issues which were of concern to them. Neighbourhood gatherings, perhaps in a park or a school, would provide people with an excellent opportunity for a rational discussion about the issues of the day as well as a visionary chats about the base of our society; health care and education. I was sure that everyone had the same intense interest in public policy as I did.

Enthusiastic, but naive!

## Reality check

My local foray into 'let's have neighbourhood chats about politics' was disappointing. I had selected a neighbourhood where our popular vote was about 65% and chose a local public school as a meeting place. Discounting my staff and local Party organizer, the event attracted three constituents. My understanding of the public's interest in politics outside of an election period was jolted.

It was rewarding to learn that many constituents desired my attendance at special occasions, such as a 50th wedding anniversary celebration. There were plaques to hand out for special events. A couple of the 90th and 100th birthdays are especially memorable. I always enjoyed delivering the plaque and having the privilege of chatting with the recipient. On one such occasion I learned that my constituent was the architect of one of the Legislative buildings. the Whitney Block. Built in 1926, it was one of the tallest buildings in Toronto at the time. On another occasion I presented a plaque to a 100 year old woman who recalled herding goats on the east side of the Don River, south of Danforth Avenue. Today the area is known as Riverdale and is a heavily populated, vibrant part of urban Toronto.

Over time I came to appreciate that while probing discussions of political philosophy and policies was rare, the vast majority of my constituents were decent, hard-working people with whom I could have a pleasant relationship.

## The balancing act

It didn't take too long to realize that a vital challenge was balancing various competing responsibilities; political and personal.

How would I ensure political success as well as a happy family life? My Queen's Park life had its own balancing. In addition to Question Period, there were caucus meetings, committee meetings, critic responsibilities, debates in the House, returning phone calls from constituents, responding to letters and so on. It was easy to get overwhelmed by the list of things to do.

Advice from the experienced Members was that no matter how important was our task at Queen's Park, we weren't elected there. We were elected in our ridings. There was usually a serious disconnect between what happened in the Legislature and the realities of every day life. Stay connected to your Riding!

"Come with me, young Warner, we are going to visit the most important room in the building," instructed Jim Renwick, a veteran Member, who would become my mentor. Jim led me to the Members' Reading Room in the Legislative Library. His advice was to take some time each day to visit this quiet haven to read. He also suggested that when things got too stressful, take an afternoon off and go to a movie. Sitting in an empty movie theatre in the afternoon, watching a good movie, is an excellent way to counter balance stress.

We were a caucus of 38, having doubled the number from the last election. The Members were from every area of Ontario. Thirteen of those seats were in Toronto. It didn't take long for me to get the sense that real or perceived, some of the caucus, especially those from the north, thought there was a "Toronto centric" ethos. It was clear to me that I needed to learn more about the north, as well as other parts of our province. Getting to know my colleagues who were from outside of Toronto would be a good way to establish a cohesive caucus.

The House sat Tuesday and Thursday evenings, with a two hour dinner break from six to eight. Dinner time was a good opportunity to become better acquainted with Members from both sides of the aisle. I learned quickly that when the evening sitting concluded at 10:30, many of the out of town members headed for The Stable near

Yonge and Wellesley, or the Jack Russell on Wellesley just east of Yonge. Lively conversation and lots of laughter was a great way to unwind after a typically hectic day. I soon discovered that I was part of a hard working caucus; individuals who were dedicated to the goals and ideals of our Party. At the same time we enjoyed each others company.

Part of the learning curve was discovering that work in the Riding involved juggling priorities; door-to-door canvassing essentially all year round, tenant meetings, individual constituents to see, community events, issues related to Scarborough City Council, team meetings with my constituency staff, and staying connected with local media. Of all my Riding responsibilities what I liked best was going door-to-door. It was a welcome change from the partisan debates at Queen's Park. Most people were friendly. Occasionally they raised issues, but mostly it was a short, cordial chat. I found that I could easily remember details about families, so that when I next appeared at their door I had an opener as a greeting. On one occasion I was invited to a 50$^{th}$ wedding anniversary reception. The happy couple had six children, all of whom were married, five of the six couples living in Scarborough-Ellesmere. Nice way to canvass!

The most important part of the balancing challenge was family. When I left my house early in the morning my two daughters, aged three and four, were fast asleep. When I arrived back home late at night, they were asleep. Saturdays were devoted to events in the riding, and canvassing. Trying to find quality time with Pat and our children was not easy. I knew I had it easier than my out of town colleagues who had lots of travel to contend with, as well as trying to cover the vast area of their ridings, but still it bothered me. I did what I could in the limited time available.

When the children were a bit older I would take them to a few of my events. One of those occasions stands out. Wendy's, the hamburger restaurant chain, invited me to the grand opening of their 500$^{th}$ location, which happened to be located in my riding. I took Sherri and Barbara along to the ribbon-cutting event. Nattily attired business men cordially welcomed me with a glass of champagne. They were genuinely surprised to see two little girls tagging along. With great aplomb, one of the executives quickly got milkshakes for my two surprised, but happy girls. Then, all of a sudden Wendy herself appeared and the two girls had their photo taken with Wendy! The event certainly helped offset some of the disappointment of not having their dad around often.

There is never enough time to accomplish all the things you need to do or want to do. What is essential if you want to be successful at balancing, is to clearly identify essential priorities, be self-disciplined, calm and patient. Top priority for me was and still is — family. One attempt by me to remain connected to my family didn't work out so well. I had an event in the riding to attend in the evening. I figured that I could leave Queen's Park and have about an hour at home before going to the riding event. Unannounced, I arrived home. My two young daughters were excited to see me. It was great to hear their laughter, see them smile and simply enjoy their company. Then I announced that I had to leave for work. Smiles turned to frowns, laughter to tears. That night when I was back home, Pat asked me to never do that again. Don't drop in for an hour. She had spent the rest of the evening trying to get these two kids, age four and five to stop crying; assuring them their father would be home later on when they were asleep.

My work week was approximately 70 hours. Occasionally there was committee domestic or international travel as well. I was able to balance the political responsibilities with my commitment to family only because of my wife Pat. It was her devotion to our family and her strong support of my political career which made it all work.

# 5

# Critic of Colleges and Universities

## 1975 - 1977

I was excited to be appointed Critic of Colleges and Universities. I suppose it was the teacher in me. Although I was never an accomplished scholar, I had always valued learning. I felt that my hop-scotching across three universities (Carleton, U of T, York), eventually achieving an English Honours degree, gave me at least a glimpse into the complexity of the post-secondary world.

Successful societies have a solid educational foundation. I needed to explore the composition of that foundation. What worked well. What didn't.

I decided that the best way to be an informed Critic was to visit each of the 40 Community Colleges and Universities. I wanted to know the concerns of administration, staff, faculty and students. What an education I received!

A visit to a post-secondary institution in a small city usually attracted a local reporter as well as a student newspaper reporter. I encountered a warm welcome everywhere, getting the impression that a visit by the Minister or the Critic of Colleges and Universities was rare. Oh, the magic of minority government. It seemed that my extensive visiting prompted the Minister, Dr. Harry Parrott, to tour around the province. What a great opportunity for the institutions to air their concerns, to be heard directly.

While writing this section I came across an interview I did with The Cord Weekly, a student newspaper at Wilfred Laurier University, "If he should inherit the ministry from Dr. Parrott, Warner would like to see several plans of his be put into action. Among them, he would like to see more accessibility of universities to senior citizens; the democratization of the system to include the voices of everyone who is affected in any way by university life, including the general population of a university town, always working through committees and the Board of Governors; the establishment of a five-year academic growth plan; day care made available where needed, for both faculty and students; the encouragement of women to higher positions within the hierarchy; better preparation of students in their early educational years." (Feb. 5, 1976) Over time most of the above has been achieved. Successive governments have done their part to ensure that Ontario continues to have a superb post-secondary system.

I did get a chuckle from a line in the interview, "He knows what he is talking about." That assertion was unique.

My extensive travelling to every area of our vast province was rewarding in terms of becoming a well-informed Critic. The learning experience also made it difficult to be a hard-nosed, tough opposition Member. It was apparent to me that our Community College system was unique, providing vision and leadership in the local communities. It is imperative to note that credit for establishing this world class Community College system goes to William G. Davis as Minister of Education in Premier John Robarts' government.

My campus visits revealed that every one of our 15 universities were institutions of excellence, some with accomplished international status. The minority government situation meant that when the Opposition brought an issue to the House or directly to a Cabinet Minister attention was paid. So, after my visit to Brock University

I raised the strange situation of Brock having its science department housed in a renovated dairy. It didn't take long for that unhappy situation to change with the promise of a new building.

Dr. Harry Parrott was a sincere, hard-working Minister who was dedicated to improving the post-secondary system. We had differences of opinion from time to time. There was one incident which I later felt embarrassed and sorry about. It was an evening sitting with not many members in the House. The Speech from the Throne, the budget and estimates are three opportunities for Members to raise issues, concerns or simply vent their frustrations with government policies. I don't recall which of above three occasions it was, but whatever I said ignited the usually unflappable, mild mannered Harry. He was livid. Storming across the aisle he invited me to step outside. I am a slightly built, short guy who has always tried to avoid violence. I took one look at this angry six foot five Harry, shook my head from side to side, while trying to make eye contact with the Speaker. I was not leaving the Chamber. Harry stood staring at me for about 30 seconds, turned and retreated to his seat. Definitely not one of my finer moments in the House. However, that episode and the more I probed the workings of our post-secondary system, the clearer it became that Dr. Harry Parrott was deeply dedicated to ensuring that Ontario would have, and continue to have world class colleges and universities.

I think that my greatest contribution as Critic of Colleges and Universities was that I spurred a more direct connection between the institutions and the Minister than they had ever had. I have no doubt that local press coverage of my visits around the province had a positive communication effect.

I certainly enhanced my education. I was being paid to learn and I loved it!

# 6

# Critic of Metro Toronto Affairs

## 1977–1979

This role was far ranging from trying to make connections with each of the component parts of Metro (Toronto, Scarborough, East York, North York, York, Etobicoke). What were the situations which should involve the province? It was a largely undefined role, yet one which was interesting. I took the position that anything in Metro Toronto which had a connection to Queen's Park could capture my attention. One dramatic incident required the involvement of the Solicitor General.

## Mounted Police — Workers — Strike Breakers with Baseball Bats

### The Becker Milk Strike — 1978

The Becker Milk Company was founded in 1957, opening five convenience stores. The chain grew to 500 stores. The main processing plant was located on Warden Avenue in Scarborough. There was a labour dispute at that plant. This wasn't however an ordinary labour disruption. A legal strike situation should mean peaceful picket lines and an attempt to negotiate a settlement. Such was not the case as the Becker Company took a heavy handed approach and so too did the Toronto Police. As the NDP Critic for Metro Toronto Affairs I took an interest in this unhappy, ugly situation.

The scene I encountered when I arrived at the Warden Avenue plant was alarming to say the least. The first thing I noticed was a group of about 50 people, which included 20 women, carrying the usual protest placards, sandwiched in-between a large tractor-trailer, one which had a driver plus two men each with baseball bats, and police on horseback. No question about the bravery of these women to stand their ground with imposing, intimidating forces on both sides of them. Clearly the company had engaged strike breakers and the police were being used to assist the company in its effort to continue business as usual.

I had a chat with the workers on the picket line, commending them on their bravery and urging them to stay strong. Then I headed inside the plant and found my way to the President's office. I identified myself as a Member of Provincial Parliament, which got me a warm greeting. The greeting went from warm to icy cold when I asked the President if he would in turn request of the Police that they remove the horses, disengage the strike breakers, and re-engage in contract talks. I was ordered to leave the building and not return.

Outside I went, to discover that the situation was worse than I had thought. Not only were there Police on horseback, there were Police on motorcycles and in squad cars just over a nearby hill. Quite a show of force to try and intimidate a small group who were peacefully engaged in a legal strike. I understood, from various reliable sources that Toronto Police had a so called "flying squad" of officers who came from different divisions around the city, none of them with a name or number on their uniform. This squad could assist companies in breaking picket lines and no one would be able to identify individual officers. This infamous squad was later disbanded.

I hustled back to Queen's Park in time for Question Period. I asked the Solicitor General to have the Police remove their horses from the Becker Milk site. That afternoon the Mounted Police unit was removed. I suggested that the Milk Marketing Board stop deliveries to Beckers for a week and during that week have round-the-clock negotiations under the supervision of an experienced mediator from the Ontario Labour Relations Board. I don't know if the attendant media publicity did the trick, but bargaining resumed shortly after this incident and eventually a collective agreement was signed.

As to the history of Beckers, the company was sold in 2006 to Alimentation Couche-Tard. The company converted the company-owned stores to Mac's Milk and later to Circle K, leaving a remnant of affiliate Becker's stores. Starting in 2013, Alimentation Couche-Tard began expanding the affiliate program. There are now over 40 stores in Ontario. The Warden Avenue plant was sold and the land now has on it a housing development.

# 7

# Life in the Caucus

38 Members of Provincial Parliament, 35 men, 3 women. 38 different personalities, varied backgrounds, half of the group having been elected for the first time in 1975. The one thing we had in common was that all of us had been elected as New Democrats. Four of the class of '75 later had the privilege of being in Premier Bob Rae's Cabinet (1990-95); Evelyn Gigantes, (Housing, Health), Floyd Laughren, (Treasurer), Bob Mackenzie, (Labour), Bud Wildman (Environment and Energy, Native Affairs, Natural Resources).

The 1975 election brought some changes to the makeup of the Legislature. Over the decades occasionally a woman was elected, but mostly the Members were white, Anglo-saxon, middle class men. Seven women were elected; three Conservatives, three New Democrats, one Liberal. To Premier Davis' credit, all three Conservative women were appointed to Cabinet (Dr. Bette Stephenson, Margaret Birch, Margaret Scrivener). The lone Liberal woman was a former Family Court Judge, Margaret Campbell. Evelyn Gigantes, Gillian Sandeman and Marion Bryden were the three New Democrat women. Breaking the ethnic barrier were three Italian New Democrats; Odoardo Di Santo, Tony Grande and Tony

Lupusella. I am glad to say that the makeup of the Legislature in the 2020's more closely reflects the cultural and religious diversity of Ontario than at any point in my tenure at the Pink Palace. Gender balance has not been achieved but progress is evident. A "fast forward" here: November 19, 1990, the day I was elected Speaker — in the media scrum I was asked if I thought that the record number of women MPPs would have any effect on debates in the House. I responded by saying that I thought having more women MPPs would bring a more civil atmosphere, that there would be fewer emotional outbursts and more reasoned debates. I don't think that answer went over well with some of the male MPPs. I remain convinced that my observation is valid.

Stephen Lewis, at our first formal caucus meeting let us all know what was expected at caucus meetings. When there was government legislation to consider, our Critic would make a recommendation, discussion would follow, then a vote. Majority vote would carry the day. Caucus solidarity was expected; that is, everyone supporting whatever the majority had decided. Stephen added, however that if the issue was a matter of principle, then the Member could abstain, just please so inform the Whip and the Leader. I never had a problem with that approach. There were only few instances which brought about a serious division in the Caucus. One contentious item did come close. And, it surprised me.

I was about age eight when I experienced the joy of my grandfather taking me to Ward's Island, one of Toronto's 15 islands, to spend the weekend at a relative's home. Added to this special treat was the opportunity to assist the Captain of the Sam McBride, the ferry boat which would take us across Toronto Harbour to Ward's Island. Grandpa took me to the Wheelhouse to meet his best friend, the Captain. While I couldn't actually steer the vessel, it was quite a thrill to stand beside the Captain while he steered the boat. Thus began a life long love of the Toronto Islands.

Imagine my surprise when I found out there were Members of my Caucus who supported Metro Toronto's desire to evict all the residents of the Islands so that the islands would be one big city park. The residents had appealed to the Provincial government. Minority government at Queen's Park meant that anything was possible. Vigorous debate in our Caucus ensured, emotional at times, with the result that the majority were in favour of the residents. The Liberal Caucus also supported the residents. In the end, the provincial government offered to mediate between the residents and Metro Council. Larry Grossman, who was a Cabinet Minister and whose riding included the Toronto Islands, played a major role in helping save the island homes.

On December 18, 1981, the province of Ontario passed a law legalizing the Islanders to stay until 2005. This kept the lands in Metro's ownership, to be leased to the City who would lease it to the Islanders. In 1993, the NDP government passed the *Toronto Islands Residential Community Stewardship Act*, which granted Islanders continued deeds to their houses and 99-year leases on the land. A Land Trust was established to handle any transfers or sales of such properties on the Islands. Since the 1800's people have been living on Toronto Islands, with about 650 people residing there today.

The 30$^{th}$ Parliament lasted only 18 months. The general election in 1977 added two Members to our caucus; Brian Charlton and Dave Cooke, both later playing major roles in the Bob Rae government. By-elections in 1979 brought in two new Members; Richard Johnston, replacing Stephen Lewis who had resigned and Colin Isaacs (Wentworth). 1977 also featured the first time a Member of the Opposition was appointed Speaker. The Conservatives had 58 seats while the combined opposition number was 67. Choosing an Opposition Member to be Speaker took away one vote from the other side of the aisle. Jack Stokes had been elected for 10 years and was deeply respected by everyone. This former railway conductor used his conductor's experience to manage the House in a no nonsense approach. He was fair but firm.

It was easy to be energized when your colleagues were so passionate about social justice issues. Each Member was a leader in his or her own right. After all they had received more votes that anyone else in their riding. While there was bound to be some highly polished egos, there was also a great spirit of cooperation and an abiding sense of team work.

The Leader of a Party is elected by the membership of that Party. During the time I was a member of the NDP Caucus it was the Caucus who elected the Chair of Caucus, House Leader and Chief Whip. Quiet campaigning took place. Lots of "let's have a chat, just you and me" and no overt persuading of one another. In 1977 I was elected Chief Whip, a coveted position for anyone who wanted to be an integral part of the Leadership decisions such as strategy in the House, negotiations with the other two Parties and proposals to the Caucus regarding which issues to focus on. There were regular meetings of the Leader, House Leader, Deputy House Leader, Chief Whip, Deputy Whip. My chief responsibility was to make sure everyone was in the Chamber for important votes. I also had to arrange to have a certain number of Members in the Chamber when the House was sitting. The majority of caucus were never thrilled about having to sit in the House for routine debates of legislation, but I rarely had a difficulty in getting Members to take their turn. Of course when there was a significant issue most Members wanted to be in the House. If it was widely known that Stephen Lewis, orator extraordinaire, would be addressing the House, just about every seat in the House was occupied.

I treasure those days in the Caucus, as I did during my time from 1985 to '87. We fought important political battles, such as achieving tenant protection, rent control, and workplace health and safety, but we also had some joyous times together.

## Life in the Caucus Included Unique Dining

*"Food brings people together on many different levels. It's nourishment of the soul and body; it's truly love."*

*— Giada De Laurentiis, Italian-American Chef*

## 1975

"I would be pleased to accept the invitation to dinner at your place." I was surprised by the invitation from John Holtby, a Clerk at the Table, and mentioned so to one of the veteran Members. He explained that John Holtby had an interesting custom of inviting some of the newly elected Members, from all three Parties, to his apartment for dinner. My colleague went on to explain that John was a gourmet cook, who took great pride in pairing wines with each of the five courses he served.

It was a memorable evening on many levels. Appetizer through to dessert, each course delectable. Each course accompanied by a superb wine. I met newly elected Members from each Party. The conversation was lively and engaging. What a wonderful introduction to some of those with whom I would be working.

## 1976

Speaker Russell Rowe invited me to dinner at Speaker's Apartment. This invitation, as it turned out, could not have come at a better time in my parliamentary education.

I had engaged in a few verbal scuffles in the House with Dr. Bette Stephenson, Minister of Education, over insufficient funding for special needs students. It didn't take long to realize that Dr. Stephenson was a tough debater. She matched my combative style with her own. It was fair to say that I wasn't a great fan of the Minister.

A surprise was in store for me. I arrived at Speaker's Apartment to discover that my seat mate for the evening was the same person I had been verbally duelling with in the House. It turned out to be an amazing evening. The custom was for the Speaker to invite three Members from each of the three Parties. The atmosphere was cheerful. Conversation flowed as smoothly as the delightful wine being served. Speaker Rowe was a superb host.

I left Speaker's Apartment with a profoundly different view of Minister Stephenson. She was witty, smart, and friendly; warmly engaging in discussion. That dinner changed my approach to debating in the House. Getting to know Dr. Stephenson resulted in a new found respect for her. While I remained resolute in my quest for greater funding for special needs students, I started listening more closely to what she had to say. By doing so, I was able to be a more effective critic, as well as contribute to a more civil atmosphere in the House.

Later I had the opportunity, as Speaker, to host dinners as a wonderful opportunity for Members, especially newly elected ones, to get to know each other as people. My guests would remain opponents, but perhaps they would be less likely to consider their opponents as enemies.

## "Will the Member for Scarborough Ellesmere come to order."

More than 40 years later I have a vivid recollection of my first day in the House. I was a bit nervous, but gloriously excited. I took my seat in the back row of Opposition side of the Chamber. I had the good fortune to be seated in between two experienced Members, Fred Young (Yorkview) and George Samis (Cornwall). I couldn't help but acquire a deep respect for the Chamber and everyone there; the Members from all Parties of course, but also the Speaker, Sergeant at Arms, Attendants, Hansard reporters and French language interpreters. At the same time, I was eager to do battle with the forces of evil! It took a while to learn that the Davis government, with a very talented Cabinet, was actually quite progressive.

I have always been someone who wants to get things done quickly and well. My lack of patience for what I viewed as a snails pace at which the government moved on issues was reflected in my (almost) daily heckling. I was mischievous, but never malicious.

A former Hansard editor, Jack White, wrote an article for the *Globe and Mail* the day after I was sworn in as Speaker, essentially pointing out that the Member who vigorously engaged in heckling now had the task of maintaining decorum in the House. Jack White referenced a sampling of my quips:

- On increasing the guaranteed income supplement: "Snails will be on the Olympic team by the time you get around to it!"
- Of the delay in raising the level of Workers' Compensation benefits: "Jelly beans roll up hills faster than that."
- "The only thing you stand firm on is quicksand."
- Of the delay in providing a dialysis unit for Scarborough General Hospital: "A centipede with fallen arches moves faster than this government."
- Of trying to understand a long drawn out response in Question Period: "It's like trying to iron out a plate of spaghetti."
- "With the dazzling speed of a herd of thundering turtles, the Minister moves towards reform," he told Gregory Sorbara, then Minister of Colleges and Universities.[2]

When my chiding of a Minister for not accomplishing a task quickly enough didn't work, I would then call upon the Minister to resign. "Resign" was heard loud and clear and at perfectly timed dramatic moments. It became my trademark as well as a note of levity in the House. One evening during a budget speech being delivered by the Treasurer, Darcy McKeough my tolerance for the perceived achievements this budget would create, evaporated. I interjected with a resounding "Resign!" A loud commotion ensued; laughter, applause and an envelope being handed from one of my caucus colleagues to a Liberal MPP. Turns out, members from all three Parties participated

---

[2] pg. A17, Globe and Mail, November 20, 1990

in a bet; at what minute and second after Darcy started speaking would the call to resign occur.

I believe in working hard, taking the task at hand seriously, but never taking myself too seriously. I fashioned tough questions in the House, trying to put political pressure on Ministers of the Crown. Intense political moments can spark uncivil exchanges, words which later are a cause for regret. Humour can often help to avoid such exchanges. I like to think that my interjections assisted. I found, to my surprise, that the quick quips made it easier to meet Members from other Parties. Perhaps it was out of curiosity; "Who is this person who keeps saying funny things?" Regardless of the reason, the end result were friendly connections across the aisle.

Jack White's article also noted, "For all his free-wheeling criticisms, Mr. Warner is well liked by his colleagues for his sense of humour, a quality he will need if he is to control an assembly with a reputation for unruliness."[3] Mr. White was spot on. Having a sense of humour was essential, especially during tense times in the House.

## Leadership — Stephen Lewis

Stephen Lewis was an inspiring Leader. His eloquent, passionate attack on issues was something to behold. Backed by a superbly talented research team Stephen would tackle an issue armed with facts and figures. When he rose in the House during Question Period I knew that all the information he needed had been memorized and therefore he could more easily make good use of his incredible oratorical skills. On occasion I actually felt sorry for the poor soul who had to take the brunt of Stephen's fact-filled barrage. The issue which I believe was closest to his heart was that of workplace health and safety.

Stephen achieved success on the issue of asbestosis as a compensable workplace disease. It was common that someone who

---

[3] pg. A17, *Globe and Mail*, November 20, 1990

had been working with asbestos would acquire a lung disease and be denied Workers Compensation if they smoked. There was no acknowledged connection between asbestos and lung disease. A focal point for this issue was the Johns Manville plant in Scarborough where there had been numerous cases of diseased lungs, all of the cases dismissed by the Workers' Compensation Board.

I vividly recall the day which likely was the turning point in this long, difficult battle. Stephen had flown to New York City in the morning to meet with Dr.Irving J. Selikoff, a renowned biomedical scientist, and returned in time for Question Period. Stephen revealed startling facts and figures so fervently and convincingly that silence prevailed. Soon there would be no denial of the truth, that those working with asbestos could contract a lung disease and if so, would be compensated.

Leadership for Stephen included allowing great latitude for the official Critics. Use your imagination, skills, energy, enthusiasm to do the job the best way you knew how. Seek advice as needed and try to adhere to Party policy. Stephen never micro-managed. In return, I would have walked on broken glass for him. His leadership was such that I was not surprised when later he became Canada's Ambassador to the United Nations.

# 8

# Medicare and the Magna Carta

## *A Clash of Kings — 1215*

Who would have thought that the life of a power hungry King would eventually result in governments being required to pass legislation in order to raise taxes! King John of England, who was also Duke of Normandy (in France), Duke of Aquitaine (in France), Count of Anjou (in France), and Lord of Ireland battled fiercely with King Phillp II of France. Wars cost money. King John ran short of cash so arbitrarily raised taxes. Again and again. The Barons, upon whom King John relied for support, rebelled. Negotiations between King John and the Barons produced, in 1215, the Magna Carta. The Magna Carta was the first document to put into writing the principle that the king and his government were not above the law. The "Great Charter" embodied the principle that taxation requires representation (legislation).

## *Medicare in Canada*

Medicare was born in Saskatchewan in 1947 thanks to the leadership of Premier Tommy Douglas. In Ontario, Premier Leslie Frost's government, in 1959, introduced a public hospitalization insurance plan which was funded through compulsory premiums and provincial and federal contributions. The premiums (single or family) were a flat amount. The premiums were not based on the ability to pay. If the government of the day decided to increase the premiums, they did so by including it in the annual budget.

## Is Medicare Premium a Tax?

*March 7, 1978*

Treasurer Darcy McKeough delivered the 1978 Ontario budget. Included in the budget was a 37.5% increase in the health care premium. Both Opposition Parties were opposed to such a large increase.

I argued in the Ontario Legislature that a health care premium was really a tax and as such required legislation. This was also a battle about fairness. Why should a wealthy family pay the same premium amount as a family with a modest income? This was a battle worth fighting.

I cited the famous agreement signed more than 800 years ago, which limited the arbitrary power of the King, hence government, particularly with respect to taxes. You want to levy taxes, bring the matter before parliament!

If I was successful, then the government could not impose a premium. They would have to bring in health tax legislation. In this minority government it was possible that a health tax would either be voted down or amended to a much lower amount than 37.5%

*March 10, 1978*

I rose in the House on a point of privilege, holding a framed copy of the Magna Carta in my hands, asking Speaker Stokes to consider that the OHIP premium increase contained in the budget was really a tax and as such required legislation. I quoted from (the English translated) Great Charter, "*No scutage or aid shall be imposed in our kingdom unless by common counsel.*" I did note that the Great Charter allowed exceptions:

*"except to ransom our person, make our eldest son a knight"* -- I don't suppose the Treasurer intends to do that — *"and once to marry our eldest daughter, and for this a reasonable aid only shall be paid."4*

Speaker Stokes responded that he would take my point of order under advisement and report back later. I left the Chamber to answer a phone call. On the other end of the line was one very excited Thunder Bay history teacher. He explained that he had been teaching the class about the Magna Carta. A student wondered why they were studying something that was so old, and not really important today. A local radio station carried a news report about the Magna Carta being used by an MPP to challenge the government's decision on health premiums. The teacher gleefully shared the news story with the class, proof that the Magna Carta, although more than 800 years old, was an important foundation for our rule of law.

*March 13*

Speaker Stokes reported to the House that I did not have a valid point of privilege. "... it is not within the Speaker's responsibilities or powers to give an opinion on the legality or constitutionality of any legislation introduced in the House."[5]

## *Two options explored*

I still wanted to test my constitutional theory. Perhaps the premium setting authority the government had granted unto itself was not constitutional. The Magna Carta is the foundation of our parliamentary system. So, I needed to explore this avenue. I turned to my mentor, a senior member of the caucus, Jim Renwick. He was a brilliant, experienced lawyer with lots of connections. The two of us visited John Laskin, a constitutional expert teaching at the

---

4 Hansard March 10, 1978

5 Hansard, March 13, 1978

University of Toronto Faculty of Law. He seemed quite delighted to take on the necessary research.

Another option was a legislative one. On March 30, I tabled a Private Member's Bill specifying legislation rather than regulation as a way to help pay for health care. I had the support of my caucus and the Liberals. The Bill, however, never came to a vote because under the Rules, a Private Members Bill can be stopped if 20 Members oppose the Bill being voted upon. The government side provided the necessary 20.

I did appreciate editorials from three important newspapers:

> The *Ottawa Citizen*: "McKeough has missed a golden opportunity to convince government that the logical way to generate more money without penalizing users is to finance OHIP with general taxation revenues. It works far Saskatchewan and Quebec; it can work for Ontario."[6]
>
> The *Toronto Star*: "The fairest way to raise the money would be to increase personal income tax since it's the only tax system that's based on the ability of people ta pay."[7]
>
> The *Globe and Mail*: "On the other hand, there is an argument that we are not referring here to a routine increase in the fee for something people can choose to buy or pass up (such as booze). This is much more. It is quite clearly a tax increase, one most people can not avoid, and a huge one at that. Shouldn't that require legislation, or at least — as suggested yesterday by NDP Leader Michael Cassidy — a resolution passed by the Legislature?"[8]

While exploring options I had buttons made, with the inscription "No Taxation Without Legislation." The buttons were quite popular

---

6 *Ottawa Citizen*, March 9, 1978

7 *Toronto Star*, March 13, 1978

8 *Globe and Mail*, March 14, 1978 — Norman Webster

with the Opposition and did attract some media attention. I don't recall seeing any government members sporting said button.

## *The path to solving an impasse*

The end of the fiscal year is April 30. The new budget takes effect May 1. So, if there was to be a change to the OHIP premium it had to happen before April 30.

In a nutshell, here is what happened between March 7 and April 25.

The issue dominated Question Period, the Liberals and New Democrats trying various approaches to undermine the government's position. It became clear that the government did not want to alter the 37.5% increase. The Liberals would settle for a 6% increase with the remaining revenue coming from various sources, including Wintario (a provincial lottery). The New Democrats wanted the revenue to come from personal income tax.

Both Opposition Parties wanted the issue sent to the Social Development Committee. This did not meet with favour by the government. Under the Rules of Procedure, however, 20 Members standing can have an issue referred to a committee, so the health care premium was whisked off to the Social Development Committee. The deliberations in committee did not produce a compromise solution.

Over the weeks there would be a non-confidence motion from the NDP, and the threat of non-confidence from the Liberals. The NDP motion was defeated and the Liberal threat withdrawn. No one really wanted a third election in two and a half years.

On April 25, Treasurer Darcy McKeough announced that the premium increase would be approximately one-half of the original.

## The fate of the health care premium

Perhaps the almost two months of focus on health care premiums was a catalyst for serious consideration about abolishing premiums.

*May 17, 1989*

Liberal majority government, Hon. David Peterson, Premier

Treasurer Bob Nixon "It is a special pleasure for me to announce to the House that OHIP premiums will be eliminated as of January I, 1990. This action keeps the promise made in 1985."[9]

*May 18, 2004*

Liberal majority government, Hon. Dalton McGuinty, Premier

Minister of Finance, Hon. Greg Sorbara, ushered in a health care premium, but this time based on the personal income tax system instead of being a flat rate. The health premium ranges from $0 if your taxable income is $20,000 or less, to $900 if your taxable income is more than $200,600. This system remains in place today.

## Reflections

I was disappointed, but not surprised when the Speaker did not rule in my favour. It wasn't the Speaker's responsibility to determine if the health care premium was really a tax. I was trying to not only bring forward an important principle, but trying to focus public attention on the issue. I think my approach worked for the following reasons: in a minority government situation the government has to be careful not to trigger an unwanted election; health care and by extension the cost thereof is always an important public issue; the novelty of using the Magna Carta to ignite a debate.

I was disappointed when John Laskin reported that the Order-in-Council authorization passed in 1971, to set premiums by regulation, met Canadian constitutional requirements.

Perhaps, since Saskatchewan and Quebec had been successfully using the income tax system as a way to help cover health care costs,

---

9 Ontario Budget, 1989, page 6

the three Parties could have used that information as a base for discussion. It might have been an avenue for compromise.

The basic principles of the Magna Carta, written more than 800 years ago, remain essential to responsible government. Well, perhaps not the part: "*except to ransom our person, make our eldest son a knight or once to marry our eldest daughter, and for this a reasonable aid only shall be paid.*"

## Minority government as a recipe for good governance

Perhaps the minority government from September 1975 to June 1977 collapsed because no one wanted it to work. The Conservatives had enjoyed majority government for 30 years so the 1975 results were a shock. The New Democrats, finishing second, felt they were in a position to become government for the first time in Ontario's history. The Liberals, I think felt that but for a bit of bad luck they would have finished second, ready to go to next level. In caucus I was a "hawk," convinced that we had the Conservatives on the ropes. We should trigger an election the moment there was an opportunity to do so. All three Parties had members itching for an election. The 1977 election saw a grand total of six seats change hands. What happened next was something which brought out the best in people and produced good governance.

In general what occurred was that in order to make things work the politicians had to trust one another. The underlying foundation: each Party would get something, no one would get everything. Key words: compromise, cooperation, listening, understanding. Cabinet Ministers reached out to their two Critics, meeting informally with them, trying to establish a good working relationship. I recall a delightful evening at the Campbell House, an 1822 heritage house which had been restored by a lawyers' group, The Advocate Society. The host was Hon. Roy McMurtry, Attorney General. Jim Breithaupt, the Liberal Critic, and a few senior staff of the AG were also present. What a wonderful opportunity to learn more about how the Attorney General's office works and of course more on a personal level about Roy McMurtry.

An essential ingredient of those four years was that the basis for any confidence motion which might trigger an election were laid out clearly. No one wanted to end up causing an unnecessary election. Of course there were differences of opinion, but rarely any outward animosity. Civility ruled the day! In my humble opinion those four years not only produced good governance, but did so in a reasoned, respectful way.

Political stability is valued by the public. Strict adherence to a political philosophy is not nearly important as the solving of problems. Politicians attacking one another personally simply undermines the public's trust in all politicians. When those we elect do not trust one another why should the public trust the politician? Broken promises, unsubstantiated accusations, denigrating of a previous government all contribute to a steady decline in voter turnout, which in turn leads to a distrust of government. Once that trust is broken parliamentary democracy is at risk.

Minority or Coalition governments have a genuine opportunity to rebuilt the public's trust. The situation of there not being a majority government dictates that Members must find a way to get along, share ideas, collectively solve problems. The road map to achieve one or the other is in front of us — proportional representation.

The "Truck Convoy" which reeked havoc in our nation's Capital in January, 2022, included neo-Nazis and other unsavoury characters, but a significant contingent were ordinary people who had lost faith in government. That convoy was a "canary in the coal mine". Politicians and political Parties have to find a way to do things differently. If not I fear that the canary will stop singing.

# 9

# Into the World of the Lawyer

## 1979–1981

I have secretly always wanted to be a lawyer. Somehow, although I had never voiced this inner thought, Michael Cassidy, NDP Provincial Leader, knew. Perhaps, along with other qualities he was clairvoyant. He asked me to be our Party's Critic of the Attorney General. I would remain as Critic of Metro Toronto Affairs as well as fulfilling my Chief Whip responsibilities. I was surprised, flattered, excited and viewed the portfolio addition as a fascinating challenge. Challenges often bring wonderful opportunities.

Pat Crowe, Toronto Star, wrote an interesting article at the time of my appointment. Reflecting on the article and my later political life, it is clear to me that being Critic of the AG helped lead me to a more parliamentary political life. My guess is that anyone who got to know Roy McMurtry (who was Attorney General at the time) can not help but learn how to debate issues without being blinded by partisanship.

Pat Crowe of the Toronto Star wrote, "The range of responsibility is likely to make Warner the second most visible NDPer at Queen's Park, a prospect he doesn't shy away from. In fact it is doubtful that Warner has ever shied away from anything.

Although relatively subdued in private, Warner is one of the most highly partisan, prickly and audible voices in the Legislature."[10]

Fast forward to November, 1990 when I was elected Speaker, and the following observation, by Jack White of the Globe and Mail, "For all his free-wheeling criticisms, Mr. Warner is well liked by his colleagues for his sense of humour, a quality he will need if he is to control an assembly with a reputation for unruliness."[11] There were a number of ingredients to my growth as a parliamentarian, not the least of which was the influence of the Hon. Roy McMurty.

Shortly after the media coverage about the first non-lawyer being appointed as Critic of the Attorney General I got a phone call from Archie Campbell, Deputy Attorney General. Archie informed me that Hon. Roy McMurtry, Attorney General would like to know if I would appreciate a ministerial briefing. I couldn't believe what I was hearing. My colleague and mentor, Jim Renwick, told me that I was being offered a rare opportunity. Take it, he said. I did. As a footnote, Archie Campbell was a very talented lawyer would was appointed to the Bench in 1986.

Archie Campbell came to my office and we spent a few hours going over a myriad of details. As he was leaving, he made another offer; informing me that I could contact him at any time if I was looking for information or had questions about policies. A short while later Roy McMurtry invited me, as well as the Liberal Critic and a few senior staff in the AG's office to dinner. It was an evening to get to know each other better. Roy viewed the role of the Attorney General to be a semi-judicial one. As such, political partisanship took a back seat.

While I was excited about trying to fulfill this prestigious position I was determined not to be so foolish as to enter into any legal debates with the AG. I was confident that I could debate legal principles, but certainly not beyond that. With that in mind, the first

10 Pat Crowe, *Toronto Star*, March 14, 1979

11 Jack White, *Globe and Mail*, November 20, 1990

issue I tackled was bail reform. I learned that the Quakers had been working on this issue for some time.

I needed to chat with those who had first hand experience. I made arrangements to meet with a group of inmates at Toronto's Don Jail. I was provided with a large meeting space and 25 inmates, all of them men, sitting in circle. I asked about the circumstances which resulted in these men being in jail, either without bail or awaiting their bail hearing. Their stories were remarkably similar; an arrest late at night or very early morning, not enough money on them for bail, having to rely on an over-worked Duty Counsel for legal representation. Often it appeared to be an arbitrary arrest. I did note that all of 25 men I met with professed their innocence of any crime.

Vagrancy, loitering, a small amount of marijuana, as well as any number of petty crimes were common grounds for a late night arrest. Poor people don't usually have a lawyer to call or even anyone else who could find appropriate legal representation. The poor person could quite easily end up in jail and if they couldn't make bail, the stay could be a while.

Bail is part of the Criminal Justice system. Any changes would need to happen in Ottawa. However, the provinces administer the Bail Act. I could advocate for more discretion on the part of the police when it comes to laying charges, and less reliance on bail for those who obviously have no money. It was clear that there was an over representation in the judicial system of indigenous people, people of colour and the poor. We must do better!

I greatly appreciated my opportunity to be Critic of the AG. It is true that a non-lawyer will have a different view of the judicial system than the professionals who work in the system every day. My former colleague, Jim Renwick, a brilliant experienced lawyer, when asked about my appointment stated: "We've been trained so long in the same mold we can't always see things in perspective. And we become disdainful of someone who tried to intrude on us."[12] That may well

---

[12] Pat Crowe, *Toronto Star*, March 14, 1979

be true but I was at a serious disadvantage. I didn't know enough about our complex judicial system to offer informed opinions about changes to the law which should be considered. In hindsight what might have worked better would be a "tag team" approach, me as the official critic teamed with a licensed lawyer, either one who was an MPP or one hired as an assistant.

The experience certainly confirmed my feeling that I would have enjoyed being a lawyer. A few years later I had an opportunity to put my interest up against aptitude. In 1995 my daughter Barbara was preparing to write the LSAT (law school admission test), and she asked me to help her by reviewing practice exams. Since a general election was on the horizon perhaps this was a fortunate opportunity to find out if I should consider changing professions, just in case I didn't get re-elected. Struggling through the practice exam provided the message to put away any notion of changing from teacher to lawyer.

I got to know and deeply admire Roy McMurtry. He was a brilliant jurist and a thoughtful, generous man with a warm, welcoming personality. Being appointed Chief Justice of Ontario was well earned, deserved. Ontario's judicial system would be well served. Roy's many accomplishments included introducing province wide Community Legal Services.

We kept in touch over the years. In the fall of 2018, it was a distinct pleasure and privilege for me, as Chair of the Ontario Association of Former Parliamentarians, to present Hon. Roy McMurtry with our Distinguished Service Award.

## Leadership — Michael Cassidy

Following the 1977 election Stephen Lewis stepped down as Party Leader a year later. The Leadership was contested by three Caucus Members; Ian Deans, Mike Breaugh and Michael Cassidy, with Michael winning on the second ballot over Ian Deans. I not only supported Michael. I managed to persuade a major labour leader to swing his block of votes behind my candidate.

Michael Cassidy was elected for one term on Ottawa City Council, four terms at Queen's Park and one term in the House of Commons. He was an accomplished academic and considered to be on the left wing of the Ontario New Democrats.

While Michael was an enthusiastic, dedicated socialist who enjoyed the cut and thrust of political debate he was in the unenviable position of following one of the most remarkable politicians Canada has ever had. There were few, if any, who could match the oratorical skills of Stephen Lewis. Michael Cassidy had a very tough time coming out of the shadow of the previous Leader.

As a member, and as Chief Whip of the NDP Caucus, I always took the position "the Leader is the Leader." I respected Michael, enjoyed his company and admired his tenacity as he worked exceedingly hard to win.

# 10

# A Winter Election — 1981

*"There is no more important commitment that a government can make than to education."*

— Bill Davis

Who in their right mind would call an election in the middle of a typical Canadian winter; deep snow and frigid cold? Well, a Premier, who after four years of minority government had read the tea leaves correctly, that's who.

I had never experienced a winter election up close and personal. Don't pine for another one! So, through February and half of March I trudged door-to-door, assuming that if I continued to work as assiduously now as I had in the past, I would be rewarded with a third consecutive term in office.

I canvassed six and a half days each week. I personally called on about one-third of the riding. The weather was brutal and it got dark early. Knocking on someone's door in the evening sometimes resulted in a guarded, suspicious response. Who would be calling when it was dark and cold outside?

My margin of victory has increased slightly in 1977 from the '75 election. I had got just over 40% of the votes. I was confident that my hard work representing Scarborough Ellesmere would result in success. As the campaign rolled along I sensed that this was going to be a tough one. I worked harder.

Election night was a shocker for me. I won't forget waiting in the campaign office for the results. When it became apparent that I was going to lose I went into the basement where I could vent my frustration by pounding on a wall. Trouping over to where my Progressive Conservative opponent, Alan Robinson, and his supporters were gathered, to concede the election and congratulate Alan on his victory was tough. It was, however, the right thing to do. Civility should always be a bedrock of democracy.

Alan Robinson was the first of three City Councillors who represented Ward Five in my Riding, who provided me with a defeat. The other two were Frank Faubert, Liberal, who later became Mayor of Scarborough, and Marilyn Mushinski, Progressive Conservative.

As painful as it was to face a room full of people who had worked hard to get me un-elected, the next stop was more painful. I had to face a room full of people whom I had let down.

I dreaded entering the hall, anticipating a crowd of mournful supporters. I did not expect a tumultuous, wildly cheering gathering. Two men, one of those who I knew was a badly injured worker, quickly hoisted me up on their shoulders, and carried me to the stage. I stood on the stage, with my wife Pat and our two daughters, Sherri and Barbara, and somehow, fighting back tears, got through a speech. Unfortunately, there was an added layer of discomfort. Ours was considered a "swing riding", hence the television cameras were there. Those camera captured, for thousands of viewers, the sight of my two daughters, ages eight and nine, crying their eyes out. That hurt me more than the loss!

I do remember the conclusion of my speech. "The fight to win back Scarborough Ellesmere starts tomorrow!"

However, the loss by 1,888 votes haunted me for an entire year.

## Self-inflicted anguish

I blamed myself for the election loss. Although I had called on 10,000 doors, I should have been able to knock on more. We had churned out six pieces of literature. The pamphlets should have been more enticing. The riding had never been fertile ground for election signs for any Party. Our total would usually be greater than the other two opponents combined. Maybe we should have replaced all the small signs with large ones near the end of the election period. And, so on. Whatever element of electioneering existed, I should have improved upon it. It all came back to me. I really beat myself up mentally. I just couldn't get past the loss.

I wanted to return to Queen's Park. There was unfinished business, especially related to tenants' rights. Rent control had been achieved, but there was much more in making sure tenants could live in well maintained buildings without fear of arbitrary eviction. My experience as Critic of Colleges and Universities had convinced me to continue fighting for the abolition of student tuition fees.

If you have never visited Queen's Park, you might find this reason for returning to Queen's Park a bit strange. I fell in love with the grand and gracious building the moment I entered the Ontario Legislature. The high vaulted ceilings, the gargoyles, corridors adorned with a wide variety of art, all contributed to creating a delightful atmosphere. That atmosphere was a calming counterpoint to the frenetic, often times emotional debates in the Chamber.

Turning to the practical side of life, the Scarborough Board of Education was terrific. Since it was part way through the academic year, a Chairperson position was not readily available. Yes, I would be happy to be a substitute teacher for a couple of weeks. Not having taught grade one, the two weeks of trying to get snowsuits on kids, and learning that a hand up in the classroom was usually a request for a bathroom break, all came as quite a learning experience. After those two weeks, the Board was able to find me a position for the remainder of the school year, as a Chairperson at Sir Ernest MacMillan Senior Public School. I was then asked where I would like to be in September. "A Senior School I could walk to from my home," was my reply. The result was placement at Henry Kelsey Sr. Public School, a 15 minute walk from our house.

# 11

# A Cliffhanger Election — 1985

***The 1985 election created a seismic shift in provincial politics.***

It was the spring of 1984. There would not likely be a provincial election for another year. After spending a year to come to terms with my 1981 election loss I had started on the comeback trail. The door knocking every Saturday, except holidays, for the past two years by a dedicated band of four had enjoyed an encouraging reception, but that was outside an election. I had a feeling that I could win this one. Then again, in my mind I had won every election regardless of the actual results. No dose of reality could dampen my enthusiasm. I asked the riding association to hold an early nomination meeting, promising that if nominated our hardy foursome would continue canvassing until the next election was called. The association agreed and the nomination meeting was called for Monday, March 26. What unfolded that evening was a surprise and gratifying.

The Scarborough Mirror reported, "Nearly half of the NDP's provincial caucus turned out Monday night to see David Warner acclaimed as the party's Scarborough Ellesmere candidate for the next provincial election. On hand was NDP provincial leader Bob

Rae and fellow MPPs Richard Johnston (Scarborough West), party house leader Jim Foulds, Jack Stokes, former Speaker, Bob McKenzie and a handful of other representatives."[13]

I didn't know my former colleagues would be in attendance or that the meeting would attract 60 people. I should have shown my gratitude by keeping my remarks brief. As noted in the newspaper article, "Mr. Warner took the opportunity to make a particularly lengthy speech in which he attacked the ruling Tory party for what he called their disinterest in social policies."[14] Verbosity aside, the solid support of my caucus colleagues was heartwarming. No one could have got a better emotional boost to keep door knocking for another year.

When, in April 1985, the election was called for May 2nd, our election team was ready and I was looking forward to campaigning, especially debating with Alan Robinson, the PC who had defeated me in '81.

Sadly, gone were the daily, full-house all-candidates' meetings of 1972 and '74. Those politically charged lively debates were replaced with a handful of sparsely attended meetings organized by a community association or a church. One of those meetings was a memorable one arranged by the Catholic Women's League.

John Lydgate, poet, wrote: "You can please some of the people all of the time, you can please all of the people some of the time, but you can't please all of the people all of the time." One of the most difficult things a politician has to do is provide an answer which he knows is not going to please the questioner. Knowing that you have been honest is the balance against disappointing the person who asked the question. Being forthright might engender respect and perhaps electoral support.

I knew before the meeting started that likely the most important issue for the Catholic audience gathered for the all-candidates

---

13 *Scarborough Mirror*, March 28, 1984

14 *Scarborough Mirror*, March 28, 1984

meeting would be abortion. I had a few options. I could ignore the elephant in the room and hope that the issue didn't come up. I could avoid answering directly about my position on abortion by stating that it is a federal responsibility. While that is true, it is also true that access to abortion, having the procedure covered by OHIP, and funding clinics which assist and counsel women about abortion is under the direction and funding of the Ontario government. I did have a third option; to meet the issue head on.

When it was my turn to make opening remarks I stated why I was running, listing the issues featured in the NDP provincial campaign. I paused, then told the audience that while the topic of abortion had not been mentioned yet, I wanted everyone to know my personal position. I explained that I understood that this was an extremely sensitive personal matter. Some will have a deeply held belief that abortion is wrong. I respect that. I have always believed that a woman should have the right to make the difficult decision she faces. I confess that I half expected to be booed or even told to leave. But no, there was polite applause. Now that I had opened up the topic of abortion, my opponents were asked for their opinions. If they skated as well on ice as they did replying to the question, they could play professional hockey! Then something I will never forget. As the event wound down and I was leaving the stage, one of the organizers of the event took me aside and whispered, "Don't worry. You will be alright." After a narrow win on election day I have to wonder if maybe some of those extra votes I needed came from the audience with whom I was candid.

The major issue of the provincial campaign was provided by Premier Davis's bombshell announcement shortly before he retired from politics. Funding for separate schools would be extended to cover grades 11, 12 and 13. This was a hot button issue which was being revisited. The 1971 election featured the Liberals and New Democrats in favour of the extended funding, with the Davis government opposed. The backdrop for providing full funding was an agreement at the time of Confederation, 1867, when Quebec agreed to fully fund protestant schools and Ontario was to do likewise for Catholic schools. Quebec had always kept its part of the bargain. Premier Davis wanted to now make good on that Confederation promise.

The public were not inclined to consider the history of the issue. There was serious push back, especially from traditional conservative supporters. At the door and on the phone, I encountered lots of anger over the decision. I explained that all three Parties had the same policy. That didn't matter. The anger was directed at the Conservatives.

The provincial campaign was unusual in that all three parties had a new leader; PC's Frank Miller, Liberals David Peterson, NDP Bob Rae. The election was unusual in other ways. Anyone born after 1945 had known only Conservative governments. There seemed to be an unwritten rule that only Conservatives should rule. Indeed, going into the election public opinion polling showed that the Tories remained strong. It seems to me that an appetite for change happened during the election period and at least two parties misread the tea leaves. First — the Tories. I liked Frank Miller. Yes, he was on the right wing of the PCs, but he was affable, a listener, had a style which commanded an audience and an engaging sense of humour. With Frank Miller's elevation to Leader came a new, young backroom team, one which did not include any people from the successful Davis era. "(The)Young advisers made a huge mistake when they ordered Miller to stick to the script and avoid talking to the press — a tall order for a man who spoke his mind and got along well with reporters. After the *Globe and Mail* criticized Miller's campaigning style, he told a key adviser, "You have destroyed my relationship with the press and my confidence in myself, and you have done it all in four days."[15]

Next — the New Democrats. The party didn't have much money. "I had to share a bus with the press," he (Bob Rae) recalled. "Someone

15 Jamie Bradburn, *TVO Today*, May 24, 2018

gave me an electric piano, and I drove them crazy with what I thought were clever songs about Frank Miller and the Tories."[16] The New Democrats also misread the tea leaves by assuming the Tories would win. The NDP aimed to finish second and got what they aimed for. Bob Rae disagreed with that approach, but as with all political leaders he deferred to the advisers.

Last (who later would be first) — the Liberals. Their new leader David Peterson created a more urban Liberal party, adopting progressive policies such as pay equity and more funding for child care. The Liberals had a new policy, one which resonated with a lot of younger voters — beer in the corner store. I recall being in line at a local beer store one Saturday evening (I never canvassed Saturday evenings) when a young man rushed into the store looking for his friend, who happened to be right ahead of me in line. "Hey! Are you going to vote?" The reply was "No. Why would I?" "Peterson is going allow beer in the corner stores." The astonished youth standing in front of me blurted, "Wow! Yeah, I'll vote for that!" I have always wanted higher turnouts in elections, but that hardly seemed like the best reason for electing a government.

In Scarborough Ellesmere we ran a vigorous campaign; lots of volunteers, signs, literature and of course continuous door knocking. Good weather was a bonus as this was a long campaign, from March 25 to May 2nd.

The air was electric on Election night in our campaign office. We knew it would be close. Would my three years of campaigning and the separate school funding issue be enough? It took an agonizingly long time for the vote count. When the wait lengthen beyond two hours, I decided to go to the hall where our campaign workers were gathered. If I was going to lose I wanted to be with those who had tried to achieve my return to Queen's Park.

Very late in the evening we got the news. I had almost the same percentage vote as last time; 37.5% in 1981, 37.4% this time.

---

16 Jamie Bradburn, *TVO Today*, May 24, 2018

However, instead of losing by 1,888 votes, I had won by 283 votes. The vagaries of first past the post election system. I was returning to the grand old building I had come to love.

Little did I know that a seismic change in the political life of Ontario was about to occur. Nor, that the next two years would be fascinating and rewarding.

# 12

# A Formal Alliance

## May 29, 1985

The results of Election Day, May 2, 1985, were as follows; Premier Frank Miller's Progressive Conservatives 52, David Peterson's Liberal 48 and Bob Rae's New Democrats 25. It appeared there would be another term of PC minority government. That was not in the cards.

We had several caucus meetings. Opinions and observations came from several sources; the New Democrat Party Executive, organized labour in general and certain unions in particular. The overall consensus of those who made their thoughts known was that this was the opportunity to end 42 years of Conservative governance. There was reluctance to trigger another election right away. There was a suggestion that we negotiate a coalition government with the Liberals. I was in that camp. I argued that since we had approximately one-third of the total Liberals plus NDP, we would have one-third of the Cabinet posts. That way, we could get credit from the public for popular programs. Those who opposed this approach argued that while coalition governments were common in Europe, the concept was alien to Canada. No one would understand or support coalition government here.

Ultimately a plan emerged to forge an agreement with the Liberals, something which would provide electoral stability for at least two years.

Rushing into an agreement with an opponent might not look good for the Party. What was being proposed had never been done in Ontario political history. It could well be that the public would not understand what was happening, especially if it all unfolded too quickly. So, for the sake of appearance and I like to think, civility, it was decided to hold separate talks with first the Conservatives, then with the Liberals.

*May 29, 1985*

There was an official signing, in public, of The Accord by Premier David Peterson and Bob Rae, Leader of the New Democrats. The agreement listed 29 items which must be accomplished and in return a promise that an election would not be called for a minimum of two years. This was the official end of 42 years of Conservative government.

## Accord Details

- Legislation on freedom of information and protection of privacy.
- Reform of the House by strengthening and broadening the role of committees and individual members and increasing public involvement in the legislative process.
- Select Committees will be established to investigate the commercialization of health and social services in Ontario and to study and report on bilateral environmental issues affecting Ontario.
- Changes to broaden the powers of the Public Accounts Committee and the Provincial Auditor to cover current and proposed expenditures and to reiterate the authority

of the Committee to direct investigations of all aspects of public spending.

- Establishment of a Standing Committee on Energy to oversee Ontario Hydro and other energy matters.
- Establishment of a Select Committee on procedures for appointments in the public sector, to recommend changes in the system of recruitment and selection of public appointees
- Election financing reform to cover spending limits and rebates, at both the central and local campaign level.
- Redefinition and broadening of the rights of public service workers to participation in political activity.
- Electronic Hansard (television in the Legislature) .
- Begin implementation of separate school funding. Release present draft legislation immediately. Introduce legislation upon a Liberal government meeting the legislature and refer to Committee for public hearings.
- Introduce programs to create employment and training opportunities for young people.
- Ban extra billing by medical doctors.
- Proclaim the sections of the Environmental Protection Act dealing with spills.
- Reform Ontario's tenant protection laws, including: Establishment of a rent registry. Establishment of a four per cent rent review guideline. Inclusion of the provisions of Bill 198 as a permanent part of the Residential Tenancies Act. Extension of rent review to cover post-1976 buildings. An end to the $750 a month exemption from rent review. Introduction of a rent review procedure to deal with costs-no-longer-borne by landlords. Introduction of enabling legislation to permit demolition control by municipalities.

- Introduce legislation for equal pay for work of equal value in both the public and the private sector.
- Include a first contract law in Ontario labour legislation.
- Introduce reforms to the Occupational Health and Safety Act including toxic substances designation and regulations to give workers the right to know about workplace hazards.
- Continue the pre-budget freeze on the ad valorem gasoline tax and establish an inquiry into gas price differentials between Northern and Southern Ontario.
- Wind up the Royal Commission on the Northern Environment and obtain release of all working papers and reports.
- Provide full coverage of medically necessary travel under OHIP for residents of Northern Ontario.
- Affirmative action and employment equity for women, minorities and the handicapped and expansion of the role and budget of Human Rights Commission to deal with workplace and housing discrimination.
- Establishment of an Ontario housing program to fund immediately 10,000 co-op and non-profit housing units, in addition to those provided for under federal funding arrangements.
- New enforceable mechanisms for the control of pollution to enable Ontario to deal effectively with acid rain and to establish the principle that the polluter pays.
- Reform of services for the elderly to provide alternatives to institutional care and a reform of the present nursing home licensing and inspection system.
- Reform of job security legislation, including notice and justification of layoffs and plant shutdowns and improved severance legislation.
- Farm financing reform, including low interest loans for farmers.

- Workers' compensation reform.
- Private pension reform based on the recommendations of the Ontario Select Committee on Pensions.
- Reform of day care policy and funding to recognize child care as a basic public service and not a form of welfare.
- An independent audit of Ontario's forest resources, and additional programs to provide for on-going regeneration of Ontario's forests.

The list was certainly one to keep all of us occupied for the next 24 months. I was excited to be part of this ambitious, progressive legislative program.

## Leadership — Bob Rae

Michael Cassidy led the Party through the 1981 election. The election results were profoundly disappointing and Michael Cassidy stepped aside. Three candidates stepped up to replace the Leader; Richard Johnston, MPP, Jim Foulds, MPP and Bob Rae, MP.

I was one of a small group of current as well as former MPPs who met with Bob at a downtown hotel in an effort to persuade him to resign his seat as an MP and run for the provincial leadership. What I saw in Bob was a very bright, charismatic leader who possessed a visionary approach to politics. He was also a great listener with a delightful sense of humour.

At the 1982 Leadership Convention Bob Rae won on the first ballot with 64.6% of the vote. In the 1985 election the Party gained only four seats, mine being one them. This poor showing prompted a Leadership Challenge the result of which was Bob Rae achieving 95.3% support.

Through the entire process of discussion, debate, negotiations and the final agreement, An Accord, I saw Bob Rae as a great listener who respected everyone's views, while at the same time being practical.

Since I lost the 1987 election I had only two years of being with Bob in the caucus. They were two remarkable years. I thoroughly enjoyed working with Bob Rae as Leader.

A tradition which goes back a couple of hundred years is that the Speaker does not attend caucus, signalling that the Speaker is neutral in conducting the business of the House. I never got to know what Premier Rae was like in Caucus or Cabinet. What I saw in the House was a Premier trying his best to be Premier of all the people, not just those who voted New Democrat. He was trying to provide inspired leadership during the worst economic times since the Great Depression of the 1930s.

There were a lot of angry New Democrats when Bob decided to take out a Liberal membership. I told Bob that if he was more comfortable playing on another team then that is what he should do. We remain friends and in 2022, as Chair of the Ontario Association of Former Parliamentarians I had the privilege of presenting Bob Rae with our Distinguished Service Award for his extraordinary global, national, and provincial service.

I consider myself fortunate to have worked with two Party Leaders (Stephen Lewis and Bob Rae) who later were appointed as Canada's Ambassador to the United Nations.

# 13

# Look Good for the Cameras

## 1986

Let the people of Ontario see those they elected at work. This was the general sentiment behind bringing television into the Legislature and why it was one of the items in the Accord. The Legislation needed to establish Broadcast/Recording passed second reading and was sent to the Standing Committee on the Legislative Assembly, of which I was a Member. The committee held public meetings and deliberated on various details. We determined that English and French simultaneous translation was essential. We also agreed, based on an excellent, informative presentation by Voice For Hearing Impaired Children that closed captioning would be included in the televised proceedings. We started with one hour per day of captioning service. By 1990 the Assembly was able to provide real time captioning of all proceedings in the House. TV monitors displaying real time captioning were installed in the public galleries. In 1991, Bill Sommerville, Director of Broadcast Recording could claim "The Ontario Legislature is a world leader in the provision of services for the deaf and hard of hearing."[17]

---

[17] Voice Ontario Newsletter, Fall 1991

Televised broadcasts of the House and one committee room began during the fall of 1986 on our own television channel. Since then, thanks to technological advances and the visionary leadership of Bill Sommerville, then Michael Donofrio, as of October 2021, the televising and streaming of all proceedings of the Legislative Assembly of Ontario began. This included the House, Amethyst Committee Room, Committee Rooms 1 and 2, the Media Studio and Committees travelling in Ontario. Whenever a Committee travels to cities or towns across Ontario, the proceedings are broadcast and or streamed live, gavel to gavel, with closed captions and interpretation. These proceedings can be found live on the Legislative Assembly's Parlance App for IOS and Android devises as well as the Assembly website.

Bill Sommerville and Michael Donofrio, as Directors of Broadcast Recording have truly provided a window on democracy in action.

In 1986 low light cameras were not available so that in turn meant Members should choose their colours wisely. White apparel could create glare. Powder blue was ideal. A single colour was better than a multi-coloured clothing. While sartorial splendour was not an objective there was an interest in looking your best for the camera. I think a few members saw this as an opportunity to showcase their wardrobe. I recall lessons on how to address the camera as well as being aware that the microphones could pick up the voice of a person sitting next to the member who has the floor.

Not every Member was excited about the advent of television in the House. There were reservations about possible negative effects. Would Members simply play to the cameras? Well, yes. Some, instead of the parliamentary practice of facing the Speaker, would turn and look directly at one of the cameras. There were five cameras, two on each side of the Chamber and one directly over the entrance to the Chamber. That camera always focused on the Speaker. When Members knew that one of them was scheduled for a speech, five or six others would sit right beside or directly behind the speech giver's chair, providing the image that the House was full. Being concerned about the camera led to more scripted questions and replies. There was a loss of spontaneity.

There were some unexpected, but nonetheless positive outcomes. The dinner break on Tuesdays and Thursdays meant that some Members would arrive for the evening sitting having consumed perhaps a glass or two more wine than they should have. Realizing that one might end up being featured on parliamentary television either curbed excess imbibing or encouraged the Member to stay out of the Chamber if they weren't on house duty. As well, knowing that people would see you on television did result in Members being more nattily attired.

There was and still is a sizable viewing audience. I recall, from my time as Speaker, being assisted by an active audience. One Member was vocally disruptive on an almost daily basis. Then, one day the Member became silent. I learned later that the Member had received phone calls from constituents who had watched Question Period on our Parliamentary channel, requesting that their Member have a more respectful demeanour in the House.

I was Speaker when I had an opportunity to reach out to an indigenous community. The Sioux Lookout hockey tournaments take place early January. It is an important local event, with thousands of people gathering in Sioux Lookout for days or even a couple of weeks. I fielded a request to have our parliamentary channel carry the hockey tournaments. There wasn't another television option for those living in the area of Sioux Lookout. Since the House does not normally sit in January this was a rare opportunity to connect with indigenous people. I gave the approval. Word travels around the Pink Palace quicker than than a prairie fire with a tailwind. At least one MPP was not happy about my decision. "What is parliamentary about televising a hockey game?, asked the member. I provided a succinct reply, "What is parliamentary is whatever the Speaker says is parliamentary." I understood the member's concern that the parliamentary channel should be used only to cover parliamentary events. Technically we might be in breach of our broadcast licence should anyone complain to the CRTC (Canadian Radio-Television and Telecommunications Commission). I was willing to take that risk. Trying to reach out to Indigenous communities was the greater good.

In return for agreeing to broadcasting I was invited to attend and drop the puck at the first game. What an honour. Bill Sommerville, Director of Broadcast Recording and I flew to Thunder Bay, then by small plane to Dryden, rented a car and drove from there.

We received a joyous, warm welcome. It was explained that although about 3,000 people would be in town for the tournaments, there were many who would not be able to attend. Thanks to use of the parliamentary channel those not attending would be able to watch the games on television. As I dropped the puck to signal the start of the first tournament I smiled. The decision to televise was a good one. The long trip to Sioux Lookout was well worth the effort. It was an even longer trip back to Toronto as our flight from Dryden to Thunder Bay was cancelled due to the pilot having come down with chicken pox and there was no substitute pilot. We rented a car and had a beautiful drive to Thunder Bay, stopping to gaze appreciatively at beautiful Kakabecka Falls.

# 14

# Seniors Independence Act

## 1986

*Caring for those who once cared for us is a responsibility and an honour.*

The sentiment expressed above was the driving force for me when I waded in to the world of elder care during my previous term in office (1977–81). First hand experiences, informed sources, research and a bit of sleuthing led me to discover shocking realities. Where I found abuses I sought redress. The more I got involved, the more information flowed my direction. I soon realized that what was needed was a public inquiry into the operation of for-profit nursing homes. There were two incidents in particular which stood out as "the tip of the iceberg."

I was contacted by a retired nursing home inspector. He was profoundly upset by what he had witnessed as an inspector and even more upset that no action was taken on the detailed report he had filed. The inspector wanted my assurance, which I provided, that his name would not be revealed for fear of potential repercussions. He went on to describe that, based on complaints, he sat in his car outside a nursing home in the early hours of the morning, waiting and watching. Sure enough, true to the complaints he'd received at about four a.m. the lights started systematically coming on, room after room until all the lights were on. Into the nursing home he went to see for himself that the residents were being woken at four a.m. to have their breakfast. The home was purposely short staffed as a way to help maximize profits. My response to the retired inspector was, "If anyone woke me up at four a.m. to have breakfast they'd be wearing it!"

One appointment I had at my constituency office was a woman who told me she just couldn't continue going to work knowing she was a fraud. The woman explained that she was trained as a Nurse's Aide and applied as such to Kennedy Lodge Nursing Home (located in my riding). The management said she would be hired provided she wore a physiotherapist badge. Of course she would be paid as a Nurse's Aide. I thanked her for the information and said I would be only too happy to follow up, however even if I didn't reveal her name the nursing home would find out it was her and she would be fired. The response reassured me that this was a person of good character. "Don't worry about me being fired. I am quitting. I can't pretend I am something which I'm not." Prior to raising this deception in the House, I contacted a reporter, revealed the story, then added that I wouldn't be surprised if the management were taking other shortcuts in order to increase profits. Would the reporter be willing to accompany me on an unofficial, surprise visit to the home. The two of us surreptitiously wandered around the building checking the posted menu (were there healthy alternatives), trying to determine if there were an appropriate number of Registered Nurses (one per floor), was the place clean etc. Our inspection didn't last long before being discovered and ordered out of the building. The physiotherapist story became public and the home had to clean up its act. Later on Kennedy Lodge was sold to new owners.

What bothered me deeply about the two episodes described above was the nagging feeling that shortcuts and abuses in the for profit homes were far more prevalent than anyone would believe. The quest for larger profits will do that. In case anyone doubted the difference in level of care between profit, non-profit and municipally run long term care facilities, the pandemic lay bare the discrepancies. An in-depth study conducted by a team of scientists and medical doctors, published in the Canadian Medical Association Journal found that, "The crude rate of deaths of LTC home residents from COVID-19 was 23.4 per thousand among for-profit homes, 18.2 per thousand among nonprofit homes, and 5.8 per thousand among municipal homes."[18]

Thoughtful loving care of our youngest and oldest is an essential part of being a caring society. Since anything which is truly important should never be entrusted to private hands, it stands to reason that child care programs and long term facilities should not be run for profit. When it comes to seniors there is so much more which can and should be done beside having not-for-profit homes. Out society seems to focus on what older people can't do instead of what they can do.

During my 1981 to 1985 sabbatical the NDP Caucus had struck a task force on care of the elderly. In 1984 the task force produced a report, "Aging With Dignity."

"Until Ontario develops a system which responds to the needs of seniors, rather than insisting that seniors respond to the demands of the system, the Ontario government will be guilty of adding unnecessary misery to the lives of our elderly."[19] The report listed 56 recommendations, all of them designed to help create a better life path for our elders.

I went a step further beyond that excellent report and researched 26 countries, most of them in western Europe. The information I gleaned from various sources was deeply disturbing. It was as if we

---

18 *Canadian Medical Association Journal*, August 17, 2020

19 "Aging With Dignity", report of the NDP Caucus Task Force, Caring for Seniors, June 1984

as a nation had decided that when someone reached age 65 they should stop trying to live independently. The information, especially from Nordic countries was quite compelling and overwhelming. It was clear that when senior citizens have the opportunity to remain in familiar surroundings, they live longer, have a better quality of life, enjoy life more, and participate more fully. They feel useful, wanted, and loved. The moment we begin institutionalizing is the moment of decline in emotional health as well as in physical health. Additionally, from a cost analysis point of view, institutional care is the most expensive form of care. The state can provide an array of services and programs which include home care, homemaker services, day care, develop local health and social service centres, support for the care givers, and the cost to the public will be less than the alternative reliance on long term care institutions. More importantly, the older person will retain that sense of independence and self worth which is so vital to a happy, healthy life.

I was satisfied with the final draft of my Private Member's Bill and excited about the impending debate. Should the Bill pass second reading and sent to Committee there was a chance during this Accord parliament for a major change in how we treat our elderly in Ontario.

May 29, 1986 The day had arrived. My Private Member's Bill was up for debate. It had been a team effort; researcher Penny Gerrie, Grant Cassidy, Head of Caucus Research, Robert Gardner, the assistant chief, legislative counsel. The Bill was a natural outcome of an NDP Task Force Report "Aging With Dignity".

## Bill 3

### An Act for the Provision and Integration of Community Based Services for Seniors

"The question is, why can seniors not live independently? We have done a very curious thing in our country. Over many decades we have found it expedient to institutionalize senior citizens. Canada has, as we all sadly know, one of the highest rates of institutionalization of seniors of any country in the world. In the early 1980's, the Canadian Medical Association reported that 9.5 per cent of people over 65 in Canada are put into institutions, compared with five per cent in the United Kingdom, 5.3 per cent in the United States and 5.9 per cent in Australia."[20] The 2011 census revealed that the figure for Canada was now 7.9%. There has been some improvement.

My Bill created a framework for the provision of community based support services for seniors and the integration of these services with established programs and facilities. The intention was that support services would give seniors greater independence and prevent their unnecessary institutionalization by giving them access to programs that would assist them in carrying out day-to-day tasks.

I was thanked by various members on both sides of the aisle for my initiative and leadership. I had strong support from municipalities around the province. Bill 3 passed second reading and was referred to the Standing Committee on Social Development. Although my Bill never made it on to the agenda of the Committee, various aspects of the Seniors' Independence Act have been enacted over the intervening years.

That said, we in Canada still not only institutionalize a frightfully large percentage of the older population, but tolerate horrible conditions in long term care facilities. The COVID19 pandemic, 2020-22 revealed those horrid conditions, especially in the for-profit sector. Our society must do better!

---

[20] Mr. Warner, Hansard May 29, 1986

# 15

# Extra Billing by Doctors

The issue of doctors having the right to bill above the OHIP rate had been brewing for a while. It was an emotional issue for those on both sides of the debate.

The ban originated in 1980 when Justice Emmett Hall recommended making extra-billing illegal because it reduced access to care for poorer patients. "If extra-billing is permitted as a right and practised by physicians in their sole discretion, it will, over the years, destroy the program."[21] In 1984, the federal government unanimously passed the Canada Health Act, which required provinces to meet certain principles in order to receive transfer payments for health care; one principle was the abolition of extra-billing.

As a backdrop to the debate about extra billing the national principles that govern the Canadian health insurance system should be noted; universality, public administration, comprehensiveness, portability and accessibility.

---

21 Malcolm G. Taylor, *Health Insurance and Canadian Public Policy: The Seven Decisions That Created the Canadian Health Insurance System and Their Outcomes* [Montréal and Kingston: McGill—Queen's University Press, 1987], p. 429

Starting July 1, 1984, the federal government would penalize provinces by withholding its payments by one dollar for each dollar extra-billed. Provinces could recover these monies, without interest, if they banned extra-billing by Apr. 1, 1987. Provinces continuing to permit extra-billing would lose the right to recover withheld funds. By June 7, 1986 the penalty for Ontario had reached 100 million dollars. This threat, coupled with widespread public opposition to extra-billing, compelled the provinces to comply.

Legislating an end to extra billing was one of the Liberal/New Democrat Accord items. Bill 94, the Health Care Accessibility Act was guaranteed passage, but not without turmoil. There were doctor rallies in front of Queen's Park, and then, on June 12, 1986, Ontario physicians walked out on strike to protest the province's imminent ban on extra-billing. It was the longest physicians' strike in Canadian history. The strike did not gain significant public support. Bill 94 was passed on July 5, 1986. The strike ended two days later.

All three Parties understood the significance of the issue, that there needed to be an open full debate. Public opinion was in favour of ending the practice of extra billing. Many doctors were angry. "Dr. William Vail, President of the Ontario Medical Association, stated, "We can hear the wolves howling. Bill 94 is perceived as a very serious threat to the physician's professional freedom, as a threat to the physician's ability to serve as a completely independent advocate for the patient and as a threat to the physician's ultimate ethical responsibility." [22]

Just as the doctors of Ontario were divided on the issue, so too were the politicians. Cabinet Ministers, backbenchers, veteran MPPs, all had an opportunity to put their thoughts on the record:

---

22 Malcolm G. Taylor, *Health Insurance and Canadian Public Policy: The Seven Decisions That Created the Canadian Health Insurance System and Their Outcomes* [Montréal and Kingston: McGill—Queen's University Press, 1987]

Minister Lily Oddie Munro, Liberal — "What do we mean by "accessibility"? We mean accessibility of patients to a health care system which is not differentiated based on socioeconomic status. Extra billing jeopardizes accessibility. It introduces the danger of a two-tiered system based on two sets of rules."[23]

George Ashe, former Cabinet Minister, Conservative — "We have a government that in the past let on it was one of the parties of the free enterprise system, a party of the people and a party of open government. Yet they come forward with this draconian, socialist legislation. That is what it is. It is down the path to socialism."[24]

Dave Cooke, Health Critic, New Democrat - "It was the New Democratic Party that in 1979 introduced the largest petition ever circulated in Ontario and presented in the Ontario Legislature, with the signatures of more than 250,000 people opposed to extra billing in this province. Today, it is very clear from polls that have been done and by talking to our own constituents that there is a consensus in Ontario and that consensus is overwhelmingly in favour of making extra billing illegal."[25]

I eagerly participated in the debate, reminding the House that in the pre-Medicare days my grandparents had to sell the family home in order to pay the medical bills associated with my grandmother's decade long serious illness. I recognized the complications of the issue, while asserting my strong support for Bill 94.

"There are doctors in Ontario who support the notion that the extra billing provision should end, and they have stated so publicly. There are doctors who maintain that extra billing should not end, that this is an infringement on their rights, privileges and freedoms and a very wrong thing to do. There are doctors who have never extra billed but support the concept and support their colleagues who do extra bill. I dare say there are some doctors who are currently extra

23 Hon. Ms. Munro, Hansard, June 20, 1986

24 Mr. Ashe, Hansard, June 20, 1986

25 Mr. D. S. Cooke, Hansard, January 14, 1986

billing who are quite prepared to live with the prospect of not being able to do so."[26]

Modern day parliaments have a myriad of issues, a seemingly endless list of legislation to consider, so debates are usually time limited. In a cooperative atmosphere the three parties come to an agreement on how much time to be allotted. I wasn't privy to the discussions regarding time allocation for Bill 94, but I anticipated that given a doctors strike and the chaos caused by the strike, there needed to be as full an airing of the issues as possible. "During the strike, clinics and emergency wards were closed, and appointments and surgeries were cancelled. Reports of patient maltreatment littered the newspapers. "Hospital turns away bleeding tot," read one front-page headline.[5] Newspapers printed advice for what to do when people needed medical care, and they published maps showing which emergency departments remained open. Physicians at York County Hospital in Newmarket, Ont., passed a motion to withdraw "all" services, even in life-threatening situations. The Ontario Medical Association condoned, as "protest strategy," the closure of intensive care units and entire hospitals. Patients waiting in emergency departments described anger, resignation and fear."[27]

Essentially any Member who wanted to participate could do so, but asked to be reasonably brief. The debate started 6:26 pm, June 19th and continued for almost 19 hours straight without a recess, concluding at 1:12 pm, June 20th. It was as highly charged an atmosphere as I had seen in my time as a Member, save for the 1976 debate on the mandatory use of seat belts in cars. During this historic debate there was a seemingly innocuous event, a note sent

---

26 David Warner, Hansard, January 17, 1986

27 Educating Future Physicians for Ontario and the physicians' strike of 1986: the roots of Canadian competency-based medical education by Hissan Butt, BA and Jacalyn Duffin MD, PhD — Canadian Medical Association Journal, February 20, 2018

across the floor, which sparked a decades long friendship. That is a story which I tell later in the book.

In the midst of overheated rhetoric from some politicians and the OMA (Ontario Medical Association) I had an unusual opportunity to use some of the political skills I had acquired of diplomacy, listening and organizing. Two Scarborough General Hospital doctors came to see me about something which had nothing to do with Bill 94. What happened next was a challenge which I fully embraced. That story will unfold in the next chapter.

# 16

# Hemodialysis

In the midst of the emotional debate on extra billing by doctors I received a call from a Scarborough General Hospital doctor. He wanted to know if, even though there was currently a dispute between doctors and the "Accord government," would I be willing to talk with him about a serious medical issue. "Of course," I responded.

Dr. Paul Tam, accompanied by another doctor arrived at my constituency office. I wasn't sure what to expect. Relations between most doctors and New Democrats was strained to say the least. The extra billing legislation and the doctors strike had taken a toll on civility.

A big smile accompanied by a firm handshake and a warm greeting was how I met Dr. Tam for the first time. He then explained that there was a desperate need for a Hemodialysis unit at the hospital. The Ministry of Health had not approved the unit. Scarborough General administration was generously supporting the doctor's unit out of unallocated funds, but what was really needed was official approval so that a proper dialysis unit could be established. "I am practicing third world medicine here," stated the doctor. "Would you come to the hospital and see for yourself?"

I took him up on his offer to visit the hospital and see the situation for myself. During the visit he explained that there was no dialysis program between downtown Toronto and Kingston, Ontario. The informative visit and Doctor Tam's passionate plea was convincing. I needed to do something to convince the government to approve the necessary funding.

I started a campaign. Over the following months I went door-to-door in the riding, asking people to sign a card urging the government to fund a dialysis unit at Scarborough General Hospital. What I quickly discovered was that the moment I mentioned this was for Scarborough General, my constituents would respond, "Where do I sign?"

"Petitioning the Crown" is a tradition dating back to 13th century British Parliament. It is a way to bring an issue to the attention of the government and the media. Time is allotted each day, when the House is sitting, for the presentation of petitions. Every time I accumulated 100 or more "dialysis cards", I would table them in the House. Day by day, month after month, I kept knocking on doors, accumulating more cards. Every sitting day, for months, I would table bundles of petition cards and announce the new total. Although I tabled more than 10,000 cards it was to no avail. I couldn't get approval for the much needed dialysis unit.

The happy ending to this story did not occur until 1997, more than 10 years after that fateful meeting with Dr. Paul Tam, an extraordinary doctor whose primary focus was on doing the best he could for his dialysis patients. Dr. Tam very graciously invited me to a celebratory dinner held at a local hotel and asked me to make a few remarks.

Working with Dr. Paul Tam was a wonderful experience. It is amazing what can be achieved even when there is a volatile political atmosphere.

# 17

# Committees are Integral to Developing Good Legislation, and Can Be a Bridge Across the Aisle

*"When you listen, it's amazing what you can learn. When you act on what you've learned, it's amazing what you can change."*

— Audrey McLaughlin

The committee stage of a Bill should be an opportunity for both the government members and opposition to consider potential improvements to the legislation. No one corners the market on wisdom. This should be a time for discussion instead of debate.

After having been a member of a dozen parliamentary committees I propose that (a) every newly elected MPP needs to sit on a committee shortly after arriving at Queen's Park, (b) every committee should travel outside of Toronto at least a few times, preferably near the start of their deliberations, (c) a commitment made that every committee will try to avoid having votes; arriving at most decisions by consensus.

Mike Breaugh, a caucus colleague, was Chair of the ABC (Agencies, Boards and Commissions) Committee. When I was about to join the committee Mike spoke to me privately, informing me that the committee tried to reach decisions by consensus. If I wasn't comfortable with that approach I shouldn't join them. "My preferred way of doing things," was my response. What followed was a great experience!

Interestingly three of the committees on which I served between 1985 and '87 had a direct influence on me when I was Speaker.

## Cross-border diplomacy

I had the privilege of serving on two committees chaired by Mike Breaugh. Mike was an absolutely superb Chair. He not only set the tone for civil discussion, but was always open to creative suggestions from committee members.

One of his initiatives was aimed at developing closer working relations with our neighbours to the south. The National Conference of State Legislatures was created by state legislators and legislative staff in 1975. This organization brought together State House Representatives and State Senators from all 50 States of the US once a year. Our committee agreed that by attending we would have an opportunity to develop a closer working relationship with a number of states, especially those bordering Ontario. So, off to New Orleans, Louisiana we went to the 1986 Convention.

The Superdome was a state of the art enclosed stadium when it was built in 1975. It was the home of the New Orleans Saints Football Team. This cavernous facility housed the Convention. The scene was somewhat overwhelming, but eventually we were able to connect with quite a few of our southern neighbours. The connections meant we could explore topics of cross-border interest.

When I became Speaker in 1990, the New Orleans experience prompted me to try and fashion a similar group, but limited to Ontario's immediate neighbours. The result was the

Midwest-Canada Relations Committee. A detailed description is found in Chapter 24: Challenges I Set for Myself, Relations with our American Neighbours.

## There are Members who care about our grand and gracious Legislature

Remo Mancini, Norm Sterling and I were three members on the Standing Committee on the Legislative Assembly who cared about the condition of our Assembly. It became apparent to a number of members that the Legislature was in need of repair. We didn't know much about restoration, but we did know that if we were to start lobbying for repairs we needed to know what we were talking about. The three of us approached our intrepid Chair, Mike Breaugh with a proposition; namely that since the three of us represented the three Parties, could we form a sub-committee and be granted permission to embark on a fact-finding mission to two nearby legislatures who had recently completed restoration projects. We would return with written reports, ones which we hoped would convince the government that restorative work on the Pink Palace needed to happen and as soon as possible.

Mike granted us permission to travel to Pennsylvania's capitol, Harrisburg and Albany, the capitol of New York State. The visits turned out to be quite instructive. The senior staff in Harrisburg explained that while preparing the area for restoration they came across some Civil War banners, those that would have been carried by the troops from Pennsylvania. Those banners had been restored. We saw them on display in the Capitol building. Staff of both Legislatures impressed on us the need to go cautiously with restoration. You never know what you will find and it is too easy to make a mistake.

During my term as Speaker we undertook a $100 million renovation and restoration; the roof, 5th floor which had been closed by the Fire Marshall in the 1940's. Our beloved Pink Palace turned

100 in 1993. One of the activities for the centennial year included the placement of a time capsule in one of the decorative copper finials on the roof of the building, to be opened in 2093. Throughout the restorative process the information garnered from those sub-committee visits to Harrisburg and Albany were helpful.

## Turned out to be an important sub-committee for me

There was an interest, mostly with the Liberals and New Democrats that it was time to have a new Clerk, and if possible one who was fluent in both our official languages. The task of finding a suitable candidate was on the agenda of the Standing Committee on the Legislative Assembly, Chaired by Mike Breaugh. Mike, in turn asked for three volunteers to form a sub-committee. The same intrepid trio who had toured two US Capitol buildings said they would be glad to take on the challenge. Being Clerk of the Ontario Legislature is a prestigious position so in short order our nation wide posting attracted quite a few applicants. In the end we settled on Claude DesRosiers who had been Principal Clerk at the Table, House of Commons in Ottawa.

On November 19, 1990 when I was elected Speaker, I was anxious about a number of things, but not about the Clerk. After all, I had hired him. He must be good!

## Visiting the "Jewel of the North"

Minaki Lodge, formerly part of the chain of Canadian National Hotels, was originally built in 1914 by the Grand Trunk Pacific Railway to be part of a coast to coast chain of luxury stopovers; Hotel Frontenac (Quebec City), Chateau Laurier (Ottawa), Royal York Hotel (Toronto), Vancouver Hotel (Vancouver), Empress Hotel (Victoria). Easy to imagine that the grandeur of these hotels greatly enhanced the journey. The train enjoyed a place of prominence until after World War Two. The combination of attractive travel options such as the automobile and airplane with the railways giving freight precedent over passenger service meant Minaki Lodge suffered financially. The Ontario government ended up owning this "Jewel of the North," reasoning that the hotel was important for tourism, hence jobs, in the beautiful but sparsely populated north-west region of the province. They ended up pouring $50 million into the hotel.

In 1985 it wasn't clear to the public and certainly not to our committee just how much public money was spent on the hotel, what loans were outstanding etc. We needed to see the place for ourselves and we needed to see the books. The visit to Minaki made it easy to understand why, after train travel was no longer "King" the hotel could not be successful. Aside from the lodge itself there was nothing else around. A ski hill had been constructed at an attempt to attract the ski crowd. The main building had some rooms, but the majority of the rooms were in a separate building with no connection to the main lodge. A modest size convention could be held in the building, but those knowledgeable about the convention business explained that usually those attending a convention like to have somewhere to meander after a full business day. It took some pressure, including the threat of issuing a Speaker's Warrant, to have the financial information produced.

I won't subject the reader to the myriad of the business complications which we unearthed. A statement by Minister Eakins, December 8, 1986, when he announced the sale of Minaki to Four Seasons Hotels Ltd cited, among other disturbing details, "The lack of diligence after the lodge was acquired extended to other matters as well. From 1974 to mid-1985, unauthorized decisions were made because of the lack of a properly constituted quorum of the Minaki board. Between 1980 and 1982, some directors were appointed without holding required directors' shares.

In 1980, the charter of the two companies lapsed because of a failure to obtain a certificate under the Canada Business Corporations Act. This problem was not addressed until January 1986, when articles of revival were filed with the federal government.

During this same period, the board's decision-making practices were also inconsistent with the Canada Business Corporations Act.

From 1974 to the appointment of a new board in January 1986, the vast majority of nominee shareholders did not sign appropriate declarations that their shares were held in trust and did not properly endorse their shares upon resignation from the companies.

From 1980 to 1986, the minute books of the two Minaki companies were not properly maintained. For example, the minutes of the two companies were not prepared into separate books and thus were not properly approved by each board of directors."[28]

It was understandably awkward for the Conservative members on the committee. The evidence was overwhelming that some bad economic decisions were made by the former Conservative government. On the good news side, there was no evidence of malfeasance, only a desire to improve tourism for the region and of course the jobs.

In addition to feeling good about coming away with a solid, detailed report, the visit to Minaki had provided an opportunity to get to know my parliamentary colleagues. A bonus was an early morning fishing trip with a couple of colleagues. One of us caught a pickerel which the chef cooked for our breakfast. Freshly cooked pickerel with freshly squeezed lime over it is absolutely delicious!

## Sunday shopping

The Retail Business Holidays Act was introduced by the Progressive Conservatives in 1975. The act was intended, as Solicitor General John McBeth noted, "to slow the growing commercialism and materialism about us."[29] Designed to act as a check on those municipalities that allowed Sunday shopping, the law established

---

28 Hansard, House document, December 8, 1986

29 Jamie Bradburn, *TVO Today*, December 27, 2018

fines of up to $10,000 for businesses that opened on Sundays or on eight statutory holidays.

Ancient history now. Shopping is possible 24/7, 365 days (add one for a leap year) in person. Of course on-line shopping has turned the retail business on its head. In 1975 however John McBeth wasn't alone in his view that family values were at risk of being severely eroded. John found support for his view on both sides of the aisle.

A Select Committee was struck to consider the legislation and I was a member. A collegial atmosphere prevailed. Political partisanship was never an issue. John McBeth, a deeply respected Member, had struck a chord which resonated with most of us in the House. When the issue was first raised I sent out a questionnaire to my constituents, asking if they were in favour of Sunday shopping. The results startled me. I had over 10,000 replies; 40% in favour of Sunday shopping, 40% against, 10% who were undecided. I had argued in the House and elsewhere that there were only so much money which would be spent shopping. If not during seven days, then six day. No need to have a seventh day available to purchase. As well, the extra day created hardships for family run businesses; either the family works seven days or has to hire part-time staff. Regardless of the decision, family life was being negatively affected.

The day I proposed to be one of the eight statutory holidays was Boxing Day. No sooner had that become common knowledge and I was the recipient of a small flood of heart-felt thank you phone calls and letters. Typical messages: "In 20 years I have always had to work December 26. It really spoiled the Christmas holidays, but I had no choice.", "My whole family thanks you!", "I work in retail. There are lots of extra hours up to the 24th, then back in to the store on the 26th. Having the 26th off is a life saver. Thank you."

Over the years corporations and individuals challenged the law in court or simply ignored the law, preferring to pay the fine. Toronto furrier Paul Magder, Edwards Books and Art, and Longo's attempted to have the act overturned, but the Supreme Court of Canada ruled against them in 1986. In his decision, Chief Justice

Brian Dickson wrote that "the desirability of enabling parents to have regular days off work in common with their child's day off from school, and with a day off enjoyed by most other community and family members is self-evident."[30]

The NDP government revised the act in 1991. Shopping on Sundays in December and on Boxing Day was still off limits, and the maximum fine for opening was raised to $50,000. But retailers continued to ignore the law — many felt that if they didn't, their competitors would come out ahead. Raising the fines had little effect, so the following year the ban was repealed, except for Boxing Day.

In 1996 the Act was found by the court to violate our Charter of Rights and Freedoms. On December 17 of that year the Ontario government ended the ban on Boxing Day shopping.

December 26 has always been a holiday for me, so there was nothing personal about having that day a statutory holiday. I believe that the reasoning I set out in 1975 holds. Families, even someone who lives alone, would be better off not having to work on Boxing Day. The Gods of Commerce reigned. My good thoughts and actions all for nought, except for a short while a well-earned respite came to some people on December 26.

## Select Committee on Health Care, Financing And Costs

### 1978

When Treasurer Darcy McKeough included, as part of his 1978 budget, a 37.5% increase in the health care premium, he created a political storm. The storm resulted in a much lower increase and the creation of a Select Committee on financing and costs. The Chair initially was Dr. Bob Elgie, a lawyer, neurosurgeon, former Chief of Staff at Scarborough General Hospital. Bob was absolutely the

---

[30] Jamie Bradburn, *TVO Today*, December 27, 2018

perfect choice as Chair. Thoughtful, knowledgeable and a great listener, Bob was never blinded by political partisanship. Unhappily for our committee, during our deliberations Bob was promoted to Cabinet. His replacement was Bruce McCaffrey who filled in most admirably.

While the committee did not reach consensus on abandoning the premium system of raising revenue I think the issue was sufficiently high profile, with both the Liberals and New Democrats pushing for a change to a revenue system based on ability to pay (ie. income tax) that a change became inevitable. Perhaps my Magna Carta approach was part of the catalyst for change.

Our committee tackled the thorny question of user fees which were seen by some as a way to prevent a frivolous use of our health care system; unnecessary visits to the doctor or the hospital. Anecdotal information of abuse of the system was presented to the committee. That information was found baseless. "On the contrary, evidence provided by Dr. Carolyn Tuohy, based on a recent survey of nearly 600 Ontario physicians, indicates that only about 10 per cent of services provided were not medically necessary in the opinion of the physician. Interestingly, the same survey indicated that a higher percentage of patients, about 12 per cent, waited too long before seeking medical attention."[31]

## Lab coat and clipboard

An ER doctor who appeared before our committee asserted that the majority of patients he saw during the overnight shift at his hospital were not in need of emergency care. A user fee would deter this inappropriate use of the hospital. I challenged the doctor about the inappropriate use of the hospital. The doctor and I had quite a

---

31 Pg. 36, Report of the Select Committee on Health-Care, Financing and Costs, October 17, 1978

discussion the result of which was the doctor saying that I should come to the hospital and see for myself. I accepted the challenge.

The overnight shift at the Emergency Ward was interesting. Wearing a white lab coat and brandishing a clip board I asked people, after identifying myself, why they were at the ER. By early morning I had results which did not surprise me. The overwhelming majority of patients were there because of a recorded message they heard when they called their family doctor, "This office closes at five pm. Please go to your closest hospital."

Our committee, with lots of relevant data reached a conclusion about deterrent fees. "The problem with deterrent fees, then, is that in general they cannot be expected to deter very much, but in particular they may deter altogether the wrong people."[32]

The committee didn't include my personal ER stint in the final report, but I felt good about meeting the doctor's challenge. When a doctor states something as a 'fact' people tend to believe it.

I thoroughly enjoyed committee work. Each experience brought something special. Top of the list for me was the Justice Committee and the Family Law Reform Act. Every committee I served on afforded opportunities to make useful legislative contributions. Committee work also provided the atmosphere conducive to developing friendships.

---

32 pg. 36 Report of the Select Committee on Health-Care, Financing and Costs, October 17, 1978

# 18

# The Most Satisfying Committee Work of My Career

The first Bill tabled in the legislature by the new Peterson government was the Family Law Reform Act. Sometimes the first Bill is a pro forma one, a Bill which will not be acted upon, but rather expresses the independence of parliament. The Bill bearing Ian Scott's name as Attorney General was no such Bill, nor was it one of the Accord items.

Ian Scott, who had a reputation as a brilliant lawyer, was elected for the first time in 1985. He would remain as Attorney General until the NDP election victory of 1990. His many reforms to the administration of justice, which included an independent panel to recommend judicial appointments to make sure the job went to the most qualified, earned him the Order of Canada in 1994. Sadly, that same year he suffered a stroke which removed his ability to speak. When I visited Ian at his home I couldn't help but think that nothing could be more cruel to a brilliant, accomplished orator and lawyer than to not have the power of speech. Ian passed away in 2006.

I knew Ian Scott from Question Period and observing him in debate. He impressed me as brilliant orator and someone with whom

I would not want to debate. He didn't suffer fools lightly, but he was a good listener. The longer our committee sat, the more impressed I was with this man who at one time considered running for the NDP. Straight forward questions were responded to in a straight forward manner. Trying to be "cute," witty or sarcastic didn't work. I soon found that I enjoyed working with Ian Scott.

Evelyn Gigantes was the NDP lead on the Justice Committee. Right from the start is was evident that Evelyn had studied the legislation closely. She could critique the Bill with great precision, clause by clause. It was easy to infer that she was a lawyer or at least had legal training. Such was not the case. That made two of us. At the risk of appearing boastful, I think our tandem approach was successful in helping to fashion an excellent piece of legislation.

Later on during this Parliament Evelyn would be successful in amending the Human Rights Code to include prohibiting discrimination on the basis of sexual orientation, a story told later on in the book — by a government MPP. It was a privilege to work along side this brilliant, determined and talented woman who pursued social justice issues with a deep seated passion.

It was maddening to hear the heart wrenching stories which revealed just how badly many women were treated and how, when they sought remedy, the legal system was of little or no help. Many of the testimonies had a familiar theme. Husband and wife were married for 10 to 15 years. The wife stayed at home and raised two or more children. The husband left the marriage for a much younger woman. If the abandoned wife was lucky she ended up with the house, but there was no share of investments, pensions or even bank accounts (other than any joint accounts). Having been out of the work force for a number of years this now single mom found it extremely difficult to acquire a suitable job. If she did find work, child care was usually a serious issue. She might get child support without going to court, but that is a roll of the dice. It didn't take a genius to realize that changes were needed. I am guessing here, but I think that Ian Scott convinced Premier Peterson that the first Bill to be introduced in this new Parliament would be the Family Law Reform Act.

Ian Scott explained to the Justice Committee what he was looking for in this reform Act, "When a couple has separated permanently, we should tell the courts what we want them to do if the court's aid is invoked to attempt to resolve the difficulties. We should not require people to go back and forth to the court more often than is absolutely necessary. We should structure it so that the judge can deal with it if it is possible, subject to appeal and subject to a variation order with finality. We should not force somebody to retain a lawyer again to get a result that everybody could have predicted in the first place."[33]

A significant reason why I enjoyed being on the Justice Committee for Bill 1 was that we discussed amendments instead of debating them. We had quite a discussion about which of these two words, unconscionable (not guided by conscience, not in accordance with what is just or reasonable) or inequitable (unjust or unfair), is best as a guide for a judge. We did agree that we didn't want wording which would limit the judge in providing a just decision. Ultimately "unconscionable" is found more often in the Act than "inequitable".

Another interesting debate was over the inclusion of common-law relationships. One position expressed on the committee was that common-law should not be included, only legal marriages. A diametrically opposed view was that there be no numerical threshold. In the end we settled on couples who cohabited continuously for a period of three years, or who have cohabited in a relationship of some permanence and have natural or adoptive children together.

A "get" is a document Orthodox Jewish men give their wives as the couple is divorcing; it seals the divorce according to religious law, meaning that the husband decides if and when the divorce is final.

---

33 Ian Scott, Hansard, pg. J22 Administration of Justice Committee, November 20, 1985

We heard testimony of situations where the wife wanted a divorce and the husband said he would agree provided his wife paid him as much as $100,000. As our committee started down this road, I could hear Jim Renwick's voice in my head, "if possible, always stay away from issues involving pets or religion". We really didn't have a choice. The task was to fashion an Act which applied to everyone.

The AG set the tone. "Let me begin by saying that in the six months I have been in government, I have never had to confront an issue that causes me more difficulty, for two reasons. The first is I believe people should get what they legitimately want and I got into politics because I believe that. There is no doubt that the community that will be affected by this amendment wants it desperately and for the sound reasons we have heard. My instinct as a politician and, I hope, as an ordinary citizen is, by and large, to give people what they want.

On the other hand, the committee may vote and the members of my party will vote as they please, but times come when the Attorney General has the greater responsibility than simply to give the people what they want. That is the right of an ordinary legislator. He has to decide, as best he can, whether what the people want is in the best interests of the law. That is a responsibility I have never expected to hold but which I hold now and therefore, I must frankly say what I think, even though I know it will cause discomfort to many of my friends and to many members of the committee." [34]

Everyone on the committee exhibited sensitivity to the impact which our actions might have on the Jewish community. In the end we agreed to an amendment which the AG considered satisfactory. "The amendment takes care of all the cases that were put to us as the damaging principle. If any man, Orthodox Jew or not, says, "I will withhold the get until you sign away this property or unless you make this deal," that man will know by section 56 that agreement

---

[34] Ian Scott, Hansard, pg. J12 Administration of Justice Committee, November 20, 1985

is worthless. It will be set aside by a court as soon as that fact is made clear. That, it seems to me, goes a very substantial way to take care of the problem that was presented to us."[35]

As we concluded our task, having considered literally every word in the Bill, Ian Scott observed, "May I say to the committee that this is the first major bill that I have been associated with and I am sure it is well known to all members who have been here in other years, but I am really impressed with the extent to which each member has been superbly prepared to engage in this presentation. The process, as Mr. Justice Grange would say, works."[36]

It is amazing what our parliamentary democracy can achieve. There seems to be a generalization in the public's mind that governments are always too slow. Sometimes moving cautiously is wiser than speedy passage of legislation. Other times, especially when political parties don't let partisanship get in the way, good things can happen quickly. Eight months after being introduced, the Family Law Reform Act became law. Years of what is best described as an unconscionable situation was remedied. Political will and an Attorney General determined to make a difference delivered much needed changes in family law. Now, in general, an equal split of all assets, other than anything brought into the marriage by one partner or the other would be the order of the day.

It felt good to contribute to such significant legislation. A few amendments to Family Law have been made over the years but the fundamental principles remain as we structured them in 1986.

It was rewarding to work with a talented, highly principled Attorney General, provided I didn't try to be "cute", witty or sarcastic. Truly one of the most rewarding experiences of my political life.

---

35 Ian Scott, Hansard, pg. J14 Administration of Justice Committee, November 20, 1985

36 Ian Scott, Hansard, pg. J36 Administration of Justice Committee, November 20, 1985

# PART THREE

# My Term as Speaker of the Ontario Legislature

# 19

# On Top of the Landslide

## *July 30, 1990*

"There's a call for you Mr. Warner," said the hotel desk clerk, when he found me sitting in the lounge. It had been a long, but a productive and enjoyable day. Time to relax and chat with my teaching colleagues.

I hesitated. Since I was at a hotel in a small town in India, I immediately jumped to a conclusion that this must be bad news from home. I picked up the phone, to be greeted by static. The phone connection was not good. Through the electronic noise I could recognize my wife's voice, then a jumble of syllables mixed with static. The only word which came through clearly was "election". I was stunned. I knew that Pat wouldn't phone to say there wasn't an election. As strange as it seemed, an election had been called!

Rumours are a constant in politics. A rumour circulating in the spring of 1990 was that Premier Peterson would call an early election. "That's crazy!" I said. "He has another year and a half. Why would he do that? Makes no sense. No need to change my plans for the summer."

The phone call from home changed everything. I had to abruptly end the fascinating Indian Project, and return to Canada as quickly as possible. "Hold on," said Pat. "What we really need ahead of you coming home is your signature on some documents so we can officially get the campaign going." I signed the courier delivered documents which arrived the following day, then focused on how to get back home from Bhopal.

There was, prior to my leaving, an important event for our team to attend. Dr. Charasia, a Christian, had arranged for our Canadian team to attend a special Hindu ceremony commemorating the 101st anniversary of the local Education College. Part of the ceremony involved the four of us squatting in a circle while the Priest spoke in Hindi. "Gulab, what did the Priest say?" I asked. "He has blessed you, that you will win the election," was the reply. In hindsight, I should have visited that Hindu Priest prior to the 1995 election!

The overnight train trip to New Delhi was enjoyable as I sat up all night chatting with the two men who were sharing the compartment; a newspaper reporter and a businessman, both of whom were keenly interested in politics. There was an overnight stay in New Delhi because British Air flew only every second day from there to London. After changing airports and airlines in London, I was able to complete the journey to Toronto. After 30 hours of sleep deprived travel I was home, anxious to be campaigning. There was a brief, but emotional homecoming greeting with my family, then I was off to the campaign office. "Give me some literature. I'm off door-to-door!" An hour later I thought I would collapse. I had pushed my body too hard. This foolishness cost me two days recuperation in bed!

The election campaign went as smooth as silk. Since Scarborough Ellesmere had, from its inception as a provincial riding in 1975, been considered a "swing riding" there was media interest. About a week prior to election day, a reporter asked if he could go door-to-door with me. I agreed and selected a street where typically I had not fared well. We called on 20 houses. At 17 of the 20, the response was a definite "I am voting for you."

"Looks like you are going to win," said the reporter.

"Not only will I win, but the NDP will form a majority government," was my response. "Strong support on a street we normally lose says to me there is something bigger going on."

Landing on top of the landslide, with over 48% of the vote, I was on my way back to my 'second home' as part of a majority New Democrat government, Bob Rae Premier.[37] I was ecstatic about returning to the 'Pink Palace', but there was another election ahead. This one for the most coveted position in parliament, Speaker of the House.

This would be my fourth term as MPP. I loved the House; the process of a Bill being introduced, energetically debated, sent to a committee and eventually becoming law. I had found it easy to get along with Members from both sides of the aisle. I didn't know for sure, but I thought that the neutral role of Speaker would come easily because of my experience refereeing soccer. The three Speakers I had known; Russell Rowe, Jack Stokes and Hugh Edighoffer, from three Parties, were excellent role models. I was sure I had the patience required as well as the ability to listen objectively to both sides of the aisle.

The Speaker had always been appointed by the Premier. During the last parliament the Parties agreed that the Members of the House should, by secret ballot, elect their Speaker. If there were more than two candidates, then voting rounds would continue until one candidate had more than 50%. The Clerk would be the only person who would know the exact vote count. Beside me, there were three others who wanted to be the first Speaker elected by his peers; Norm Sterling, PC, and two Liberals; Jean Poirier and Gilles Morin. We were invited separately by each Caucus to explain why we were best suited to be Speaker. My guess is that each of us

---

[37] 1987/1990 results: NDP 19/74, Liberal 95/36, PC 16/20.

tried to convince our colleagues that we would firm and fair. On November 19, one day after my 39th birthday, I was elected on the 2nd round of balloting, to be the 33rd Speaker of the Ontario Legislature. Two Members, one from each side of the house, "dragged" me to the Speaker's Chair. Facing the House for the first time as their Speaker, I recited the famous quote of Speaker Lenthall, in 1642: 'May it please Your Majesty, I have neither eyes to see, nor tongue to speak in this place, but as the House is pleased to direct me, whose servant I am here…'[38]

After I was elected Speaker, Premier Rae invited the Liberals to select a Deputy Speaker. They chose Gilles Morin. The Conservatives were asked to choose a second Deputy Speaker. The PC choice was Noble Villeneuve. The three of us worked closely together and became good friends, a friendship which continues to this day with Gilles and did with Noble until his passing February 28, 2018.

In the scrum outside the Chamber reporters were interested in my view about the oft times noisy atmosphere in the House, and whether having a record number of women elected will make a difference. "I think …… when the issues are being debated that most women parliamentarians will use calm, reasoned, logical approach and many male politicians tend to resort to an emotional response — name calling and so on. …. In accepting the position, Warner told the Legislature that the public expects less rambunctious behaviour from politicians and that he intends to rule with that in mind."[39]

Shortly after the election the answer to "Why would Peterson call an early election?" became apparent. Premier Peterson sensed that a recession was on the way. I am guessing that the reasoning went this way: call a snap election, which would result in another majority government, then ride out the recession. Four years should be sufficient to weather economic turmoil and the public would be ready for another Liberal government. The plan might have worked

---

38 History of the Speakership, UK Parliament, www.parliament.uk

39 Derek Ferguson, *Toronto Star*, November 20, 1990

if Premier Peterson had provided a solid, believable reason for the early election call. He didn't. Couldn't really. He would not have wanted to state publicly that an election was being called because a recession was on the horizon.

The New Democrats took office in September, 1990, the first NDP government in the history of Ontario, excited about trying to fulfill a progressive agenda. Soon to learn that job number one would be "fight the recession." For me, November 19, 1990, marked the beginning of an extraordinary five years.

# 20

# No Instruction Book for this Job

"Congratulations! Here are the keys to the building and the keys to the car. Good luck!" It was his usual warm smile and firm handshake. The outgoing Speaker, Hugh Edighoffer, met me in Speaker's Office, following the vote and the ceremony conferring upon me the title of Speaker in the Chamber. After a short chat, Hugh was on his way. I turned my attention to the Clerk, Claude Des Rosiers.

As explained in an earlier chapter, I was a member of the three person sub-committee which recommended hiring Claude DesRosiers as the Clerk of the Ontario Legislature. There were a lot of unknowns ahead of me now, but one great source of comfort would be working with someone I recommended for the position of Clerk because of his experience, dedication to parliamentary democracy and non-partisanship.

"So Claude, is there a manual or guide book for this new job of mine?" I asked, expecting the Claude would produce a book or a binder.

"No," was the reply. Claude went on to explain that what I had to do was maintain order in the House and rule on points of order. He added, "You should review the Standing Orders tonight and start memorizing the names of the Members as well as the name of the Riding the Member represents."

In 1975, when I first took my seat in the House, I pulled out the Standing Orders from my desk and started memorizing them. Tommy Douglas had said one time, "Know the rules, then make them work for you." I thought that was great advice. However, seated near me was an experienced Member who had a reputation of often being told by the Speaker to take his seat. This member, after observing what I was doing, said, "Don't learn the rules. If you learn them, they will want you to obey them." Well, now I had to not only know the rules, but be able to enforce them!

In this initial chat with the Clerk, I wanted to know about points of order. How would I know what was a valid point of order? Claude patiently explained that he was there to assist, especially with points of order, however there would be times when I would be on my own. I realized that I needed to be a patient listener as well as firm and decisive.

Claude Des Rosiers turned out to be a great source of strength. His wisdom, experience and understanding of parliamentary practice and precedents served me exceedingly well during my five years as Speaker. He also saved my parliamentary career. More about that later.

On November 19$^{th}$, one day after my 49$^{th}$ birthday, I was elected as Speaker. The next day was the opening of parliament. I have always enjoyed the first day of a new parliament. You don't have to be on the government side to appreciate the pomp and ceremony. Everyone is wearing their finest. There will be special guests seated on the floor of the Chamber. The Speaker's Gallery will have close friends and family of the Speaker, as well as former MPPs and possibly some visiting dignitaries. The Press Gallery, located directly above the Speaker's Chair, will be full. At the other end of the Chamber, above the entrance to the Chamber there will be a row of television cameras. There is an air of excitement. The Lieutenant Governor will arrive at the Legislature in full regalia, ready to deliver the speech from the Throne, a document which will outline the government's plans for this parliament.

By noon on the 20th I had a made-to-measure, all black outfit of trousers, vest, and cloak, along with several tailored white shirts. After donning the black tricorn hat I picked up my white gloves, ready to be in the procession from Speaker's Office to the Chamber, then to Speaker's Chair.

Every opening of parliament is special, with lots of happy, excited people around. This opening has a higher level of buzz. Today is the official start of the first New Democrat government in the history of Ontario.

The Sergeant-at-Arms, carrying the Mace, the symbol of the authority of parliament, lead the procession into the Chamber and up to the foot of Speaker's Chair. He stepped aside, as did I. The Lieutenant Governor, the Hon. Lincoln Alexander, came forward, offered a slight nod in my direction, then stepped up to the Chair, turned and started to sit down. Lincoln Alexander is a tall man, well over six feet. At five foot five, I am a great deal shorter than the LG. My attire wasn't the only thing attended to overnight. Speaker's Chair had been altered. A few inches had been sawed off the legs, my predecessor being quite tall. When Lincoln Alexander sat down his chin touched his knees. He looked at me and smiled. Not a word was said. Dignified calmness!

After the Speech from the Throne the government introduced Bill 1 "An Act to amend the Retail Sales Tax Act", a Bill which followed up on proposals made by the previous Liberal government. Formalities completed, it was time for socializing. As much as I enjoyed the afternoon and the festive occasion, I was thinking about what came next. The following day would be back to the business of parliament, including Question Period. It would be "showtime" for me!

A footnote: Pat was able to attend the opening, but not my daughters. Sherri who was in her last year at high school joined us at the apartment late afternoon, while Barbara was attending Encounters Canada at the Terry Fox Centre in Ottawa that week. By coincidence the week was themed "law and politics" and Barbara was selected by her peers to be the Speaker in their mock Parliament!

# 21

# Showtime

The Clerk solemnly advised that the Members would give me a day or two, but very quickly I would need to know the names and match them with the Ridings represented. Since I knew my own name and Riding, there were only 129 more to commit to memory. While I knew many from previous terms in office, nearly half of the Members were first term Members. As I set about memorizing names, faces and places, I remembered a specific advantage of having a good memory for Member names connected with Riding names. "The Member for Scarborough Ellesmere knows that heckling is not allowed, but if you are going to heckle, at least do it from your own seat," would be the admonishment from the Speaker. It was quite common that during times when House business was less than electrifying, Members from both sides of the aisle would wander across to sit beside a colleague for a chat or find that was a good opportunity to have a moment with a Cabinet Minister. Then, without warning, a comment by the person who had the floor would cause an interjection from a Member who wasn't in their seat.

I was excited about my first day presiding over Question Period. The Speaker's procession started at my office, led by the

Sergeant-at-Arms, followed by the Clerk, then two table officers, with me at the end of the line. There were Assembly staff standing along the corridor, wishing me good luck. Along the first floor hallway the entourage walked then up the Grand Staircase. As we proceeded toward the Chamber I kept wondering what it really would be like to sit in Speaker's Chair and exercise the authority which comes with the position. Through the entrance to the Chamber went our parade, and up to the Chair, all Members standing, most of them smiling and quietly whispering "good luck". The procession stopped. I came forward and moved up the steps, where I turned, bowed to the Sergeant-at-arms, who then turned and marched back to his desk which was situated close to the Chamber door. Once all the formalities were out of the way, it was time for the first Oral Questions of the 35$^{th}$ Parliament.

That first Question Period went quite smoothly. There was generally a convivial atmosphere; respectful and restrained. I looked forward to day two.

By day three I had a pretty good grasp of all the names and Ridings. So far, so good. This job may not be so difficult after all.

# 22

# Honeymoon's Over

Day Four, the honeymoon was over! Question Period, a reasonably polite affair for the first three days was suddenly a group shouting match. There was heckling which originated on the government side of the aisle, something quite rare when I was an ordinary member. I had learned early on that the accepted practice was for government members to not initiate heckling, but certainly respond. The interjections were often quite funny. Rarely personal or malicious. I felt that I needed to cut these new members some slack. Most of them were not sitting beside an experienced member who could offer advice about standards of conduct in the House.

I felt that I was being tested to see if I knew how to maintain order. Being a teacher by profession came in handy. That however, was balanced by the fact that basically I am not by nature an authoritarian. I am not inclined to tell people what to do. I prefer to guide, letting people use their intelligence to figure out what should be done. Clearly that philosophic approach was not going to work in the rambunctious situation I was facing. I quickly adopted an approach which was mostly successful.

The 60-minute Question Period is highly valued by the Opposition Parties. It is an opportunity to confront the government on current issues in front of the tv cameras. New Opposition MPPs learn quickly not to ask a question without already knowing the answer and new Government MPPs observe that Cabinet Ministers provide replies, not answers. As one Speaker reminded a rookie MPP, "It is Question Period, not question and answer period."

Staff at the Clerk's Table have control of the clock. The clock can be stopped by the Speaker at any time. I decided that when it was too noisy to hear what was being said I would stop the clock if the government side was the cause of the disturbance, but keep the clock running if the Opposition were to blame for the disorder. Both sides of the aisle caught on quickly to how I would handle the noise in the House. Even this approach was tested.

Some days were quieter than others. Often, the noisiest days were Tuesdays. The three Caucuses met Tuesday morning. I remember those weekly caucus meetings serving as an energy boost for a lively Question Period. Each morning the House was sitting I would meet with the Clerk, two table officers, Deputy Speaker Gilles Morin and second Deputy Noble Villeneuve. Gilles and Noble both were in a more awkward position than I was when it came to inside information. The Speaker does not attend caucus meetings or have anything at all to do with his Party. Gilles and Noble would never betray a caucus confidence, but tried to help me. So, 'might be a bit lively today Speaker' was a well received early warning of trouble ahead.

There was a day when the early warning was a prelude to my resolve being tested. When the volume was such that it was impossible for anyone to hear what was being said, I stood and signalled for the clock to continue running. Usually that would cause silence in the Chamber. Not this day. The noise continued. I continued standing, clock running. The Opposition was losing valuable Question Period time. I stood for seven minutes. Then, the Official Opposition Liberals, apparently unhappy with how I was handling Question Period, decided to walk out. The entire caucus got up and walked out of the Chamber. Since the majority of the noise was gone, I motioned to the Third Party Conservatives that Question Period was all theirs. Those members were ecstatic. They would have far more questions than they normally got. Meanwhile, the Liberals who had gathered in the Opposition Lobby, watched the proceedings on the monitors. A short while later the Liberal Caucus came very quietly back into the Chamber.

I had demonstrated my resolve to control the House. However, the unusual episode did not result in a less raucous atmosphere. Day after day angry voices could be heard in the Chamber. I interpreted much of the clamber in Question Period as an attack against me.

I tried to not let the unhappy atmosphere of that hour be a distraction from my other duties. There were functions to attend, out of country visitors to greet, administrative responsibilities and of course paying attention to my Riding. The time zipped by and after a few late night sittings, it was a deeply welcomed Christmas break. I had survived the first session.

# 23

# "I Quit!"

A new year. A new sitting of the House. A fresh start. Question Period would be highly spirited, as it should be, but everyone would be respectful of each other and the Chair. That was dreaming in technicolour! Letting the clock run, stopping the clock, having to remove a couple of members because they wouldn't withdraw unparliamentary remarks all contributed to what was becoming for me the most unpleasant hour of the day. There was anger and frustration in Question Period and it was being directed at me. It all came to a head one day. As I recall, the events were not any worse than other days. This particular day was the proverbial "straw which broke the camel's back."

"I don't need this anymore. I quit! I will do something else for a living." was what I exclaimed as I stormed into my office, simultaneously tossing my tricorn hat across the room and my robe on a nearby chair. Close on my heels was Claude DesRosiers, the Clerk. Claude swiftly and silently closed the office door. In a soft, calming, yet firm voice he told me that I was not going to quit. He asked me if we could find a nice quiet spot, have a drink and chat. As far as I was concerned, the quietest place in the building is Speaker's Apartment; situated on the 3rd floor, north-west corner of the Legislative Building, far removed from the Chamber. Once seated in a comfortable chair, drink in hand, I started to relax. "Now that I think about it," I began, "today wasn't any worse than any other day in the House. Today was the final straw. I think I am doing a good job, but I seem to be a target. If it is something I did or didn't do, I haven't a clue." I paused, looked at Claude and stated, "Maybe they want me gone."

Claude, with his usual calm, reasoned approach, explained that I was a target, but not because of anything I had done or hadn't done. His observation was that the Opposition was upset and angry because they had lost the election and the person who called the election wasn't there. Everyone knows that the Speaker is in no position to fight back. Claude then advised that what I needed to do was to keep doing my job the best way I knew how. He reiterated that I was not going to quite, thanked me for the drink and stated that he needed to get back to work.

I realized Claude was right. I had been taking the daily commotion in the House personally. The secret ballot vote to become Speaker had resulted in me feeling that I was being judged every day. I accepted that as appropriate. What I wasn't doing was separating out the political animosity across the aisle which had been a result of the last election. I needed to re-focus! If it hadn't been for Claude DesRosiers I would have ended my political career that spring day in 1991. During the rest of my five year term in office I observed how Claude applied the same calm, reasoned, visionary approach in the daily running of the Legislative Assembly with its more than 300 employees to manage. In 1986 we had hired well!

# 24

# Challenges I Set for Myself

## November 20, 1990

I sat at my new desk, in my new office. The Office of the Speaker. The previous day was one of excitement as well as deep appreciation. I had been elected by my peers to the important position of Speaker. My family and close friends were there to share in the joy.

Presiding over proceedings in the House was essential. I wanted to make a meaningful contribution beyond the Chamber. I wrote a list of what I thought were significant topics where the influence of the politically neutral Speaker could make a difference.

- Improved relations with Quebec
- Strengthen the use of French in the Legislature
- Enhanced connections with our bordering states
- Literacy
- Improved relations with our indigenous population
- International friendship

I put the list where it would be handy, in the top desk drawer. Periodically, I would make notes on the list. When I left office in

1995, I turned that list with the notes into a summary which I thought might be helpful for the new Speaker.

## Improved relations with Quebec

In 1976, the Parti Quebecois, a Party pledged to achieve Quebec independence, formed a majority government in Quebec. The following year Bill 101 was passed by the Quebec National Assembly declaring that French was the only official language of Quebec. The next step would be a Quebec referendum on sovereignty in 1980. The Ontario Legislature would hold a debate on the subject.

In an effort to gain greater knowledge about this quest for independence, the NDP Caucus sent a delegation to Quebec, to meet with politicians, business people, labour leaders etc. I was a member of that delegation. This was a unique opportunity to learn more about Quebec's culture, history and politics. Reading, discussions, caucus meetings. I was ready to participate in this historic confederation debate.

I had grown up knowing there were 10 provinces, the 10$^{th}$ one having joined Canada when I was six years old, and two territories. The thought of one of those provinces opting out of Canada was unfathomable. While I was a staunch supporter of a Canada which included Quebec, I was also aware of the English domination of the French in *La Belle Province*. The English had firm control of the economic levers in that province. English was the language of business. Retaining the French language was becoming increasingly difficult.

Canada's governance is complicated. We are officially, an English/ French bilingual nation. Each province, however, can decide if they wish to be bilingual. Only New Brunswick has made that declaration. While Ontario is not officially bilingual, the Courts offer trials in either language. The Legislature provides simultaneous translation and all statutes are printed in both French and English. There are francophone MPPs in each of the three Parties.

## Strengthening the status of the French language at Queen's Park

Day two of my Speakership I asked staff to check all the signage in the Legislative precinct to ensure that they are in both English and French. I also had a quiet chat with Jean Poirier, a Francophone Member who was one of my opponents for the position of Speaker. "I will do my best to create a welcoming atmosphere for all Francophones. I have started with the signage in our buildings. If there is more which should be done or I have missed something, please let me know." Jean and I worked well together. I was later rewarded when attending a Francophone Summit held in Quebec City. Jean introduced me to visiting parliamentarians from France this way: "Our Speaker is not a Francophone, but he is a Francophile." The visitor couldn't help but notice that I was grinning from ear to ear!

I hadn't passed grade 9 French. Never too old to learn, I thought. So, I got a tutor. She was a highly skilled French language teacher and very patient. Her skills and patience were not enough! I did manage to read the French titles of Bills in the House. While I never did accomplish even conversational French, my appreciation and support of the French language became evident. I did whatever I could to encourage greater use of French in the House.

*1991*

I thought that a Parliamentary Association between Quebec and Ontario would provide a valuable opportunity for Members from both provinces to learn more about each others' political and social culture. Dialogue between Members from both provinces might help to offset some of the nasty incidents which had occurred in Ontario. When you set fire to a Quebec flag in the main street of an Ontario town, that is news right across the province of Quebec.

There was a Parliamentary Conference in Halifax early in '91. Speaker Jean-Pierre Saintonge and I met to discuss my proposal.

He quickly and enthusiastically agreed. Two meetings, each two days duration, were arranged; to meet first in Quebec City, then Toronto. A framework was put in place for annual meetings with topics of mutual interest for discussion. Jean-Pierre and I developed a warm friendship.

The first test of this new found Ontario-Quebec relationship came later on. The salient feature of a parliamentary association is non-partisan discussion; the promotion of listening to others and considering differing points of view.

Speaker Saintonge called me on a Friday, explaining there was an Ontario-Quebec cross-border labour dispute which was causing headaches for both provinces. Could Members from the three Parties in Quebec have a meeting with our Members the coming Tuesday. "Of course," I replied. On Tuesday, the Ontario Minister of Labour, one Liberal and one Conservative MPP met with the Quebec MNAs in Speaker's Apartment. The issue was aired out in a calm, detailed, cordially interactive manner. Two days later the Premiers of Quebec and Ontario chatted on the phone. The issue was resolved to the satisfaction of both provinces.

In 1992, the Quebec Assembly celebrated 200 years since the passage of The Canada Act. The Act which created Upper and Lower Canada was passed in 1771, but the first sitting of the new legislatures occurred the following year. I was offered the privilege of addressing the National Assembly from the Chamber floor. My speech was written in French and I spent untold hours memorizing, determined to pronounce the speech properly. I received quite an enthusiastic response from the Members. A reception line followed. One MNA spoke excitedly to me in French. The stunned look on my face told him I didn't understand a word he was saying. "Your speech was so good, I was certain you spoke French fluently!" I guess you can fool some of the people, some of the time.

I am exceedingly glad to know that the Ontario-Quebec Parliamentary Association continues to this day.

In 1996, to my surprise, I was awarded Order of La Pléiade by the Government of France. The medal was to recognize my promotion of the French language in Ontario, in the spirit of cooperation and friendship. The ceremony, for me, was enhanced by the fact that there were just three of us being so honoured; Hon. Bob Rae, Marc Garneau, former Astronaut and me.

## Relations with our American Neighbours

Canada and the United States have long been neighbours, allies and friends. Ontario is bordered by seven states. In the natural course of events, there will always be challenges and opportunities between bordering jurisdictions. Why not create a non-partisan committee of MPPs, State Congresspeople, State Senators to meet those challenges and opportunities.

The Legislature's Protocol Office put me in touch with Ilene Grossman, Assistant Director of the Midwest Legislative Conference, Council of State Governments. Ilene was gracious, hard-working, diplomatic and effective. Her expertise and guidance ensured success. She introduced me to State Senator Gerald Conway of Nebraska, Chair of the Midwest Legislative Council, who shared my interest in developing cross-border discussions. The result was the creation of the Midwest-Canada Relations Committee.

Our small, fledgling Committee focused first on getting to know more about each others' political system. This morphed into conferences. At the same time we reached out to include Manitoba in the Committee. One of those conferences focused on the shared challenges of the Great Lakes port cities. All 32 port cities had the same problem, that of needing to dredge to handle larger shipping vessels, but dredging might stir up chemical wastes etc.

Interest in the annual conference, one year being held in Toronto, the next in a neighbouring state, increased dramatically over the years. Today, it remains a success story of helpful, civil discussions across the US-Canada border.

## All-Party Literacy Committee

Literacy is a topic which crosses partisan politics. My teaching background was the catalyst for creating an all-Party Literacy Committee. It was easy to get a volunteer from each of the Parties. Together we embarked on a few projects, the most ambitious being a "library bus", filled with 10,000 books, shipped to Trinidad and Tobago. The kindness and generosity encountered during the project was amazing. The school bus was donated by the Scarborough Board of Education. Volunteers from the Scarborough Board removed all the seats, replacing them with shelving. The Toronto Public Library donated the books, which we stored in the basement of Queen's Park until the bus was ready for shipping. The Consul General of Trinidad and Tobago found a shipping company to supply free transportation of the library bus.

Once everything was in place; the bus, filled with books ready to head south to the Caribbean, we invited Speaker Occah Seapaul, first woman elected to the Parliament of Trinidad and Tobago, to visit for an official send off of the library bus. The library on wheels was destined to roam the rural areas of the country, focusing especially on helping women to break the literacy barrier.

Our Literacy Committee launched a program at Queen's Park designed to reinforce the importance of reading; if important people read, reading must be important. MPPs were asked if they would participate in reading to a visiting school group or reciting poetry. The catch was that being on the roster meant they might be reading to children who were not from their Riding, that an MPP from another Party might end up reading to children from their own Riding. This was to be a non-partisan program. Initially we had about 40 Members volunteer. Year two of the program that number rose to 65.

One day, as I walked past a room near my office I could hear a voice I recognized. I looked into the room. The children were sitting quietly, mesmerized, as MPP Alvin Curling, who later was elected Speaker, had the group hanging on every word as he recited poetry.

During my term as Speaker, the Legislature participated in "Share a Story." This exciting event was hosted by Mila Mulroney, wife of Prime Minister Brian Mulroney and Arlene Perly Rae, wife of Premier Bob Rae and Lieutenant Governor Hon. Henry Jackman. His Honour was one the many personalities and celebrities who read stories to groups of children. Other celebrities included Steve Paikin, Sarah Polley, Lambchops, Babar the Elephant, Astronaut Dave Williams, Al Waxman, Sandy Rinaldo, Polkaroo, Fred Penner. It was an exciting worthwhile event. What a marvellous day! Children everywhere; authors, celebrities, politicians reading to the children.

The message that reading is important was delivered in exciting fashion!

## Relationship with Indigenous people

I had an uneasy feeling that scant attention was ever paid to our Indigenous people. I was aware that Toronto had the largest indigenous population of any place in Ontario. Yet, I couldn't recall having seen any indigenous person in the building. I asked an indigenous friend to make some discreet inquiries to find out why. The answer which came back was very disturbing. "We are not welcome. We should not be entering Queen's Park."

The thought that our First Nations people were not welcome in the place which represents democratic governance was embarrassing and distressing. I again relied on my friend for advice as to how I could try to right this wrong.

"A good start might be through art," was the response.

I was excited to host and have curated the first contemporary Indigenous art exhibit to be held at Queen's Park. Amazing works of art were on public view for six months. Next was a most fortuitous opportunity. The Assembly was being granted its own Coat of Arms. A ceremony in the Chamber was in order.

The Members were invited to this special ceremony on Monday, April 26, 1993. Not all Members attended. A few declined the opportunity; as rumour had it, objecting to having a non-elected person speaking from the floor of the House. I had asked Mr. Gordon Peters, Ontario Regional Chief, Assembly of First Nations, to be our key note speaker. Chief Peters delivered a riveting speech. The part which stood out so vividly for me was his reflection about decision making; stating that when you make an important decision ask yourself what will be the effect seven generations from now. I couldn't help but think at the time, "we don't ask what the effect will be seven days from now!"

Admittedly, what I did was only a modest beginning toward undoing mistrust and misunderstanding. Later, Speaker Levac, a Metis, turned Room 228–230 into "Gathering Place," a curated, permanent Indigenous Art Exhibit.

In 2016, as a result of the findings of the Truth and Reconciliation Report, there was a meeting of Indigenous Leaders and Party Leaders. Two years later an all-Party Committee and Ontario Regional Chief RoseAnne Archibald selected an artist to create a wood carving to be installed in the Chamber. In 2021 Speaker Arnott unveiled the beautiful carving created by Indigenous artist Garrett Nahdee, who is from the Walpole Island First Nation in southwestern Ontario. The carving, which showcases the Seven Grandfather Teachings was placed above the interior Chamber entrance. Perhaps, as Members exit the Chamber they will reflect on the values embodied in the animals of the carving; Love, Wisdom, Truth, Humility, Respect, Courage and Honesty.

As non-indigenous politicians tread the path to find truth they will do everything they can toward reconciliation. Political will and leadership which goes above and beyond partisanship is essential to engage the entire population in the process of reconciliation.

# 25

# International Friendship

There are more than 100 consulates in Toronto. Much of the world comes to our doorstep to conduct business. The Consul Generals are generally posted here for three years. Some have never been to Canada. Some countries, for economic reasons, opt to have an Honourary Consul, a local Canadian. They too, in addition to processing visa applications, have an abiding interest in international trade.

I embarked on a plan to provide Members an opportunity to get to know each other, and at the same time provide Consul Generals newly arrived to Canada an opportunity to meet MPPs and of course some of their international colleagues. I would invite six Consul Generals or a mix of Consul Generals and Honorary Consuls, and three MPPs, one from each Party, to dinner at Speaker's Apartment. In terms of the invitation, I had but one rule; no two countries who shared a border. Even great neighbours can have issues.

The feedback from the Consular Corps was rewarding. The dinners were a wonderful introduction to Canadian parliamentary life, as well as a unique opportunity to meet MPPs and other diplomats. While all the evenings were excellent, one in particular stands out.

One evening the group assembled were particularly relaxed and convivial. The discussion at the dinner table somehow turned to poetry. I suggested we could recite our own poetry or that of someone else. Turned out that the Consul General of Granada was a poet. After he recited a poem he had written, Alvin Curling then provided a beautiful recitation. What a delightful evening.

The population of Ontario reflects the composition of the United Nations. We have responded to this reality by officially being a multi-cultural society. That brings a responsibility for those who are elected to understand as much as they can about various cultures and religions. A good way for a Parliament to accomplish this is through exchange visits of lawmakers. I selected three countries, each for a different reason and in each case a specific province; Cuba (Havana), Pakistan (Sindh), China (Jiangsu) to see if I could establish Province to Province Friendship Agreements. Those Agreements would provide a framework for exchanges; opportunities for Members to learn first hand the cultural and religious foundations of each others society.

# 26

# Friendship Agreements

## *Cuba*

What is life like in an economically poor, Communist country? What are the realities in terms of culture, society and economics.

In 1992 I led the first of four parliamentary delegations to Cuba. Between '92 and '95 we twice visited Havana and twice to Santiago. The visits were designed to be all-Party delegations. The Conservatives declined without explanation each opportunity to participate.

We were afforded the opportunity to explore every facet of Cuban life and engage in lively discussions about trade, culture, economics and politics. It became evident that mutual exchanges involving not just politicians could be great learning opportunities for both Cuba and Ontario. Case in point: a child care centre has staff which includes a nutritionist and a medical doctor on call. For every five children at the centre there is one child care worker. All child care workers are university trained. The emphasis is on early childhood education and the centres are able to care for youngsters from age six months to five years.

Their universal health care system is focused on using the hospital as a last resort. Local clinics staffed with a doctor and a nurse conduct routine checks on their roster of approximately 800 people, trying to provide the care needed without relying on the hospital.

US Laws prevent American businesses from engaging in trade with Cuba. Quite an opening for Canadians, provided the Canadian companies don't mind being banned from doing business in the US (Cuban Democracy Act, 1992). Sherritt Mining, a Canadian company entered a number of deals to mine nickel and cobalt in Cuba, refining the ore in Fort Saskatchewan, Alberta.

The Cuban officials clearly welcomed Canadian trade and investment. MPP Jim Henderson, who had encouraged me to organize the visits to Cuba, explained that the Cubans were good business partners. Everything would move slowly, but honestly. Jim said the Cubans were always very polite, had a special spot in their heart for Canadians. Prior to the parliamentary delegation of 1992 Jim had led several delegations of Canadian business people looking to do business in Cuba. Jim described how Cuban politeness caused confusion. A Canadian businessman reported to Jim that it had been a few months since he had presented his proposal and had not heard back. Could Jim find out what the hold up was about. Jim reported later that the Cuban officials were unsure how they could diplomatically explain that there wasn't a market in Cuba for NHL hockey cards.

At the end of that first visit to Cuba it was clear that closer ties between Ontario and Havana Province would help a country which was struggling against their powerful unfriendly neighbour. There was a lot we could learn as well. So, after returning to Ontario, I proposed a Friendship Agreement between the Legislature of Ontario and the Assembly of Havana Province. The Agreement, accepted by Havana, provided a framework for parliamentary exchanges.

Cuba is not a democracy although there are democratic elements in their governance structure. Perhaps one day there will be a multi-party parliamentary democracy. In the meantime peacefully sharing space on this planet requires accepting differences and celebrating that which we have in common.

## *Pakistan — January 1994*

What is life like in an economically poor, Islamic country? What are the realities in terms of culture, society and governance. In 1947 India gained independence, and separate countries of Pakistan and Bangladesh were created. Since then Pakistan has experienced parliamentary democracy and military rule. The period between 1988 and 1999 was one of those democratic times and as luck would have it Speaker Maher of Sindh Province, Pakistan visited Queen's Park. He was warm, friendly, outgoing. The two of us hit it off. An additional ingredient in my decision making was the fact that Canada was experiencing a significant emigration from Muslim countries. There wasn't one Muslim elected in the Ontario Legislature. Establishing a Friendship Agreement with a framework for reciprocal parliamentary visits could be of great value to both parties.

My itinerary is a week in Pakistan, then on to a Commonwealth Parliamentary Conference in New Delhi, India. I had two major objectives; a Friendship Agreement with Sindh Province and the establishment of a small Commonwealth Committee to tackle the status of the disputed territory, Kashmir.

Nestled in the Himalayas, Kashmir, a tourist destination with a population of only four million has been a disputed territory from the 1947 India/Pakistan partition to this day. While the area is predominately Muslim, India has always laid claim. Fighting has erupted periodically over the decades. It seemed to me that perhaps the most reasonable, fair thing to do would be to let the people of Kashmir decide for themselves in a referendum which provided three choices; join India, or Pakistan, or be an Independent State. The Pakistan portion of my visit started in Karachi. At a press conference held after the official ceremonies were concluded

I responded to questions about Kashmir by suggesting that Pakistan and India should consider a referendum. Let the Kashmiris decide the status of their territory for themselves.

One result of the press conference was a body guard assigned to sit outside my hotel room all night. Later, when I arrived in New Delhi my personal security arrangements would be upgraded considerably.

Meetings in Karachi with the Pakistan Chamber of Commerce, groups of MPs and diplomats bolstered my initial impression of a lively interest in a Friendship Agreement as a way to further develop the ties between Ontario and Pakistan. Then it was on to Lahore, the Capital of Punjab Province where a spirited discussion with large group of Members of Parliament underscored one of the most important reasons I was pursuing a Friendship Agreement. The topic was the war in Bosnia (1992–95) with Bosnian Muslims being victimized by both the Serbs and Croats, because of religious prejudice.

Art, music, poetry are avenues which can lead to a deeper appreciation of a different culture. The local museum was interesting, so too Lahore Fort, but what impressed me the most was the tomb of Mazar-e-lqbal, Pakistan's national poet. Impressive that a country would pay such reverence to a poet.

Speaker Maher's village is in a remote, rugged hilly area not too far from Mohenjo Daro, an archaeological site which dates back to 2,500 BCE. It was impressive to see how so long ago people were able to devise a water and sewage system. After the tour it was on to the Speaker's village for a feast. A sumptuous array of food and lively music provided a welcoming atmosphere. The assembled group numbered about 75. The fact that all were men brought home a cultural difference, one open to discussion when we have a Friendship Agreement.

The official signing ceremony was a joy for me. A small step, but a good one in trying to establish understanding and appreciation of the cultural and religious differences. It was cause to celebrate that which we had in common, a deep commitment to parliamentary democracy. Members of Parliament can have a positive effect in their communities. In Canada those MPs can play an important role as new comers adjust to a different life in a very different country. Now, on to the Commonwealth Parliamentary Conference in New Delhi.

I must admit that at the time I had not an inkling that I had poked a hornets' nest. I thought being whisked directly from the plane to a private lounge, having someone take my passport away briefly, returning it and then being escorted to a limo was all standard for visiting dignitaries. It was when the first person I met at the hotel wasn't another delegate, but Mr. Mahinder Singh, who introduced himself as my PSO (personal security officer) that I realized that the press conference in Karachi where I shared my reasonable, constructive suggestion regarding Kashmir had caused a stir. I never felt that I was in any danger. Obviously my Indian hosts did. Opening my hotel door the first morning I was greeted by two soldiers, each with rifles, standing on either side of the door. An over-reaction I thought. I asked if we could tone it down a bit. After that morning I didn't see the soldiers again. Mahinder and I got along quite well. Turned out that Mahinder was a senior New Delhi police officer who knew the city extremely well. He seemed quite delighted to find a lovely, non-tourist restaurant where another delegate, Marcel Parent, Member of the Quebec National Assembly and I could enjoy delicious, authentic Indian cuisine.

I was afforded an opportunity to present my proposal to create a Special Commonwealth Committee to examine the Kashmir situation with a goal in mind of finding a peaceful solution, to the General Assembly of the Conference. Predictably there was mixed reaction. Some Indian MPs were visibly upset. There were suggestions that the Canadian should try to solve the independence question of Quebec before wading into Indian affairs. A couple of newspapers had a negative take on my presentation. That was day one of the Conference. By day three however a different tone appeared. An Indian MP asked permission to revisit my presentation and when granted the opportunity said that perhaps the group was too hasty in dismissing my suggestion, that maybe Indian and Pakistani politicians were too close to the situation to view it objectively.

That evening I was able to arrange a dinner meeting of four people; Speakers Ramay and Maher, both of Pakistan, myself and the Indian Minister of Foreign Affairs. No staff. Just the four of us to chat about Kashmir. I was told later that it was the first time in years that Indian and Pakistani politicians had sat down together to have a civil discussion. Sadly, nothing ever came of that dinner, except that I was convinced more than ever that conversation is better than confrontation.

## *China — July, 1994*

*"Wu shi Wu Da Wai, an sheng yiz hang. Xie xie nimen qing wo lai."* (I am David Warner, Speaker of the Ontario Legislature. Thank you for inviting me here.) 17 hours of flying, toss in the time zone changes and I am meeting the Mayor of Shanghai for lunch, hoping that my attempt at speaking Cantonese will offset my somewhat dishevelled appearance. A rumpled suit and dress shirt is to be expected when you are wearing the same clothes you had on when you left home more than 24 hours earlier and your luggage has yet to appear. I am able to introduce my wife Pat, *"Wu pei zhen."*

A side story: Our daughter Sherri was learning Chinese at the University of Toronto. When she told the professor about her parents pending trip to China, the professor volunteered to provide Pat and I will some phrases and names which would be significant. Wu is a Chinese family name and it also represents the province we will be visiting, Jiangsu. I chose this province for our official visit as Ontario has had a long standing trade relationship with Jiangsu, one of the most economically developed provinces in China. Although our daughters would not be on this trip they were given Chinese names; Sherri is Wu Jiang and Barbara is Wu Su.

The top of my curiosity list was the question "What is life like in a Communist/Capitalist country?" Closely followed by "What are the realities in terms of private business, international trade, individual rights?" At the end of 10 days I was a bit wiser, but didn't have clear answers to those questions. All the more reason to have regular reciprocal parliamentary visits. China 1994 was developing into a formidable world power. Today they are a dominating force in the world.

Shanghai, a city of 13 million, looked like one gigantic construction site. Office buildings, apartments, financial centres, warehouses and factories were springing up faster than weeds in a spring garden! We were shown three dimension model boards of what the end result should look like. Today Shanghai is an industrial giant in the world. In terms of trade and commerce, a capitalist gem!

Now for the Communist part of the equation, a visit to Huaxi, a village Collective of approximately 1,400 people. Those who had been farmers are now factory workers. There is a small steel mill as well as other enterprises. Everything in the village has been purchased from the profits of the village's economic activities. A typical house, which appeared spacious, had three levels; bottom floor for grandparents, middle and top floor for parents and children. If you desire a car put your name on a list. End of year village profits determine how many cars can be purchased, then comes seniority on the list.

Coming from a young country I always find it fascinating to learn more about the cultural history of countries which are thousands of years old. Over the course of our visit we were entertained with traditional Chinese opera, classical vocal and instrumental music, ballet, juggling and magic. We observed two sided silk embroidery being created and tried our hand at brush writing.

It was in Nanjing, the capital of Jiangsu Province, where I broached the details of what a Friendship Agreement might look like, with Madame Wu, Vice-Chair of the Standing Committee of the People's Congress for the Province of Jiangsu. It was interesting to learn at the outset that a working relationship existed between

Jiangsu Hospital and Toronto's Sick Kids Hospital. I listed items which I thought were important for Members from Ontario and Jiangsu Provincial Assembly to discuss:

- our legal systems
- market economy
- bi-lateral trade
- education
- rights of women

Flying home from Beijing was an excellent way to conclude the visit, not just because it is the Capital of China and we could visit the Forbidden City, the Great Wall, but we could walk in Tien An Men Square. A chilling reminder that this Communist Capitalist juggernaut is an authoritarian regime.

A few months later I hosted a Conference at Queen's Park, one feature of which was the official signing of a Friendship Agreement between the Assembly of Ontario and the Assembly of Jiangsu Province. The two topics accepted by Madame Wu from the list I had suggested for the Conference were "Examining the Canadian Justice System", and "Achieving Gender Equality".

Our baby Sherri is getting her first experience with door-to-door canvassing for the 1972 Federal Election. Although door-to-door wasn't Pat's favourite activity, she was always a great source of strength.

I was proud that my daughter Sherri served as a Page in 1985.

Bob Rae was the third Leader I worked with (1985–1987).

I admit to being a bit nervous facing the House for the first time as Speaker (November 19, 1990).

The unveiling of my portrait was a proud moment. Left to right: Margret Warner, Sherri Warner, D.W., Barbara Warner, Pat Warner (November 20, 1995).

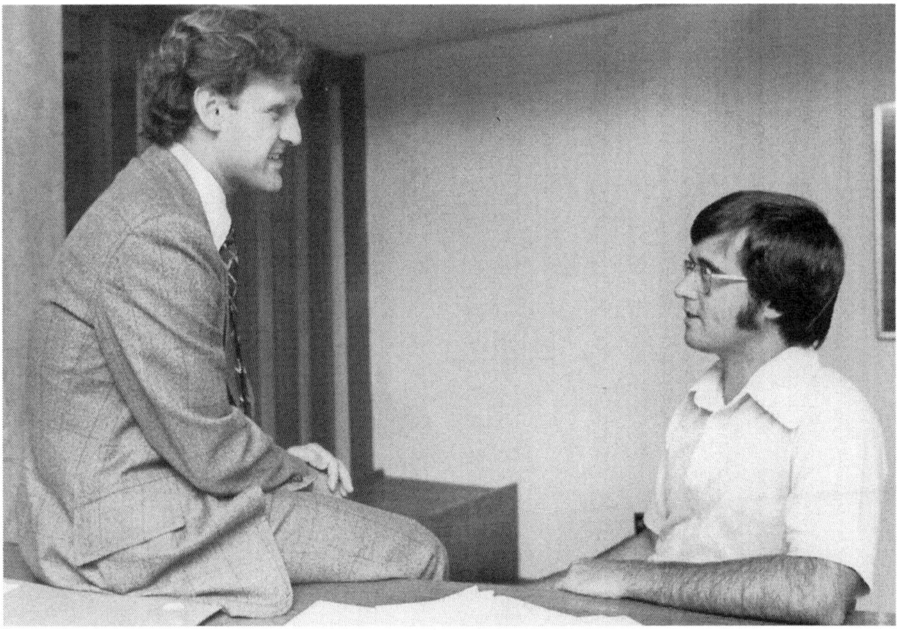

I always listened intently to Stephen Lewis, Leader of the Ontario NDP from 1970 to 1978. Photo taken in 1977.

It was a great honour to participate in the Bicentennial Commemoration at the Quebec National Assembly (May 23, 1991). I rehearsed for hours to deliver my entire speech in French.

With Speaker Jean-Pierre Saintonge, Quebec

As Chief Whip, I often met with Michael Cassidy, who was our Party Leader from 1978 to 1982. Photo taken in 1980.

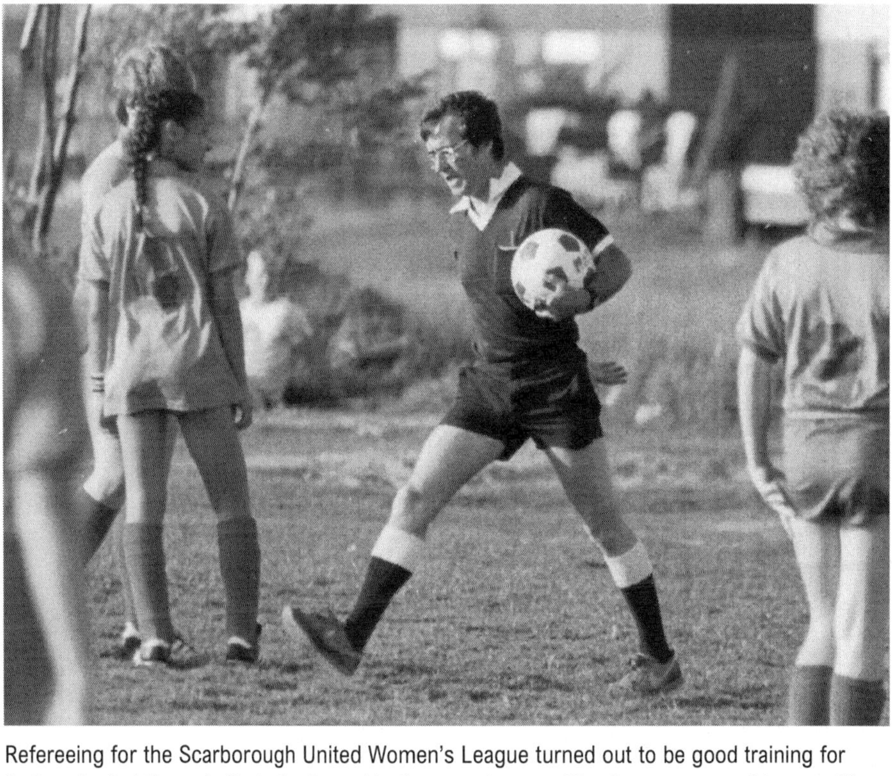

Refereeing for the Scarborough United Women's League turned out to be good training for "refereeing" at Queen's Park. I refereed both rep and competitive leagues, ages 5 to over 50, from 1981–1985.

At the opening of the Oncology Unit at Scarborough General Hospital (1993). From left to right, front row: Dr. Jackie Gardner-Nix, David Warner, Dr. Bob Frankford, MPP.

The Breakfast Club at 2180 Ellesmere Rd. was a great way to help children start their school day without hunger. Photo taken May 6, 1994.

It was exciting to break ground for the not-for-profit Squirrel's Nest Child Care Centre on Ellesmere Road near Brimley Road (1994). To my right are Mayor Joyce Trimmer and Councillor Marilyn Mushinski. A year later, Marilyn Mushinski defeated me, but we remain friends.

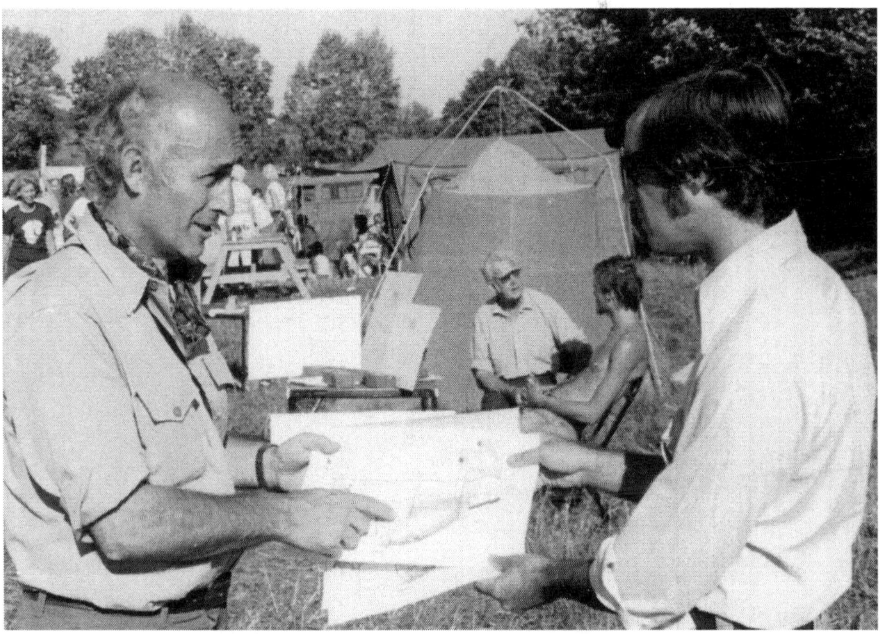

Dr. Charles Godfrey explains the People or Planes protest strategy to me at a rally to stop the proposed Pickering Airport in the summer of 1974. Dr. Godfrey was later elected MPP for Durham West, and the Pickering Airport project was halted.

Signing the Friendship Agreement between Havana Province and Ontario in Havana, Cuba (January 1993)

With MPP Jim Henderson (to my right) and TTC buses donated to Cuba (September 1992)

# 27

# The Commonwealth and the Francophonie

Canada is a unique member state of planet Earth, a country which holds a special position in the world. We have a long proud history of being peace makers, peach keepers (awarded a Nobel Peace Prize in 1957 for promoting UN Peacekeeping in the Suez crisis — Lester B. Pearson, Prime Minister), a robust parliamentary democracy and we are a middle power, not likely to attack anyone but always willing to defend other democracies against invasion. What elevates "special" to "unique" is that by virtue of being a bilingual country we belong to two international organizations, the Commonwealth and the Francophonie, whose combined membership equals more than 130 countries. A collective voice which spans the globe could be an effective voice for peace.

My 1993 visit to London and Paris had a number of objectives, one of them being a proposal to the Commonwealth Parliamentary Association and the Organization internationale de la Francophonie that we coordinate our resources to assist emerging democracies, monitoring elections and establishing the infrastructure of democratic governance. My proposal was warmly received by both

Secretary Generals. Generally large organizations are slow to make changes and I was asking both large organizations to meet the challenge of collaborative decision making. So....as far as I know these two excellent international organizations continue to do their good work, but on their own. There truly is an untapped source of strength in the quest for making this a better world.

## Commonwealth Conferences

I was surprised at how valuable I found the CPA (Commonwealth Parliamentary Association) conferences to be. The topics were timely and important. Discussions were frank yet courteous. Occasionally I had the opportunity to present a paper. Sometimes the sessions motivated me to write something for The Parliamentarian, The Journal of the Parliaments of the Commonwealth.

It was at the Cyprus CPA Conference that I first thought about suggesting the use of small, multi-nation committees to tackle difficulties encountered by Commonwealth member states, a Special Affairs Committee. At that conference local concerns were raised by Fiji, Gibraltar and Cyprus. A Special Affairs Committee, with regional representation, might be able to find acceptable solutions. It was that approach which inspired me to tackle the Kashmir situation. The Commonwealth, especially with the leadership of Prime Minister Mulroney of Canada, helped end apartheid in South Africa.

I had the privilege of serving on the CPA Executive for a short while. The dedicated leadership of the Chair, Mr. Colin Shepherd, MP (UK) confirmed for me that a family which spans the globe can solve problems within the family as well as beyond the family. Imagine how much good could be accomplished by two international families working together.

# 28

# A Speaker's responsibilities

The day to day functioning of the Assembly with a staff of more than 300 is in the hands of the Clerk. Should anything go wrong, from the Parking Lot Attendants, to the Post Office, cafeteria, accounting, maintenance, library, security etc., the Speaker is held responsible. In taking this aspect of the job seriously I did a "walkabout" at least once a year, visiting every department. I was accompanied by a couple of senior staff who would take notes, then later meet with department teams. "Do you have any suggestions as to how we can do things more effectively and efficiently? What might be done to make your job easier?" were the questions I asked every employee.

Over the years security had become a more serious matter. The majority of Members, me included, wanted the public to feel welcome in their building; to be able to wander in if only to enjoy the amazing art collection. What changed my mind was when, as Speaker, I was shown the security files. At the time the OPP (Ontario Provincial Police) had a detachment at Queen's Park. They were in charge of security.

"Would you like to see the bomb threats first or the death threats?" asked the officer. There were file cabinet drawers full of both! Of particular note was a death threat against a Member whose office was just a few steps inside the Legislature's East Entrance. The officer explained that no more than 30 seconds would be required for someone to enter the building, leave a briefcase containing an explosive device in the Member's office, then exit the building. That wasn't going to happen. Changes to how we did security had to happen.

It didn't really seem appropriate to have the OPP as security. It wasn't ordinary police work. Mostly it was public relations. Security staff needed to be individuals who were trained to be watchful regarding security threats but at the same time could interact with the public in a diplomatic, helpful way. Meeting with the Sergeant-at-Arms for the House of Commons in Ottawa was very helpful. So too was the visit with the UK House of Commons Sergeant-at-arms. That meeting was one part of a larger agenda. More about that later. It became clear quickly that what we needed was our own Security force. As it turned out the OPP were only too glad to close the detachment. They could use the personnel elsewhere. This was the time to establish our own recruitment, training and career advancement programs. I knew that upgrading our security protocols would be appreciated by some Members, not so much by others. Whether the changes would be popular or not I was determined to minimize security risks as much as possible.

The order of precedents in Ontario is Lieutenant Governor, Premier, Chief Justice, Speaker. Diplomacy is an important responsibility of being Speaker. In addition to my initiative as described in Chapter 25: International Friendship, the Speaker is often the host of visiting dignitaries from various countries around the world and occasionally members of the British Royal Family or their Canadian representative. I recall a delightful visit from Governor General Ray Hnatyshyn around the time the Ontario Legislature received its Coat of Arms.

The visit of Prince Charles and Lady Diana was a joyous occasion. The Royal couple attracted crowds wherever they went. They were enormously popular. A tumultuous crowd gathered at

Queen's Park to welcome them to Toronto. Of course the Lieutenant Governor, Hon. Lincoln Alexander hosted an official welcome. Pat and I were fortunate enough to be included in a selected group of about 70 people to meet Charles and Diana in the Vice-Regal Suite. I was immediately taken by how gracious and warm they both were and how easily they circulated the room, taking time to chat with everyone.

The Lieutenant Governor and I were standing at the entrance to the elegant reception room, watching the Royal couple as they engaged various people in conversation. Lincoln turned to me and whispered, "Look how he works the room. Charles could be elected." My response was, "I agree. I think Diana could also be elected." What a wonderful, memorable event!

The responsibilities of being Speaker is serious business, but the holder of this important position should not take themselves too seriously. Enjoy the inevitable lighter moments.

# 29

# My Last Hurrah 1995

*"If you never encounter anything in your community that offends you, then you are not living in a free society."*

— Kim Campbell

## Recession fuels a mood for change

The first New Democrat government in the history of Ontario started their mandate with an inherited recession. Plants were closing at an alarming rate. The unemployment rate was over 11%. Canadians were facing the worst recession since the 'dirty thirties'. In the Legislature, the Opposition Parties, as they listed the latest plant closures, demanded answers. "What was the government going to do about the closures and widespread unemployment?" There were Opposition Members who went so far as to accuse the New Democrats of having caused the recession, knowing full well that the recession had begun before the NDP took office. As is so often the case during partisan political battles, truth becomes a victim.

The 1987 election had resulted in the Liberals capturing 95 of the 130 seats. Premier David Peterson's huge plurality should have meant a stay in office until 1991 or '92.. Instead, just

18 months into the mandate Peterson announced a general election set for September 6, 1990. "Why?". The government's economic advisers were privy to information that the economy was weakening, a recession was on the horizon. It seemed to me that Premier Peterson's political advisers reasoned that by calling an early election, ahead of a full-blown recession, the Liberals could hold on to their majority and ride out the recession. Since most downturns in the economy usually last only a couple of years, the recession would be over before it was time for another general election. In other words call the election in the summer of 1990 and get re-elected with a majority. The recession would likely be over with good times restored by 1993 and forgotten by 1995. The logic was good. What was missing was providing the public with a valid reason for an early election. That turned out to be a fatal error! I encountered puzzled voters as I went door-to-door in the 1990 election. "Why are we having this election?" was a common question. The 1990 election saw the Liberals going from 95 seats to 36 and the NDP jumping from 19 seats in 1987 to majority government with 74 seats.

These were tempestuous times in the House, especially during Question Period. I dutifully fulfilled the Speaker's historic role as referee and observer, cognizant of the precedent which was set way back in 1728 when Speaker Arthur Onslow, of the British House of Commons, set the standard that the Speaker of the House should withdraw himself from his Party, and not attend caucus or any caucus functions. To this day, that precedent is followed. So, of course I wasn't privy to decisions arrived at in the NDP Caucus regarding the government's efforts to battle the recession. As an observer what I saw was a government struggling to find ways to offset the pain and suffering caused by severe job losses.

The Rae government's response was in three major ways; increasing various taxes, investing a significant amount of money in infrastructure projects and imposing a "social contract" on all public sector employees.

The tax increases included increasing personal income tax on most income earners, except for low income earners whose tax was decreased. A surtax was applied on high income earners and an employer health tax introduced for those who were self-employed.

The infrastructure projects created jobs in the private sector by repairing schools, libraries and other community facilities as well as building affordable housing, long-term care facilities and child care centres. Work was begun on constructing four new subway lines in Toronto.

The philosophy of the "social contract," dubbed "Rae Days," was that if every employee in the broader public service (nurses, teachers, etc.) worked a few unpaid days there would be thousands of jobs saved as well giving the provincial treasury a boost. The Premier's approach was the concept that we are all in this together, let's try to share the burden. In fact, the measure saved about 30,000 jobs and the treasury netted nearly 2 billion dollars. As well intentioned as it was, the Rae Days would be an albatross around the neck of every NDP candidate in the '95 election.

Plant closures with the resulting unemployment caused a severe decrease in government revenues. The investments in infrastructure were expensive. The result of revenue being down and expenditures being up was that when Treasurer Floyd Laughren tabled his first budget there was a 10 billion dollar deficit. The ensuing accusation in the House and in media scrums of reckless spending was a prelude to a major election theme that an NDP government means tax and spend. Interestingly, I don't recall plaudits after there were three successive balanced budgets. Such is the nature of partisan politics.

The Legislative Assembly was also bound by the Social Contract. As Speaker, I was the "CEO" of the Assembly and therefore obliged to negotiate or simply impose unpaid days. The maximum number of unpaid days was 12. However, a provision in the legislation allowed the opportunity to offset those unpaid days with productivity savings. Senior staff worked hard to find those savings, and they did. The result was that the balance owing was five unpaid days. I proposed that those days be taken between Christmas and New Year's. The staff agreed. About two years later, as I was walking along a downtown street I was stopped by a man I didn't recognize. He thanked me warmly, saying that the Rae Days were the best thing that had happened to him in a long while. He was able to spend a whole week with his family at Christmas time, and the loss in pay was hardly noticeable.

Thousands of people were out of work. Families were struggling to make ends meet during these were tough economic times. A predictable result was an angry and frustrated general public. But, then, Mike Harris, Leader of the Ontario Progressive Conservatives, delivered a message of hope. He introduced the "Common Sense Revolution." His platform promised tax cuts and a solution to the deficit. The NDP government, trying to soften the blows of the recession, had boosted social programs. Tough times had created an atmosphere which made it easier for Mike Harris to sell the idea that cutting social programs was a good way to balance the budget. He was aided in his fight by a campaign of misinformation (who knows where or how it started). Unsubstantiated stories giving the impression that large numbers of people were receiving welfare payments they didn't deserve circulated. A sample of such misinformation is the following tale from the trail:

The woman who answered my knock at her door, smiled and politely took the literature. A bit of small talk ensued, but I could sense there was something she wanted to say, yet was reluctant to speak. I did what I was taught not to do: ask, *"Are there any issues of concern?"* Everyone has an issue, so the moment you ask about issues of concern, you are likely to get an earful. Perhaps issues you would rather not discuss. Your time is better used by moving quickly from one house to the next. You simply want to register your presence with the voter.

*"As a matter of fact, there is. There is far too much welfare money being given to people who aren't entitled to it."*

I was a bit weary of hearing the same old, unverified story, so did the second thing which I had been taught not to do: challenge a constituent. The moment you challenge a constituent you put them on the defensive, resulting in a negative connection with a voter. You are making it tougher on yourself to get their vote.

*"That's terrible. Not right. Give me the name or names and I will make sure that if they aren't entitled to welfare, they will be cut off."*

*"Well, I don't really know the name. I heard about it from the neighbour behind us."*

My response was to ask for the address and name of the neighbour so I could follow up.

*"Well, actually, I am pretty sure she heard it from someone else. Sorry."*

I then did a third thing I had been taught not to do: instruct a constituent. This will likely come across as a lecture. It is easy to imagine that the voter now thinks "I don't need this guy telling me what to do."

*"In future, it would be helpful to verify accusations. Social assistance is vital to a lot of people, especially during these tough times. Rumours are not helpful."* I moved on to the next house, being pretty sure that my three canvassing errors would send that woman's vote to my Conservative opponent.

Capitalizing on an atmosphere of uncertainty, bordering on fear, Mike Harris included in his platform a number of other populist items; reduce the number of MPPs, deregulate university tuition, and weaken unions with new anti-labour laws. The political climate was perfect for launching regressive policies.

While province-wide polling predicted the NDP would be tossed from office, I was sure that losing government would not include me losing my seat. I had worked exceedingly hard, accomplished a great deal for Scarborough Ellesmere and had distinguished myself as Speaker. There is one additional ingredient in the mix, something I had relied on since my first election campaign in 1972 — the *David Warner Happiness Scale*. This scale, applied in all nine elections, predicted a victory each and every time. The reality was very much different. However, what it did do was to energize me because I believed I would win!

## David Warner's Happiness Scale

(How to interpret responses when canvassing door-to-door)

- ✓ "I am voting for you."
- ✓ Smile + "I wish you good luck"
- ✓ Smile + "I have voted NDP in the past"
- ✓ Smile + person accepts literature
- **?** Opens door, accepts literature
- **X** No smile, clearly hostile

I have always enjoyed going door-to-door, chatting with people. Friendliness is good for the soul and for capturing votes, so I thought. I eventually learned that most people were polite and often less candid with me than with my campaign workers. Some people outright lied about their voting intentions, while others, perhaps basically kind, not wanting to hurt my feelings, fudged the truth about their voting intention. Perhaps it is simply easier to smile than make a commitment about voting.

While my happiness scale provided me with nine election victories, the reality was: I lost the federal elections of 1972 and '74, won the provincial elections of 1975, '77, '85, '90 and lost the provincial elections of 1981, '87 and '95.

## Hard work is always politically rewarding (or so I thought)

Heading into the 1981 election I assumed that my good work in the Riding would be rewarded. I had completed six years in office (1975–81) during which I had created an excellent media profile on a wide range of issues, both local and province wide.

News stories, with large bold headings and even the occasional supportive editorial painted a picture of an energetic, devoted MPP. Media coverage was bolstered by my regular door-to-door visits. I always had a strong community presence. The following newspaper headlines are a sampling of the extensive coverage I generated. I had a caucus colleague tell me one time that I had more media coverage than anyone in the Opposition, except our Leader, Stephen Lewis.

> Nursing home abuses ignored?[40]
> Stricter Rent Control wanted, MPP's poll finds[41]
> Reject Interchange at Brimley, 401 Scarborough urged[42]
> 10,000 families seek homes help — MPP[43]
> 'Skittish' horses at Becker's strike dangerous — MPP[44]
> Fare cut urged for TTC/GO commuters[45]
> Raise school board grants, cut property taxes, MPP says[46]
> Protecting lawyer-client relationship[47]
> Warner decries wiretapping
> Youth plan must get grant[48]

The most important issue I had during my first two terms as MPP was the needed expansion of Scarborough General Hospital.

There had been complaints about long wait times and overcrowding at Scarborough General Hospital Emergency Ward

---

40 Charlotte Montgomery, *Toronto Star*, November 25, 1977
41 *Toronto Star*, May 23, 1978
42 *Toronto Star*, April 20, 1977
43 Dorothy O'Neill, *Toronto Star*, May 4, 1977
44 *Toronto Star*, April 15, 1979
45 *Toronto Star*, March 17, 1980
46 William Bragg, *Toronto Star*, October 30, 1978
47 *Scarborough Mirror*, March 5, 1980
48 Kathleen Harford, *Toronto Star*, May 5, 1980

for some considerable time prior to 1981. I needed to validate the claims first hand. On March 4, 1979, with the permission of the doctor on call, I donned a lab coat and carried a clipboard. I put in an overnight shift in the Emergency Ward, always identifying myself, and assuring the patients that I was not a medical doctor. I asked where they were from and how long they had been lying on a gurney. The survey results were stunning. There were patients from small towns and villages an hour or two drive away. Many had been lying in the hallways for a couple of days. Around 4 am, I hustled off to my office, wrote a press release and got it to the Toronto Star. It ended up as a front page story the following day, illustrating that a new Emergency Ward was needed. I raised the issue in the Legislature every chance I got for the next two years.

> Hospital care 'sickens' MPP blames cuts[49]
> MPP Lambastes Queen's Park health funding[50]
> Warner call for expansion of SGH in first campaign speech[51]

The first of two shrewd moves by the Conservatives occurred in the midst of the election. I was contacted by one of my supporters, letting me know that a press conference was being held at the hospital. A new Emergency Ward was being announced by the Conservative candidate, Alan Robinson. I arrived at the hospital at the end of the press conference. An obvious conclusion was that the Board of Directors of Scarborough General had no intention of notifying me. Alan Robinson and the Davis government garnered the credit for this essential project. An editorial in the Scarborough Mirror, March 4, just two weeks ahead of Election Day, stated what turned out to be reality.

---

49 *Toronto Star*, March 5, 1979

50 Kathleen Harford, *Toronto Star*, March 12, 1979

51 *Scarborough Mirror*, September 17, 1980

A little vote buying?[52]

"The PC's have blatantly adopted a Buy-A-Majority platform. .... Scarborough Ellesmere, now held by NDP incumbent David Warner, is on the Tory hit list. Fair enough. But what really grates is the way in which the Conservatives are going after the riding — trying to purchase the seat with taxpayers' money. ..... Mr. Warner is now all smiles. It's common knowledge in this borough that he has pestered Mr. Timbrell (Minister of Health) for months about the overcrowded conditions at the hospital's emergency ward."[53]

The second shrewd move which contributed to my 1981 defeat and was a factor in other closely contested ridings, was when hospital workers went on strike. The moment that strike was labeled illegal by the government, public opinion shifted dramatically. It was as if illegal was equated with immoral. By extension, since the New Democratic Party was supporting the strike, they were backing something which was immoral. I remember being on the picket line at Scarborough General. The hospital workers were glad to see me, but those a bit more savvy than I remarked that being there was not going to be politically helpful. They were right!

Overshadowing whatever I may have done in the riding were the provincial campaigns of each Party. Post-election analysis made it clear that the election was more about greater trust in Premier Davis than in the NDP Leader, Michael Cassidy or the Liberal Leader, Dr. Stuart Smith. It took me a very long time to accept that my work in Scarborough Ellesmere was nowhere near as important as the province wide campaigns by the Party Leaders.

---

52 editorial, *Scarborough Mirror*, March 4, 1981

53 excerpts from the editorial, *Scarborough Mirror*, March 4, 1981

## Hard work plus a prestigious position is politically rewarding, (or so I thought)

Entering the 1995 election I thought the added prestige of being Speaker would ensure my success. There were constituents who were proud of the fact that their MPP was Speaker of the House. I was at a well attended tenants meeting when someone stood up and addressed the group by announcing that he was proud of the fact that their MPP was the Speaker of the House. I admit being pleased, but embarrassed by the standing ovation I received. To those who expressed concern that being Speaker meant their MPP could not fight for issues important to the Riding or to them personally I offered an assurance that I was as vigorous in my representation as in the past; only my approach had to be a bit different. While I couldn't raise issues in the House or issue press releases regarding local issues, I could approach the senior bureaucracy for assistance as they understood the unique situation of a Speaker.

Of course, the proof was in the pudding. I had succeeded in getting a new not-for-profit child care centre, and new affordable housing which included a low rise apartment building for people with special needs. The infrastructure investment in my riding during my five years in office was second highest in the province. Tangible, remarkable results should equate with electoral reward. Right! Wrong!

In the end I got the lowest percentage of my seven provincial elections, 28.5, losing by more than 5,000 votes. In visiting the PC election headquarters to congratulate Marilyn Mushinski, I realized that I was getting quite good at delivering congratulatory speeches to opponents. Experience will do that for you.

The polls were right. On June 8, 1995 the New Democrats were swept from office, going from 74 seats to 17. A majority Progressive Conservative government, led by Mike Harris, was elected, going from 20 seats to 82.

## Anguish to acceptance - the psychological impact of each of the three provincial losses

The loss in 1981 was devastating. Lots of self blame. The 1987 loss was less traumatic. More frustration than anything else. The two years had gone by quickly. Lots of unfinished business. No self blame this time, but a determination to return to the Pink Palace. The 1995 loss was more a feeling of disappointment than anything else. I felt that my initiatives in International Friendship Agreements, the Quebec Ontario Parliamentary Association, Midwest-Canada Relations Committee, All-Party Literacy Committee, and relationships with Indigenous communities were all in their infancy. So much more to be done and I had no idea if my successor would continue the work. Would the next Speaker even read the detailed notes I left?

The Scarborough Board of Education let me know that I would retain my Chairperson status and would be assigned a school for September. A staffer at Queen's Park offered to have his travel agent daughter, who was living in Lisbon, Portugal, organize a three week Portuguese vacation for Pat and I. Carla, the travel agent, arranged an amazing three weeks. Pat and I, after spending time in Lisbon, traversed much of this beautiful country. The highlight was five days at a 17th century manor house in the mountainous Douro River region. Using the wise advice from Clerk Des Rosiers of never making a decision when you are upset or tired, I used the restful five days at the delightful manor house in Portugal, overlooking vast vineyards, to contemplate my future. I had a decision to make. Would I continue this revolving door political career or should I open a new door?

Logically, rationally, losing the '95 election was not my fault. I have always accepted being elected as a personal commitment to both myself and those who supported me, so there was a feeling when I lost, of letting down those who believed in me. I couldn't help but feel I had failed. If I decided to not run again, it would be walking away from a challenge. It would be admitting defeat.

However, I needed to calmly and objectively consider two options; seek returning to Queen's Park or go back to teaching.

My love for Queen's Park had never waned. The grand and gracious hallways, magnificent art and of course the green carpeted Chamber remained a lure. I would love to have another term as Speaker to continue the various projects I had started.

I had always enjoyed teaching, so returning to the classroom was not a hardship. While teaching full time, I could also use my acquired political skills to good use, connecting with community based organizations.

The essential question was whether I wanted a political life badly enough to commit to two or three years of political activities, planning, and door knocking prior to the next election. In the end I realized that I didn't have it in me to continue my revolving door career.

While I had made the decision to not run again, I felt an obligation to not abandon those who had steadfastly stayed with me for the past twenty-three years. The Riding Association had been loyal and supportive. I had never faced a challenger for the nomination, either federally or provincially, in those nine elections. Boundary changes for the '95 provincial election resulted in Scarborough Ellesmere disappearing, to be replaced by Scarborough Centre. Potential new candidates needed to be found, a critique of the past election to try and understand what needed to be done to regain the riding and a new executive for the new Riding. I offered to help with the transition and was elected Chair of the new Scarborough Centre Riding Executive, a position I kept until 1998.

I decided that the next chapter in my life would be full time teaching, and volunteering in three organizations; Scarborough Centre NDP Executive, Churchill Society for the Advancement of Parliamentary Democracy, and the Canadian-Cuban Friendship Association. There would be more family time which would include more travel. I certainly didn't anticipate that beyond the next four years of teaching a new path would present itself.

# PART FOUR

# The Non-Elected Years

*"We should encourage civic engagement and active participation in our democratic processes."*

— Hon. Brian Mulroney

# 30

# The 1972 Election Loss Sparks Community Leadership

## *Community, Family, and Teaching*

In the '72 election one of the all-candidates meetings was at Stephen Leacock Collegiate, our local high school. Someone one in the audience must have been impressed with my performance. I was approached later by Doctor Bruce Phillips about being on the Board of Agincourt Community Services (ACSA), an organization founded in 1970 to address the hidden pockets of poverty in Agincourt. Eight local faith groups had come together to build on the work that Holy Spirit Catholic Church had been doing to assist local residents who were in need. Reverend Bruce Scott from Knox United Church devoted much of his time in launching ACSA. There was a special focus on youth. In truth, what I learned was a shock; sad circumstances which I didn't know existed in my community. ACSA had one staff, an Executive Director, Lorna Prokaska. She was so amazing at organizing, being able to connect with individuals and groups in our community, that when I was elected as MPP in 1975, I asked her to be my Assistant.

Bruce Phillips announced in '73 that he would be leaving for a post in Geneva, Switzerland with the World Health Organization, his specialty being cancer research. I was invited to be ACSA's Chair. No hesitation on my part. In the short time I had been on the board I had come to realize the challenges in Agincourt and the emotional reward of making a difference.

The "Glorified Tree House" was an amazing ACSA project, whose end symbolized misplaced priorities. On the north-east corner of Finch Avenue and Birchmount stood an abandoned one-room schoolhouse, vintage 1850's. On the south-east corner of the same intersection was a public housing project consisting of a high rise apartment building and a couple of rows of townhouses. In an era where drop-in centres were in vogue, the Scarborough Board of Education let us use the schoolhouse as our drop-in centre. With a grant from the federal government we hired an older teenager who lived in the housing project, someone we knew was seen as a leader, to be in charge of the program. Providing a place for teens to gather, and chat, without an adult telling them what to do, was a huge success; that is until the City of Scarborough decided that it was more important to straighten the intersecting roadways to align perfectly. I made an impassioned plea at City Council that providing a safe haven for young people was more important than straightening the roadways. The heritage building was moved to another location and our program collapsed.

A different kind of political experience came along in '73. I was approached to be on a Steering Committee, Scarborough Branch, of Committee For An Independent Canada (CIC). This was a national, multi-party organization, conceived as a citizen's committee to promote Canadian economic and cultural independence. The founders, Walter Gordon, Peter Newman and Abraham Rotstein, well established, respected Canadians, in turn recruited a famous publisher, Jack McClellan and Claude Ryan, politician and director of *Le Devoir*, a daily newspaper in Montreal, as Co-Chairs. The CIC was launched in 1971 and immediately petitioned Prime Minister

Trudeau demanding limits to foreign investment and ownership. Many CIC ideas were eventually incorporated into law, e.g., the establishment of the Canadian Development Corporation, Petro Canada and the Foreign Investment Review Agency; controls over land acquisition by nonresidents; tougher rules regarding Canadian content on radio and television; and the elimination of *Time*'s and *Reader's Digest*'s tax privileges. I felt strongly about Canadian independence, believing that bit by bit our country was being taken over economically and culturally by the United States. I remained an active Scarborough member until deciding to seek the nomination for the 1975 provincial election.

In 1973 I was teaching full time, on a career path with my first promotion, devoting time to ACSA, CIC and the local Riding Association as well as a role with the NDP provincially.

August 21 was singularly the most unnerving day of my life. I had come into the house for a cold drink to find Pat, pregnant with our second child, in great pain. She said quite simply,"We need to go to the hospital." It was a frantic drive to Centenary Hospital, where shortly after we arrived, Barbara Elizabeth Warner came into this world, three months early and weighing just two pounds. A week later a semi-retired pediatrician recognized there was something wrong, ordered an ambulance to transfer Barbara to Sick Kids Hospital. She had meningitis. The incredible medical staff at Sick Kids saved her life. Three months later we were able to bring our baby home. This tiny, premature baby with a life-threatening ailment would go on to a full scholarship at university and graduate as a lawyer.

1973 certainly was a memorable year. What was next?

# 31

# The Aftermath of the 1974 Federal Election

The rest of the summer could now be devoted to family time. It was so good to spend time with Pat and our two daughters; picnics, short trips and some time at a friend's cottage.

I certainly had a busy life. Chairing Agincourt Community Services, as it continued to meet the needs of vulnerable people in our area with new programming as well as being successful in connecting the various social service agencies with each other was hugely rewarding. I devoted time to strengthening our local riding association and was elected to the Provincial Council of the New Democrats. As busy as I was, I couldn't turn down an amazing, unique opportunity. A retired Family Court Judge invited me to a meeting with a retired police officer, a social worker and a retired school principal. They wanted to establish a not-for-profit, peer mentorship program for at-risk youth, ages 6 to 15, pairing one on one with senior high school students. I jumped at the chance to be part of the founding group. 45 years later Youth Assisting Youth continues to have a 98% percent success rate of keeping kids out of the criminal justice system and in school.

In June, during the 1975 Provincial election, I was promoted to Chairperson and assigned to Joseph Brant Senior Public School, starting in September. I had truly enjoyed being an Audio-Visual Teacher Consultant, especially because my boss encouraged me to use my imagination. The promotion however put me one step closer to administration — if that was what I wanted. I was on two pathways, which was not a good idea. At some point, likely sooner than later, I would have to decide — a path to being a Principal or a path to being elected.

My situation at Joseph Brant Senior Public School was wonderful. Ted Richardson, my Principal was a superb administrator. I was one member of a team-teaching foursome, and the other three were talented, dedicated teachers with engaging personalities. I enjoyed my new responsibilities as Chair of a department, overseeing programmes and providing leadership. The path to administration was appealing.

# 32

# A Significant Community Contribution

(during my unsolicited sabbatical 1981–85)

Out of the blue, a phone call from someone who said she was in the process of putting together an application to establish Scarborough Community Legal Services. Would I like to be involved. I jumped at the opportunity.

It was during the 1977–81 parliament that Attorney General Roy McMurtry created community legal clinics. The clinics had a four point mandate: legal services, legal education, community development, and law reform. Interestingly there were some private bar lawyers who objected to the clinics on the basis that these "no fee" clinics would take away business from private law firms. Of course the clients of community law clinics are people who could not afford the fees of a private law firm.

In Scarborough the need was obvious. Our city of 500,000 did not have a legal clinic. There were literally thousands of people who could use legal assistance and did not have the means to pay for a lawyer. There was a pressing need for tenants to be organized so they could lobby effectively for better living conditions in their apartment buildings. Tenant organizations are better able than individual tenants to fight back against landlords who attempt to circumvent rent control laws. Advocacy for marginalized groups, and those with disabilities could lead to law reform.

Our application was successful. Four talented, hard working community legal workers, an Administrative Assistant, and two superb lawyers were hired. A community based board of directors was created and I was elected Chair, a position I held until I was elected Speaker of the Ontario Legislature in 1990.

It didn't take long to realize the complexity of what we were trying to do. The myriad of services we offered included laws related to housing, income-maintenance (including employment insurance, the Canada Pension Plan, welfare, family benefits, and workers' compensation), work-related issues (including employment standards, and occupational health and safety); and consumer and debt problems. We initiated immigration legal assistance.

A major initiative we undertook was to help establish a women's shelter. In Scarborough there was no place of protection for women who experienced abuse at the hands of a husband or partner. After more than a year of planning the Emily Stowe Shelter for women and children opened. It is sad that the shelter is needed, but vitally important there is a safe haven for abused women. A major accomplishment by our organization.

We had an amazing staff of talented, experienced community workers and two superb lawyers. The standard format for a community legal clinic was one lawyer, who was the Director, two community workers and one secretary. Our group of six, which after a year or so became a group of eight, consisted of two lawyers, one secretary (who was really an Admin. Assistant) the rest being community workers. There was no Director. Our group functioned as a collective. The result was a dynamic, creative team totally dedicated to the mandate of our clinic. Their enthusiasm was infectious. We had a board of directors who were equally committed to the goals of the clinic.

I certainly was using the political skills I had learned over the past six years. Combined with my experience, especially during my time as Critic of the Attorney General, our Community Legal Clinic was able to help thousands of people. The ten years I had as Chair of SCLS were deeply satisfying.

# 33

# Refocused on Family

Without the extreme hours of an MPP, I had an opportunity to be a more attentive husband and father. As summer approached, daughter Sherri expressed an interest in playing soccer. I was delighted. I had coached the school soccer team when teaching. I loved the sport. So, Sherri signed up for community soccer. Part way through the season I was approached by one of the league's organizers, who informed me they were short of referees. Would I consider refereeing. I enthusiastically agreed. Sherri participated for one season. I stayed on, as a referee for the Scarborough United Women's Soccer Association until the 1985 election. It was great fun. I called games for every age group, from age five to the over 50. Apparently, I was particularly appreciated by the over 50 group as I blew the whistle quite frequently, allowing the women a chance to catch their breath.

After a year of agonizing over the election loss, wallowing in self blame, I accomplished two things. I had found a satisfying normal life of teaching, chairing the legal clinic, refereeing community soccer and spending time with my family. I had also come to the conclusion that the only sensible thing to do was to put the 1981 election behind me.

Family has always been paramount for me. I have never been able to escape the image of Sherri and Barbara crying uncontrollably in front of the tv cameras election night 1981. Now I had an opportunity to put the extra time to good use in developing a deeper bond with my two daughters. The four of us travelled; a camping trip down east to the Atlantic provinces, a trip to Disneyland and in 1983 a month long journey visiting friends and relatives in the UK, a week long, whirlwind coach tour through Belgium, Netherlands, Germany, Luxembourg and France, then a week in a village high in the Swiss Alps. We spent every waking hour together, dining, sharing learning opportunities as well as recreational pursuits. We created a marvellous atmosphere. I got to really know my children as individuals.

Approaching 1985 I experienced an emotional "push-pull." I was truly enjoying life; a significant community involvement, a satisfying teaching experience and delightful family times. I also felt there was more I could accomplish by being elected. I could not escape the bug bite of Hemptera Politicus. The decision to re-enter the political arena was made easier by knowing I had the solid support of my loving family.

# 34

# A Road Back to the Pink Palace

In the winter of 1982, I approached the riding executive with a plan. "I want to win back this riding. I propose that every Saturday until the next election, excepting holidays or totally miserable weather, I will knock on doors. A simple, basic piece of literature is needed and a small group of volunteers. Who is with me?"

An enthusiastic "Count me in!" came from Kaarina Luoma, a young woman new to the riding executive. Next was her boyfriend Mark Crowe then Pat Maye-Chandler, both equally excited. Kaarina didn't need to check with her mom about using their house each Saturday. The Luoma family had always been staunch supporters.

I looked forward to gathering each Saturday. Coffee, donuts, then off to knock on doors. Our plan was simple; houses only, starting with the polls which had been best for us in the last election. Gaining access to apartment buildings was tricky. The law had been changed prior to the 1977 general election, allowing campaigning in apartment buildings during the official election period, but without an election you had to either sneak into a building or have a tenant let you in. We would leave the apartments to sometime in 1985. While we had contacts in a lot of buildings we also realized that the tenant turnover was about 25% year to year. Best to focus on houses where the turnover was minimal.

"Hello, it's David Warner, your former MPP," I would say as I handed the person at the door a card which had my name, Party and contact information on it.

"Is there an election?," was the most common (and genuinely surprised) response.

"There is always an election," was my rejoinder.

It was rewarding to find out that despite having lost the previous election, support remained strong. I had not been forgotten. Many, all of whom we noted, stated "Call me when the election is on. We'll take a sign." or "Glad to support you again, once the election is on."

Of course we ran into people who had voted Conservative, but no gloating, boasting or hostility. The Saturday forays were worthwhile. Those Saturdays also convinced me that Kaarina, with her superb organizing skills and infectious enthusiasm would be the perfect choice as Campaign Manager.

I was on my way back and feeling good about it!

# 35

# Another Unsolicited Sabbatical 1987–1990

*"My dream is for people around the world to look up and to see Canada like a little jewel sitting at the top of the continent."*

— Tommy Douglas

## Under the landslide

Both the Liberals and the New Democrats held up their end of the bargain. The items listed in the Accord were accomplished. Two years without an election was honoured. Now, Premier Peterson turned to the voting public for a majority mandate. And did he get one! Provincially, the Liberals went from 48 seats to 95, the New Democrats from 25 to 19 seats and the Progressive Conservatives sliding from 52 to 16.

Would the results have been different if the New Democrats and Liberals had entered into a coalition government instead of the Accord? We will never know of course, but perhaps the NDP would have got credit for some of what was accomplished in the two years; that credit translating into more seats.

In Scarborough Ellesmere, my vote percentage went up from 37 to 40%. I had won by 283 votes in 1985, to lose by 472 votes two years later. I was surprised with the results, although in truth I always thought I won, regardless of the reality. As with the previous election night it took a long time before the outcome was evident. After dejectedly making my way to where the Liberal candidate Frank Faubert was celebrating, to congratulate him, I headed for the union hall where our disappointed supporters were gathered. My spirits were lifted with the raucous response to me shouting, "The next campaign starts tomorrow! We will win back this Riding!"

**"When you come to a fork in the road, take it."**

— Yogi Berra

Perhaps it was the dark days following my election loss in 1981 and the subsequent soul searching, or the 1985 win substantiating a conviction that it was always possible to bounce back. Whatever the reason, I found it easier this time to accept the ballot box defeat. I could slide back into a life of teaching, community involvement, full time parenting, social life and travelling. I also knew that always lingering was the life long effect of having been bitten by the "Hemptera Politicus" bug. After winning three elections and losing two, I had reached a fork in the road.

1985 to 1987 had been two years of frenetic legislative activity. Lots to celebrate, especially being on the Justice Committee which passed the Family Law Reform Act, but also some unfinished business. It was tempting to call an end to my political career and slide back in to a comfortable, enjoyable life. However, if you want to make changes you need the power to do so. There were two issues I passionately wanted to keep working on; a Hemodialysis Unit at Scarborough General Hospital and community based services for seniors. I needed to be back at Queen's Park come the next election in order to at least fight for those two issues.

The first issue was one I felt could be solved by applying my political skills more effectively. If the Liberals remained as government come the next election then I had to find a way to get past the partisan barrier. I needed to make this dialysis campaign appear more of a community appealing to government for a needed service than a personal political campaign.

The second issue, that of Community Based Services for Seniors, was trickier.

My Bill 3, formerly known as "An Act for the Provision and Integration of Community Based Services for Seniors," which I dubbed as The Seniors Independence Act, passed second reading, but never ended up on a Committee's agenda. I had a deep conviction that the essence of the Bill was absolutely the right way to go in providing a longer, better quality of life for senior citizens. If the Bill was enacted properly, hundreds, if not thousands of older adults would be living independently, not having to be 'housed' in a nursing home.

When an election is called, everything on the Order Paper dies. I would need to re-introduce my Bill. I needed a new game plan; different strategies to get the support needed so that my "Seniors Independence Act"became law. I would reach out to certain Members in the other two Parties to gain their support. The strong support I had gained from various municipalities around the province could be a springboard for a wider range of support. I could embark on a province wide campaign.

To accomplish what I had set out to do in the last Parliament I needed to be elected. I had bounced back before. I could do it again. Majority government meant no election for four years, so in the meantime I could enjoy a normal life and lay the groundwork for a return to the Pink Palace.

## Sabbatical starts with a picket line

Voters went to the polls on September 10, 1987. Eleven days later the elementary teachers of Toronto went on strike. After winding up the Constituency office, cleaning out my Queen's Park office and attending to necessary paper work, I was in time to join the picket line at Henry Kelsey Sr. Public School. The Scarborough Board had asked me, and I happily agreed, to return to the school I had taught at from 1981 to '85.

The withdrawal of service by the elementary teachers of Metropolitan Toronto was centred on the issue of appropriate preparation time. Being on the picket line was a great opportunity to get reacquainted with the Kelsey staff. The month long strike which ended October 18, achieved an agreement on preparation time; initially 100 minutes, later 120 minutes per week of preparation time. I looked forward to being immersed once again in something I had never considered a job; the joy of working with children.

## Normal life once more

No agonizing about the election result this time. I felt good about returning to teaching, and being fully involved in the life of the school. Both daughters were in high school. I was able to attend their drama productions at Leacock Collegiate as well as their Scarborough Band performances. It was wonderful to enjoy theatre nights and play bridge with our friends. I didn't have to give away Blue Jay tickets because of a last minute political engagement. I planned family vacations; the most memorable of which was our first ever Mediterranean cruise. I was now a full time parent!

## Community commitment

The time I had spent since 1981 as Chair of the Scarborough Community Legal Services had quite an impact on me. I came to deeply appreciate how important the legal clinic was to the community. Not being elected gave me time to be more deeply involved as Chair of SCLS. It was satisfying to work with a dedicated Board of Directors and our team of highly skilled lawyers and legal workers. Every one of them embodied passionate commitment and compassion.

I enjoyed my unexpected sabbatical. Yet, I instinctively knew that the effect of the "Hemptera Politicus" bug bite had not worn off. While my new "normal" life was satisfying I would want to plot and plan for a return to Queen's Park. I had four years to figure out how to get back to the Pink Palace. Well, I thought I had four years!

## 36

# Politics Follows Me to India

Early in 1990 I applied to Project Overseas, a collaborative teaching development program operated by the Canadian Teachers Federation. I was accepted to be part of a four member Canadian team who would be working with a three member Indian team, from mid-July to mid-August. We would be working with newly graduated teachers, with a focus on the creative use of audio/visual equipment. My experience as an AV Teacher Consultant would come in handy. I was excited about the opportunity, especially my first visit to India.

The teaching experience in India was amazing, at least until July 30. Our Canadian team was led by Evelyn, a retired elementary school Principal from Edmonton. The other two women, both secondary school teachers, Chris from Vancouver and Bev from Ottawa. I was the only male and the only one without international teaching experience. Not necessarily intimidating, but certainly humbling. It didn't take long to realize that the three women were talented, creative experienced teachers with a deep passion for education. The three person Indian team was headed by Dr. Gulab Charasia, the founding President of the Council for Teacher Education, India, an educator with his M. Ed. From Columbia University, USA. He and

I became friends, keeping in touch until he passed away in 2009. The remaining Indian team members were both experienced male teachers.

Working with enthusiastic, freshly minted teachers was delightful. The instructional sessions in Bhopal and Jabalpur were excellent, especially when we were invited into someone's home for dinner. We had dinner at a hotel only once! Since I enjoy Indian cuisine, having authentic, home-made meals was special.

One experience in particular stands out. A severely rugged road meant that our 120 km drive from Jabalpur to the village of Katni took much longer than we thought it would. It was a blistering hot day, and we were about two hours late. Would the students still be waiting for us to judge their science fair projects.

What happened next could have been a scene from a Hollywood movie. As our van crested a hill we could see two rows of students, perhaps 400 in total, half on each side of the road. Every student was waving a home-made Canadian flag. The four of us stared in disbelief, then tears started to flow. I recalled an earlier remark by Dr. Charasia. "Do you know the difference between the Americans who come here and the Canadians? The Americans always ask for their flag to be flown. Canadians never ask, but you will always see Canadian flags." After exiting the van we were escorted by a pipe and drum band to a courtyard where a tribal group performed traditional dancing on stilts. The dancers formed a circle around a man who gyrated on foot. The energetic dancer then invited me to join him in the circle. I did my best to keep up, feeling the energy and the sheer joy of the tribal group, also thankful that I wasn't asked to try dancing on stilts.

Eventually we got around to judging the science projects. The teachers had narrowed the choices down to six. We were to select first, second, etc. Nervously, our group huddled to ponder the situation. This was a political situation. We were four foreigners in a tribal village. Every child in the village attended this school. Unwittingly we could stir up an unhappy situation among the children. Our unanimous decision was to declare that these six projects were all so remarkable that it was impossible to place one ahead of the others. All six were first place winners! Such celebrating I have rarely witnessed. Our reward was a sumptuous feast. Tired, but joyously happy, we returned in the wee small hours of the morning to Jabalpur.

The Indian team knew that I had been a Member of Ontario's Provincial Parliament. This turned out to be a source of discomfort for me. I was not the Canadian team leader. I was, in fact, the junior member of the team. So, when Dr. Charasia asked me to participate in a national radio program devoted to education, I tried diplomatically to suggest that our team Leader, Evelyn, should be the radio guest. Dr. Charasia would not take no for an answer. He wanted the former MPP. Not for the first time, I realized that politics would follow me wherever I went, whatever I did.

# 37

# A New Path

## 1995–1999

*"Don't be afraid of the future," he begins. "Regret is the most useless of human emotions. And there's something happy around the corner every day — just go find it."*

— David Peterson

I stood by the windows of my classroom, staring out at the empty schoolyard, holding a bag lunch in my hand thinking about how quickly my world had changed. One day I was presiding over Ontario's Legislature, responsible for the management of 300 employees, meeting and greeting heads of state, travelling the world seeking ties of friendship and the next day I am in charge of a grade seven class at Anson Park Public School in Scarborough. The fine dining is gone but I am sure I will enjoy the peanut butter and jam sandwich I made for myself.

As it turned out no one could have selected a better school for what turned out to be the last of my teaching years. Anson was a small community school; one class per grade, kindergarten to grade eight. Since the school was too small to have a Vice Principal, I filled that role as Chairperson. John Sexton was the Principal and in his last year prior to retirement. He was wonderful to work with. Then came Ernie Mee, in his first year as a Principal. I soon discovered that in addition to being a superb Principal, Ernie was a professional musician, had a sailboat, and reconstructed old cars. The two of us hit it off immediately, went from colleagues to a friendship which continues today. The staff were friendly, making me feel welcomed right away. Teaching students age 12 and 13 is always an adventure, but a rewarding one. The Anson Park students were delightful and the parents supportive. I settled in quickly to my new reality. I was enjoying the new path I was on.

The bubble burst in the fall of 1997. What teachers want is to be left alone to teach. They chose the noble profession of teaching, took teacher training, and were hired to apply their skills and training. First the Bob Rae government imposed a social contract whereby they forfeited three to five days pay, a unilateral move which was deeply resented. Now the Mike Harris government would impose serious budget cuts, making their teaching life more difficult. Adding insult to injury was the clear impression that Premier Harris had little if any respect for teachers.

No amount of discussion between the teachers' unions and the government made a difference. The deep budget cuts, with their serious consequences such as music programs which couldn't keep going because there was no money for instrument repair, continued unabated. In January 1997 Bill 160 was introduced. "Under Bill 160, responsibilities for multiple aspects of school administration would be transferred from local school boards to the provincial government. In particular, the bill would grant the province the ability to determine school funding, class sizes, the levying of school property taxes, and the number of hours allotted for teacher prep time; it would also permit non-certified teachers to instruct in public schools, and implement standardized testing for students. While the government stated that the purpose of Bill 160 was to "improve the performance of Ontario schoolchildren", critics of the bill argued that its true aim was to diminish the power of school boards and teachers unions, and that the passing of the bill would amount to CAD$1 billion in cuts to the province's education system and layoffs for up to 10,000 teachers."[54]

Jobs were on the line. The teachers of Ontario responded to the assault on education by going on strike. The largest teachers' strike to ever occur in North America started on October 27 with walkouts by over 126,000 teachers resulting in the closure of nearly all of Ontario's 4,742 public schools. Although the teachers had solid support from the public the Harris government refused to budge. The teachers' unions called off the strike on November 10. The cuts would continue unabated.

Walking the picket line was an interesting experience. The same teachers who had opposed the Rae government Social Contract were now looking for the NDP to support their fight against the Harris government. The support of the parents and the community was reassuring that we were fighting a just cause. I was most grateful to a parent who lived across from the school. She told us that her front door would be open from 6:30 am for anyone who wanted to stop by for a coffee, get warm or use the washroom.

As 1999 rolled around I had reached another fork in the road. Having taught 25 years should I choose to retire this June I qualified for a 50% pension. On the other hand I liked where I was. I had been in and out of teaching too often to consider climbing back on the promotion ladder, but I would continue to have my Chairperson status, which provided the extra responsibilities I appreciated. What tipped the scales toward retiring were two factors. The public opinion polls during the spring of 1999 showed the Conservatives and Liberals close. My instinct was that Mike Harris had a better chance of winning than the Liberals under Dalton McGuinty. Continuing to teach under a Mike Harris government was not attractive.

---

54 "Why Ontario teachers went on a province-wide strike in 1997", Canadian Broadcasting Corporation, February 21, 2020.

The other factor was a desire to use my political experience and skills in ways which could be of benefit to civil society. The end of June, 1999, was the end of my teaching career. I loved teaching. I have shared my thoughts about the joy of teaching in a later chapter.

## Churchill Society for the Advancement of Parliamentary Democracy

> *"We shall fight in France, we shall fight on the seas and oceans, we shall fight on the beaches, we shall fight on the landing grounds, We shall never surrender."*
>
> — Winston Churchill

I had always been in awe of Winston Churchill. As a teenager I tried to imagine what it would be like to have the oratorical ability to galvanize an entire nation in a desperate fight to save their country. My two federal election forays, with a total of more than sixty all-candidates meetings, average attendance 1,000, whetted my appetite for more political debate.

After winning the 1975 election, I had visions of being a revered orator at Queen's Park. That vision vanished when I sat in the Chamber listening to electrifying speeches from Stephen Lewis, James Renwick, Jim Bullbrook, Darcy McKeough, and a few others. I would have to be satisfied with presenting well reasoned, substantive arguments and witty interjections.

During my term as Speaker, Donald MacDonald, former Leader of the Ontario New Democrats, came to see me. He suggested that I might enjoy joining the Churchill Society for the Advancement of Parliamentary Democracy, saying that while there were a lot of Conservatives in the group, they did good work in promoting parliamentary democracy.

I hadn't reached Churchill's level of oratory, but I could learn more about the man who inspired a nation in their hour of greatest need. I joined the Churchill Society in 1995 and was promptly asked to serve on the Executive. It turned out to be a wonderful experience. There may well have been a lot of Conservatives in the group, but I wouldn't know it from the work we did together. There was never a politically partisan moment.

The Society had an impressive list of accomplishments which included having a statue of Sir Winston sculpted, then erected at Toronto City Hall. No mean feat! There were a number of initiatives involving young people, all aimed at developing a greater understanding and appreciation of our parliamentary democracy. Financial sponsorship was provided to the Ontario Legislature's Internship Programme and the Teachers Institute on Canadian Parliamentary Democracy. A high school essay contest focusing on parliamentary democracy was launched, offering a cash prize. All of these initiatives required planning and fund raising. As a politician I was no stranger to fund raising. The combination of my political experience and teaching background was being put to good use. I served on the Board of Directors for three enjoyable years.

## A Canadian's Love of Cuba

As a result of my visits to Cuba when I was Speaker I had fallen in love with Cuba. Not the endless stretches of white sand beaches or the lively, joyous Havana night clubs. It was the people. Their genuine warmth, kindness and determination to be independent.

The irony of Cuba's situation is striking. A successful revolution in 1959 rid the island of a military dictatorship as well as drugs and gambling, both of which were controlled by a US based mafia. That should be cause for celebration for anyone who doesn't favour dictatorships. Instead of celebration, decades long American government animosity.

Russian missiles on Cuban soil in 1962, at the height of the Cold War, prompted the US to apply an economic blockade. Sixty years have passed and the internationally illegal economic blockade remains. Each year, for the past 30 years, there is a resolution presented at the United Nations, condemning the blockade. The resulting vote is usually the same; almost every country supporting the resolution and two countries against; United States and Israel. In 2022, the vote in the 193-member General Assembly was 185 countries supporting the condemnation, the United States and Israel opposing it, and Brazil and Ukraine abstaining.

## Democracy in Cuba

It is easy to understand that "top down" governance was needed in 1959. Schooling was almost non-existent for Cubans. Life expectancy was age 60. Universal health care did not exist. Fidel Castro's first National Congress of the Cuban Communist Party was determined to create an excellent public education system and a universal health care system while ridding the country of drugs, gambling and prostitution. Within a decade they accomplished all of the above, except ending prostitution. During our parliamentary visits in the 90's we were often told that there was an interest in political change, but that as long as the United States continued to treat Cuba as an enemy, the Cuban government needed to remain unified, speaking with one voice. Political plurality would serve to undermine Cuban sovereignty.

Cuba is not a democracy, but there are democratic aspects to the system. Individuals can run for local town or city Council. No Party label required. Once elected there is a publicly held accountability session every six months. Constituents, if unhappy with their local councillor, can vote to hold a new election. The current councillor is obliged sit out that election, but can run in a following election, at the end of a two year term. The system at the local level appears to provide an effective way to meet local needs.

It is still one Party rule in Cuba, that of the Communist Party. I wonder how things might have progressed differently had the

United States engaged in meaningful, friendly dialogue instead of trying to starve the island nation into submission.

## Canada Cuba Friendship Association

Dr. Jim Henderson, MPP, was the organizer of the parliamentary delegations I led to Cuba. On one of the trips he suggested that when I was no longer elected I consider joining the CCFA, Toronto. He told me that they were a very active non-profit group who were focused on developing friendship between Canada and Cuba, organizing humanitarian aid and protesting against the United States economic blockade of Cuba. I should know, he said, that there were a number of communists in the group. There may well have been a number of communists in the group, but I wouldn't know it from the work we did together. There was never a politically partisan moment.

The decision to join CCFA in 1996 was an easy one. The unique opportunity of an in-depth view of Cuban culture, history, economy and political structure revealed a proud people who cared about each other. Politics aside, Cubans wanted to be part of the world. A vivid example for me was our visit to Tarará, a city outside of Havana, where children who survived the Chernobyl nuclear disaster were being cared for. The setting for residency, treatment for the effects of the radiation suffered, schooling in their first language and recreation was located at a former seaside holiday resort.

I was excited about using my political experience and skills in a battle against the illegal US Blockade of Cuba. That Blockade had caused billions of dollars damage to the Cuban economy and with the collapse of the Soviet Empire in 1991, had sparked a significant international humanitarian effort.

Since I had created Friendship Agreements with Santiago and Havana, being on the board of the Canadian-Cuban Friendship Association seemed a natural fit. I was soon elected Chair, a position I held for nine years.

## Raising the Cuban flag at Toronto City Hall — 1996

An effective way to raise the profile of CCFA would be to hold an event at Nathan Phillips Square. Make it a celebration, with Cuban music, food and beverages available, perhaps teach salsa dancing. Raising the Cuban flag, for the first time at Toronto City Hall, was the icing on the cake. Approvals were sought and granted.

The Cuban Ambassador, Cuban Consul General in Toronto, a City Councillor representing Mayor Barbara Hall, and members of the CCFA executive gathered in the rain to sing "O' Canada," then Cuba's national anthem, as the Cuban flag was hoisted on a City Hall flagpole.

Over the next decade I had the privilege of being MC for the joyous celebration of Cuban culture at Nathan Phillips Square. Each year there was a band on the stage, singers, dancers, free salsa lessons, speeches by the Cuban Ambassador, Toronto City Councillors, MPPs, MPs and of course the Chair of CCFA. The annual festivities always started with the raising of the Cuban flag, and our flag, followed by singing the Canadian National Anthem, then the Cuban National Anthem, both led by a very talented opera singer.

A culturally rich Cuba remains economically poor. Literacy, longevity, infant mortality all comparable to Canada. This small Caribbean country of 11 million has a long list of accomplishments, especially in the field of medical science research. Most of the world has a friendly, working relationship with Cuba. Should the United States decide to shake hands instead of waving fists, there just might be a better chance for a fully democratic Cuba.

## The Song of Cuba

Life in a rhythm of independence,
a heartbeat stronger than the incessant
Latin beat, or the muse's verse.

A rhythm singing freedom,
framed with caring and sharing,
caressing every child with love's
soft, sweet breeze.
Sway to a pulsating rhythm,
the pulse of a proud people.
Rhythm which is life itself.
See their love with your soul.
Hear their voices with your heart.
Touch love with love.

# PART FIVE

# My Life After Politics — Political Skills Connect with Civil Society 1999–2022

*"If you want to go quickly, go alone.*
*If you want to go far, go together."*

— African Proverb

# 38

# Forum For Young Canadians

Ernie Mee, the amazing Principal of Anson Park Public School, arranged a joyous retirement party at a waterfront pub. Ernie was the bass player of the trio which entertained everyone. Scrumptious food, drinks, music, singing, laughter. What a wonderful celebration with colleagues, friends and family. A new chapter in my life was about to unfold.

I was retiring at age 57; young, healthy, energetic. I also had something quite valuable, an asset which few possess, political experience. I treasured my gift of good health. Jack Warner, my dad, died at age 55 and Pat's dad, Gord Draper, passed away at age 65. Neither man had a retirement life. I now would have no direct responsibilities other than to Pat and my family. More time to travel, read, and spend some leisure time with friends and neighbours. There was however something more important than personal gratification waiting for me.

It turned out to be a perfect fit! In the fall of 1999 I was offered an opportunity to be a Trustee on the Board of Directors of Forum For Young Canadians. I jumped at the chance. I was soon to discover that I could ably draw on both my political and teaching experiences.

The program, whose patron is the Governor General, brings young people together from every province and territory in Canada for a week in Ottawa. They have an up close and personal look at how parliament functions, engage in mock sessions, visit the Supreme Court, meet MPs and senior staff. The highlight of the week is the MP's Dinner. There are usually 40 to 50 Members of Parliament each seated with a student who is from their riding. I recall one of those dinners which was attended by Justin Trudeau, MP. The moment he entered the room quite a few young women excitedly formed a line to get his autograph.

In addition to the 100 or so students, there were a dozen high school teachers who were from every province and territory, none of them connected to the attending students. The teachers' program dovetailed with that of the students. I volunteered to be a resource for them. I always looked forward to the end of the day when I would get together with the teachers to review what they had experienced and answer questions. I was able to witness the student program first hand as well as connect with the teachers. I always returned home energized having experienced both teachers and students excited about our parliamentary democracy.

The board of directors was also from across Canada and with a varied background. I quickly learned that this diverse group were deeply committed to the concept of bringing young people together to deepen their understanding of Canada and learn from one another while growing their confidence and commitment towards democracy and civic engagement. Deep commitment to Forum was also evident with the staff, led by the Executive Director Clare Baxter. Augmenting Clare's superb organizing skills was her warmth, enthusiasm and an amazing ability to get the students to connect with each other. One special ability which we didn't get to hear often was her fiddle playing. Too bad as in the summers she taught fiddle playing at Gaelic College, Cape Breton.

## The magic of Forum

Bringing young Canadians together from every part of Canada provides a unique opportunity for contrasting and comparing regional experiences. Understandably those from Canada's far north have the most profound differences. One of the weeks I attended included a heart warming incident, one which involved an Inuit student from a small village in Nunavut.

The session on the Role of the MP was held in the Press Theatre that day, a small, intimate room with blue curtains and flags in the background, a room normally used for press conferences. The speaker was MP Jack Layton. When it came time for the Q&A, the student from Nunavut identified where he was from and asked Jack a question. A few questions later, another student asked Jack why he had chosen to join the NDP. Jack related his response to the student from Nunavut, explaining to the rest of the students that the cost of living in the North is outrageously higher than in the rest of Canada. He cited examples such as the extremely high cost of food, fresh milk (which he said is why so many people in the North drink powdered milk or soft drinks, both of which last longer than fresh milk), toothpaste, gas, etc. Jack said that he chose the NDP because he wanted to fight for equality in the cost and standard of living for everyone in Canada, no matter where people happened to live. The students burst into applause at Jack's response. This discussion left a lasting impression on the students, especially for two of them.

Just before the start of the (students) First Ministers' Conference at the end of the week those two students spear-headed an idea to create a surprise "care package" for the Nunavut student, to be presented to him at the Closing Banquet a few hours later. They asked the Director of the program, Clare Baxter for permission to embark on this mission. Permission was granted, along with a donation from Clare. The two students quickly and quietly collected donations while the student from Nunavut and other "First Ministers and Prime Minister" were engaged in a simulation exercise in another room. Everyone wanted to pitch in. Enthusiastic, overwhelming support!

The two students, accompanied by their Group Leader, went shopping. The generosity of the group resulted in there being two huge, very heavy boxes of items for their Nunavut friend and his family; everything from toothbrushes and toothpaste to powdered milk, soap, gas cards, school supplies, Easter chocolates, etc. Clare Baxter called the airlines, explained why there would be so much additional luggage for the Nunavut student on his return flight and asked that any additional baggage fees be sent to Forum. Impressed by this remarkable story, the airline representative waived the luggage fees.

The presentation was made to the Nunavut student by the two organizers of this "care package project" at the Closing Banquet. Thunderous applause. Not a dry eye in the room. The appreciative student from Nunavut was overcome with joy, deeply touched by the friendships cultivated with every person in the group, who were from every part of Canada.

This anecdote is but one of the numerous times I witnessed the "magic of Forum". There is no doubt in my mind that more opportunities need to be developed for Canada's youth to get to know each other better, from coast to coast to coast.

Forum has expanded over the years to take advantage of technology but the core message of inspiring youth to deepen their understanding of Canada and the national decision-making process remains. Forum is a remarkable program and it was a privilege to have been part of it for more than a decade.

# 39

# United Nations Association in Canada

*"The United Nations is our one great hope for a peaceful and free world."*

— Hon. Lester B. Pearson

"Better late than never" so goes the saying. In this instance more than 40 years had passed from my first opportunity to join a United Nations Association. In the 1950's a United Nations Club in a high school was common. There was one at my school, Agincourt Collegiate, but I was too wrapped up in being the school DJ, attending football games and just hanging out with my pals to have time to join a UN Club. Ironic really because at home almost every dinner time included a discussion about world events.

In 2000 I joined the Toronto branch of the UN Association in Canada (UNACTO) and was promptly elected Chair. There were a number of factors contributing to my decision to join this important organization which was created in 1946, just after the United Nations came into existence. One significant factor was that I was impressed by the legacy of Lester B. Pearson. He was instrumental in drafting the UN Charter and served as Canada's ambassador to the UN from

1945 to 1957 and his efforts in resolving the Suez Crisis through the creation of the first-ever UN peacekeeping force earned him the Nobel Peace Prize in 1957. Another factor in my decision was my experience in achieving three Friendship Agreements. Overarching these factors was my profound belief that every conceivable effort must always be made to create peace and a more just world.

The executive was small in number but energetic and devoted. We undertook a number of initiatives aimed at promoting the UN Association and significant global issues. One year into my term as President I was asked to seek election as a Regional Vice-President, which I did and was elected. The next step was in 2002 when I was elected as a National Vice-President, a position which I held until 2005.

One of our Toronto projects was to assist in publicizing the Land Mines Ban Treaty, an important peace measure, initiated by Canada and signed by 122 countries in 1997. Civilians, especially children, are safer when landmines are removed and countries less likely to go to war over casualties caused by the landmines. Setting up a kiosk at Toronto's Eaton Centre, handing out literature and asking people to sign a petition sure is a lot different than electioneering. Unlike a political campaign we did not meet any opposition to our efforts. There were many who were unaware of the Land Mine Treaty so took the literature but didn't sign the petition. There were others who were quite happy to sign. There were a few who were either too busy or simply shrugged in passing as if this issue was too far away from Canada to have any relevance to their life here. The selection of the Eaton Centre for our little campaign was by design. This famous shopping mall is a major tourist attraction in a city which is a preferred destination by a lot of Americans. The United States at the time had not signed the Treaty. As of 2022 the US remains one of the thirty-two countries who have not signed the treaty. There are two other permanent members of the United Nations Security Council: China and Russia who have yet to sign a Treaty which is designed to save lives.

The global challenges of climate change, regional wars, food and water scarcity, population displacement, to name only a few, are overwhelming. The one remaining great hope for a free and peaceful world is the United Nations.

*2005*

I had reached another fork in the road; follow the suggestion that I seek election to be National President of UNAC or follow a new path, that of helping establish a not-for-profit debt counselling and debt management organization. The UN Association was inspiring and worthwhile. I believed passionately in the aims and ideals of this vital global organization. I knew from my constituency work that not only was individual debt a significant problem for a lot of people but also that there were vultures out there, masquerading as debt management experts who actually made the problem worse. The venture being proposed could be of immense help in Toronto and beyond.

# 40

# InCharge Debt Solutions

*"Debt is the slavery of the free."*

— Publilius Syrus, a Roman slave

It is easy to get into debt. Credit cards are readily available and purchasing with those cards helps avoid the reality of how much you are really spending. A while later the credit card statement arrives in the mail. The card company is generously giving you an option of paying a nominal amount now and paying the balance later. The later part can be at 24% interest (higher or lower related to current economic times). By choosing to pay just the minimum you have unwittingly fallen down the debt hole. There is a good chance that you don't know how to climb out of the hole. Don't think for a moment that this sad story is confined to people of modest means. There are those with six figure incomes deeply in debt. Money management is an elusive skill for a lot of people. Enter credit counselling.

I got to know Greg Gogan during the 2004 federal election. Greg was the NDP Candidate in Scarborough Centre, provincially my old riding Scarborough Ellesmere. He was a chartered financial planner with experience in the world of finance and deeply concerned about the plight of so many people who fell into debt and didn't know how to climb out of the hole. Canvassing together door-to-door during the election was a great opportunity to learn more about each other and share ideas. Greg lost that election and a short while later called me saying he would like me to meet an American who was a board member of InCharge Debt Solutions, a large not-for-profit debt counselling organization headquartered in Florida. After meeting Lonnie Ritzer, lawyer and board member and engaging in quite a few conversations I was convinced that InCharge was a first rate company and that starting a 'sister' company in Canada was a good idea. There certainly was a need here. Greg and I were determined that over time the Canadian operation would morph into a 'stand alone' Canadian company.

"How is a not-for-profit service able to meet the expenses associated with a business; rent, salaries, advertising?" I asked. Here's the explanation I received:

Banks and credit card companies like to get their money back. If someone defaults on paying there is an option for the lender to go to court. That is an expensive route and there is a chance that the individual simply has no assets and will declare bankruptcy. This is where InCharge is of benefit to both the lender and debtor; negotiating a debt repayment plan over a number of years, usually four, at a greatly reduced interest rate. The lender will get back their money, albeit over time and our client will be debt free! Since the financial institutions benefit from our intervention they donate to InCharge.

Developing a plan to retire the client's debt is one part of our service. A concurrent part is money management counselling.

## The latte factor

"How much do you spend on coffee each day?" This is a good place to start. Turns out quite a few people are spending $10.00 or more per day at a coffee shop near where they work. That computes to at least $200.00 per month.[55] Options are suggested; a coffee fund at work, bring a thermos. Counsellors take the client through an exhaustive list of regular expenses such as haircuts, clothing, food etc. determining in each case if there are less expensive alternatives. If the situation is severe; disconnect from the internet and use the local public library, cancel your credit card and use cash or a debit card. As a footnote, I was shocked to learn we had examples of individuals who had maxed out more than 40 credit cards!

## Success stories

There are literally thousands of success stories, people who were able to shed huge debts and never have to look back, now able to successfully manage their money. Our AGM (annual general meeting) always featured stories of accomplishment. As I listened to some of the stories I couldn't help but think how easy it is to fall into the 'debt hole'. Learning how the person climbed out of the hole brought tears.

The credit counsellors are talented, knowledgeable people; patient listeners, empathetic, and skilled at leading the client to just the right path for them. Below are two of the countless "Thank You" letters we received:

"I have struggled with financial well being for my entire adult life. My habits with money reflected an attitude of 'lack' and irresponsibility. My counsellor helped me to acknowledge and take ownership of that. I can be financially strong if I take things step by step. It's not EASY but it's SIMPLE...A-B-C. Your organization is an empowering and empathetic resource. Thank you!"

"My counsellor is absolutely incredible. I had the pleasure of working on a Debt Management Program with her 2.5 years ago. She taught me financial skills, budgeting, learning to work with my money, and motivated me to reach my goal. I paid off $10,000 in

---

55 Figures as of 2007

debt in 9 months. Today, after my 2-year mark, she wrapped up my account and helped me with credit building options for the future. I am so relieved, grateful and happy!"

InCharge Debt Solutions had an excellent, dedicated board of directors and an efficient management team. We were successful in establishing satellite offices and effective working relations with smaller credit counselling organizations. By about year 2012 we realized that instead of competing with for profit companies we were actually, especially in Toronto, competing against Credit Canada, a not-for-profit established in 1966. It made sense for us to amalgamate and so we did the following year. I then served on Credit Canada's board of directors for a year to make sure the transition was a smooth one for our staff.

Those six years were rewarding. The banking world presented a learning curve for me. I can't claim to have become an expert, but I came away a lot more knowledgeable. Learning how many people are deeply in debt and don't know how to escape that debt had inspired me to do everything I could to make InCharge successful. It was satisfying to chair an organization which had dedicated, talented professional staff who had helped so many people create a better life.

I came away with some concerns. Our society isn't doing a good enough job in making sure everyone is financially literate so they don't get into debt so easily. Some debts are acceptable, such as purchasing a house or a car. But it is how one manages the debt which can spell the difference between financial success or failure. The payday loan places, which levy outrageous interest rates, exist because we do not have a banking system which serves everyone. That needs to change.

I certainly had a wonderful opportunity to use my political skills when connecting with the banking industry. All told, it was a great experience. The amalgamation with Credit Canada meant that my time with Credit Canada was winding down. That was when another path opened up.

# 41

# The Ontario Association of Former Parliamentarians

On May the 10th, 2000, the first Bill in the history of Ontario to be introduced by a committee was passed into law, with unanimous support of the House. Rev. Derwyn Shea who had served one term (1995–99) as the Member for High Park-Swansea had the concept and was the driving force to establish an Association of Former Parliamentarians. The catalyst for Derwyn's passionate quest to create an association whose primary aim would be to support each other was the tragic death of Han Daigeler, a former MPP who just five months after his defeat in the 1995 election committed suicide. Essentially a politician's life is measured in victories and defeats. Losing can be totally devastating, something which I experienced in 1981. Acceptance of defeat is not easy. Derwyn reasoned that those who best understand an election loss are former Members. He was right. Derwyn also realized that an association of former Members could do more than be there for one another.

OAFP was established with the following objects:

- to put the knowledge and experience of its members at the service of parliamentary democracy in Ontario and elsewhere;
- to serve the public interest by providing non-partisan support for the parliamentary system of government in Ontario;
- to foster a spirit of community among former parliamentarians;
- to foster good relations between members of the Legislative Assembly of the Province of Ontario and former parliamentarians; and
- to protect and promote the interests of former parliamentarians.

As with most of the former MPPs I was happy to join the Association. I would attend the annual general meetings and at each AGM Derwyn would approach me about joining the board. He was a very persuasive fellow, but I begged off each time, citing other commitments.

In 2012 with the amalgamation of InCharge and Credit Canada behind me, I was ready to readily accept Derwyn's invitation to join the board of OAFP. I admit that at the time I did not realize just how rewarding would be the experience.

Derwyn Shea was an excellent Chair, setting a harmonious tone. The three Parties were equally represented on the board and everyone adopted a non-partisan approach to our work. This was definitely going to be enjoyable and stimulating.

## Back to school

"Politics is not a science. It is an art." This opening remark in front of a university political science class invited lots of discussion. It had been a very long time since I had been at university, but just looking at the eager faces, quizzical looks and hands in the air I felt the years melt. Along with a colleague, who was of a different political party, we were participating in OAFP's Campus Program. Former Members engaging in a two hour session with post-secondary students is a good way to reinforce the importance of parliamentary democracy. Over the next couple of years I visited on one or several occasions U of T, McMaster, Seneca College and Toronto Metropolitan University (formerly Ryerson). The session at TMU was particularly memorable.

Sean Conway (former Cabinet Minister) and I were asked to talk about health care costs. We had served together on a Select Committee on Health Care Costs[56] Sean's story of how the mixing of health care and religion is a recipe for upheaval was told against a backdrop of a provincially mandated Health Services Restructuring Commission whose work ultimately resulted in (among other things) "ordering amalgamations and "takeovers," creating larger hospital organizations capable of greater quality and economies of scale; closed 31 public, 6 private and 6 provincial psychiatric hospital sites, prompting major expansion, province-wide, in home care and facility-based longterm care"[57] Sean represented a riding which included the town of Pembroke. The town had two hospitals, the publicly owned Pembroke Civic, and a Roman Catholic hospital,

---

56 Committee on Health Care, Financing And Costs June 19, 1978 — October 23, 1978

57 Riding the Third Rail - The Story of Ontario's Health Services Restructuring Commission, 1996-2000
Duncan Sinclair, Mark Rochon and Peggy Leatt August 15, 2005

Pembroke General. The Commission decided to close the Civic and consolidate health care services at the General. As Sean was telling the story advice from a former colleague, Jim Renwick, was dancing around in my head, "Always try to avoid issues which involve cats, dogs or religion." Predictably a lot of people in Pembroke were very upset, some because of an attachment to the civic hospital and others because of a concern that a Catholic hospital might have challenges providing reproductive health services for women.

It is a tribute to Sean Conway that he was able to steer his way through an emotionally charged political situation. The Pembroke Civic Hospital closed December 31, 1997. Despite the political turmoil, Sean Conway was re-elected in 1999. My guess is that being of sterling character, bright, articulate, honest and hard-working accounted for eight straight election victories. He was trusted through good times and bad by the constituents of Renfrew—Nipissing—Pembroke.

The students were amazed by the story. So was I. I don't think these political science students had ever considered the intersection of politics, hospitals and religion and thankfully I had never encountered such a situation.

# 42

## David Warner, Editor

Perhaps secretly I always wanted to be an editor. I enjoyed writing and came to appreciate journalism when, as an MPP, I became acquainted with the Press Gallery. Now as a board member I had an unexpected opportunity to be an editor. Derwyn Shea was emailing a newsletter, The InFormer, usually eight pages, periodically. He asked me if I would like to take over the publication. I agreed but only if I could send it out quarterly and expand the newsletter. That was the start of a decade long journalistic journey.

Alexa Huffman was our intern, a fourth year Journalism student from Ryerson. She was brilliant, but if I was to accomplish what I wanted to do, I needed two interns. I wanted to expand the scope of the publication to a quarterly, full colour, 32 page published magazine. An electronic version would be sent out at the same time we mailed the magazine. I was determined that nothing was going to be printed until we had reached a professional standard — which we did by 2017 with our first Special Edition. The printed quarterlies came a bit later, in 2020.

The interns I worked with were amazing. They were bright, enthusiastic, talented and creative. It was a joy to work with them. A couple of exceptional interns, Victoria Esterhammer and Lauren

Malyk, after they had graduated, volunteered to edit my children's novel. More about that later.

My concept was to make this publication interactive and educational. While interviewing former Members would always be the central part of each edition the members would be asked to contribute. I set out to develop a wide variety of subjects.

As knowledgeable as those elected tend to be, I thought there were places around the world about which few retired MPPs had knowledge. The world lives here so why not explore some of those places represented by Ontario MPPs. I always looked for the connection to Canada. One interesting example is Bhutan a Buddhist kingdom on the Himalayas' eastern edge, a land of monasteries, fortresses (or dzongs) and dramatic topography ranging from subtropical plains to steep mountains and valleys. The country is bordered by China, Burma, Nepal and Bangladesh, has a population of about 770,000, is a constitutional monarchy and a member state of the United Nations. The Canadian connection is a unique one. When the country moved from an absolute monarchy to a parliamentary democracy the Speaker of the Canadian House of Commons assisted in the transition. Canadian officials oversaw the elections and Chief Justice of the Supreme Court, Hon. Beverley McLaughlin helped write Bhutan's Constitution. The package we printed would include an interview with the Consul General in Toronto, a map of the country, facts and figures and of course the "Canadian connection."

Many of those we elect to be representatives at Queen's Park have impressive backgrounds in the arts and sport. What I quickly realized that given our Canadian approach to life, modesty has prevented our colleagues from learning about those accomplishments. Fascinating stories flowed from the interviews. Hon. Roy McMurtry, a talented landscape painter was a student of A. J. Casson, a member of the "group of seven."[58]

---

[58] Hon. Roy McMurtry MPP and Attorney-General 1975-85, Chief Justice of Ontario 1996-2007

Who better to describe an area, town or city than the MPP who is the representative. One phone call was all it took to have a former member write an article which included the history, importance, attractions, why someone would want to live there. Karen Haslam[59] even included some beautiful photos of past and present Stratford.

We interviewed Lieutenant Governors, covered special events at Queen's Park and generally tried to connect the former members as much as possible with those things which had been a part of their parliamentary life.

## The InFormer — Special Editions

Between 2017 and 2022 we published six Special Editions, all of them distributed to both former and current MPPs. The first was a 32 page "Women and The Vote — 1917–2017." The approach was to take a look at the past, present and future, with lots of photos as well as interviews. We released the publication to coincide with commemoration events at Queen's Park. Among those who expressed their appreciation for this publication was Premier Kathleen Wynne.

## "Leadership — Walter Pitman" and "Leadership — Dr. Bette Stephenson"

Leadership is so much more than being the Leader of a political party. I embarked on what I thought would be an interesting series providing an in-depth look at deceased former members, who were noteworthy in leadership roles beyond politics. I completed two. Time is such a precious commodity and it turned out I simply didn't have enough of that commodity to expand the series.

The 56-page magazine about Walter Pitman focused on his contributions in politics, education, the arts and social justice causes. This recipient of the Order of Canada, Order of Ontario and

---

59 Karen Haslam MPP 1990-95, Mayor of Stratford 2000-03

numerous other awards left an indelible mark in education with his leadership at Ryerson (now Toronto Metropolitan University) and in the arts with his transformative work as Chair of the Ontario Arts Council.[60]

The 52-page publication about Dr. Bette Stephenson focused on her leadership in both domestic and international education and her remarkable achievements in medicine. Dr. Bette Stephenson was a trailblazer, especially in the field of medicine. Her numerous awards include the Order of Canada, Order of Ontario and being inducted into the Canadian Medical Hall of Fame.[61]

Dr. Bette Stephenson and Walter Pitman illustrated what I believe to be a moral imperative of taking your political experience and skills and applying them to the betterment of civil society. These two were diametrically opposite in their political beliefs, but both were determined to make a difference, to help create a better society.

## The Artists Who Created The Art At Queen's Park

"You realize that Queen's Park is really an art museum, but we do allow the politicians in here from time to time," I would quip to visitors as I was happily showing them what had been my home away from home. At the end of a late night sitting I would wander my way to Speaker's Apartment taking lots of time to admire the paintings. Just stopping and staring at them for a while was calming, relaxing. While I admired the art I wasn't particularly knowledgeable. Going from interest to deeply enthusiastic came years after I was no longer elected, 2009.

In the summer of 2009, Pat and I took our eight year old grandson, Sebastian, on a holiday to Paris. We had spent a few hours in the Louvre and were ready to call it a day. Sebastian however seemed fixated on the ceiling. "Look up, Grandpa. See the beautiful

---

60 Walter Pitman was MP 1960-62, MPP 1967-71

61 Dr. Bette Stephenson was MPP 1975-87

frescoes on the ceiling." That prompted more art museum trips; each one eliciting excitement from Sebastian. If an eight year old is this enthralled by art there must be more to it than I thought. So began my journey into the world of art.

It struck me one day that while Queen's Park has lots of information about the remarkable art collection, there was little information about the artists who created the art. In 2017 with Sebastian as photographer (he had his own photography web site for photo cards at age 10) I set out to write about 32 artists, interviewing eight of them. The result was an 80-page magazine. The project was made possible because of the generosity of a wonderful patron of the arts, Hon. Henry (Hal) Jackman, former Lieutenant General whom I got to know when I was his "landlord". The book launch at Queen's Park was special. I wanted the focus to be on the artists so all eight I had interview were invited and asked to talk about art, in whatever way they wished. Wine, hors doeuvres, two jazz guitarists — a delightful event!

## Remembering Bill Davis

William Grenville Davis was the most consequential Premier in Canada in 100 years. His remarkable listening and negotiation skills resulted in the patriation of our Constitution as well as creating Canada's Charter of Rights and Freedoms. His vision, commitment and determination resulted in an Ontario rich in educational opportunities, an arts and culture awakening and an economically prosperous province which embodied compassion. When Bill Davis passed away August 21, 2021, I wanted to publish a Special Edition focusing on photos and stories which reflect his leadership, wisdom and humour.

The response to the email I sent to former members was swift, voluminous and heart-felt. In short order we had a 36 page publication. When Pat and I delivered extra copies of "Remembering Bill Davis" to Mrs. Kathleen Davis I was rewarded with a cup of tea and a delightful chat, sharing memories about someone who for me was the most likeable political opponent one could ever have. Someone who made a significant difference in Ontario and in Canada.[62]

## We Will Meet Again

It came swiftly and silently. It seemed that almost overnight a lethal amorphous cloud shrouded the globe. COVID-19. This coronavirus disease 2019 came from Wuhan, China. The understandable involuntary reactions were incomprehension and fear. As the infection spread the medical message became crystal clear; stay home, wash your hands vigorously and often. Political leaders across Canada sang from the same song sheet. "Follow the Science" with the refrain "stay calm" almost became a national anthem. And, it was time for snow birds to fly north. Those adventurous Canadians scattered around the globe were urged to return home immediately.

We were in a war! Not a military war, but a life and death struggle with an invisible enemy. As with any war, courage and determination are essential qualities in the quest for victory. Calmness in the face of a frightening situation along with a collaborative approach has to be the order of the day. We are in this together. We will win this together.

Mid-March, 2020 Canada was in lockdown, coast to coast to coast. If you weren't in hospital or seriously ill at home you likely were lonely. Fearful. We couldn't connect in person but we could bridge that physical gap electronically.

Arrangements were made for OAFP's Administrative Assistant Mobina Bhimani to work from home and she could email 300 former MPPs. In World War II a popular singer, Vera Lynn sang an inspirational song, "We'll Meet Again". This would be our survival banner. I was determined that everything everyone wrote and everything we printed would be positive. The only victim here would

---

62 William G. Davis MPP 1959-85, Premier 1971-85

be negativity. Every day for forty days I sent out poems, stories, articles and in return encouraged members to respond in kind. We celebrated William Shakespeare's birthday, National Chocolate Eclair Day, explained why the dandelion was a flower, paid tribute to Bob Dylan and Joni Mitchell and pondered how confinement could widen your world.

Prior to the end of the 40 days, at which time the accumulated material would be turned into a 46-page magazine, I asked members to share their thoughts about what was positive in their lives. Some wrote that they looked forward each day to see what I had sent along.

I treasure the email I received from former Premier, Hon. David Peterson, "I never thought I would see the day when David Warner was my therapist."

I am not a therapist, but the project was therapeutic. Dozens of us were sharing positive messages and humourous stories every day. Whether we realized it or not at the time we were supporting each other through the worst time our country had known in 100 years.

## We wanted to go far so we went together

The Special Editions had the professional appearance of magazines available at a book store. This was the result of remarkable team work. Each publication engaged a pair of Interns; Victoria Esterhammer and Victoria Shariati, David Cassels and Cassandra Earle, Lauren Malyk and Ramisha Farooq. While I did most of the writing, meticulous editing was provided by (retired) Professor Helen Breslauer. She wasn't able to edit one of the editions so three former Members stepped up; John Parker, Linda Jeffrey, David Neumann. In an effort to guard against errors Mobina Bhimani, OAFP's Administrative Assistant checked. We had additional help at the printing stage. Ira Danchyshyn at Print City has an exceptional aptitude for catching flaws. I always felt comfortable that the printing would be perfect because Ashok Jain with his 35 years of printing experience was overseeing it.

## Obituaries

The audience I had in mind for the obituaries was the former members and the family of the deceased member. Sitting in the House with someone, even being in the same caucus doesn't mean that you know much about your colleague. My approach was to certainly list the details of their parliamentary life, provide background information about what they did before being elected and post Queen's Park; their hobbies and interests. Adding tributes from three members, one from each party, was easy. Generosity of spirit prevailed. This unique obituary was sent to all former members, included in the next publication and most importantly sent to the family.

I appreciated the opportunity to create unique memorable obituaries.

# PART SIX

# Political Travelling

# 43

# Fact-Finding Mission in Nicaragua March 13–23, 1987

An earthquake in 1972 shook the foundation of Somoza's dictatorship. A revolution had been brewing in Nicaragua for a while, but in the aftermath of the earthquake when international aid was not distributed properly and there were accusations of corruption, support for a revolution gained traction. The Sandinista National Liberation Front (FSLN) ousted the dictatorship in 1978–79, and governed Nicaragua from 1979 to 1990. Fighting, known as the Contra War, continued during that entire time. The Contras were a collection of right wing groups backed by the United States.

That was one narrative. This was, however, still the era of the Cold War between Russia and the U.S.A. A second narrative floated around that the Sandinistas were a front for the Soviets and this war was really an opportunity for Russia to gain a foothold in Central America.

Who really were the Sandinistas? What was this war actually about?

Richard Johnston, New Democrat MPP, organized an all-Party fact-finding mission. Members from all three political parties signed up. We had briefing sessions about what we might expect to find, who and what we were going to see and the usual travel information needed for travelling to Central America. At the last minute the Conservative Members of the group reported that they were not allowed to participate. While I can't confirm the details, it seems that the Conservative Club on campus at the University of Toronto who were supporting the Contras, applied pressure on the Ontario PC Party to have their MPPs removed from the fact-finding delegation.

My travel mates were New Democrats Karl Morin-Strom, David Reville, Richard Johnston, Liberals Joan Smith and Christine Hart, as well as two reporters; Pauline Comeau, Toronto Sun and Derek Nelson, Thompson News Service, an Ontario Legislature Committee Clerk, Doug Arnott, two interpreters; Jeff House and Vernon Crawford, Shirley Darling Toronto Star Researcher who assisted with the logistics of our trip, as well as Leonard Epp, a prison chaplain. Although a disparate group in many ways, a camaraderie emerged. Lively guitar music, as well as some beer and rum in the evenings may have played a part in developing a wonderful group atmosphere.

It was ten days of dedicated learning, some surprises, engaging political discussions and an opportunity to know something about a small, economically poor country.

## From cows to coffee we traverse a rugged, beautiful country

- Canadian cows at an efficiently government run farm, producing milk for Managua. Bulls born here will go to independent farmers.
- Momotombo, a geothermal power project built with Canadian economic assistance
- A playoff baseball game. Each team had a musical band. Thousands of happy, cheering fans. Final score was 6 to 2. Unfortunately, I didn't record the team names.
- My first visit to a coffee plantation. This one situated beyond the City of Matagalpa, high up in the mountains.

- Mass at a Roman Catholic Church. The priest pleaded that the North Americans in the gathering take a message to the United States that Nicaraguans want peace. Many dramatic paintings in the church, including one of Archbishop Romero who had been assassinated by the CIA in El Salvador in 1980
- Meeting with two of the six opposition Parties represented in the Assembly. There is proportional representation. Both Parties acknowledged that Nicaragua is developing a political pluralism.
- A meeting with Sergio Ramirez, Vice President of Nicaragua, who explained the extent of the economic war being waged by the USA. There is not only a blockade of goods and services, but a blockade of money from the International Development Bank, the International Monetary Fund and the International Americas Development Bank.
- An impromptu baseball game. Our group stopped where some children were playing baseball and asked to join them. They didn't have a real baseball, but a rock covered in oil cloth. It was fun until a sharply hit line drive struck David Reville squarely in the eye. He received medical attention at a local hospital and we continued on our way to Esteli, a small city near the fighting.
- Tour of a maximum security prison, which turned out to be dramatically different than what I had expected. There is an emphasis on acquiring literacy skills and practical skills so that the individual is better equipped for the real world. A reward system provides time off the sentence based on degree of cooperation and willingness to acquire new skills. Prefab houses are built, then go to families in need of housing. Those working building the houses are credited wages, with the money going to their families.

- A meeting with Carlo Nunez Tellez, President of the National Assembly. There is excited mutual interest in parliamentary exchanges which would include staff.

## A remarkable revolutionary

She strode swiftly into the room, dressed in battle fatigues, then stood in front of a large map of Nicaragua. Using a military chart pointer, she proceeded to explain how her Ministry of Health would inoculate the entire country against diseases in only two days. As I listened intently to the interpreter, I simply stared, mesmerized. This energetic, slight of stature woman at the front of the room is the one, at only age 23, who was second in command of the FSLN, winning a major battle in 1979, spelling the end of Somoza's dictatorship. I am looking at Comandante Dos, Dora Maria Tellez.

It is clear from Dora Maria Tellez's presentation that the Sandinista government identifies public health care as a high priority. When asked if her medical training is why she was appointed Minister of Health, Tellez responds that the Minister of Health doesn't need to be a doctor. It is more important to have good health experts and a determination to rebuild health care institutions.

I came away from this fascinating session with the feeling that the delivery of an efficient, effective health care system is in good hands. What a remarkable woman!

## Another remarkable revolutionary

"90% of us in this country are Christians and this is a people's revolution. It is a whole people who are both Christian and revolutionary." Those were Father Fernando Cardenal's opening remarks, as he went on to explain the difference between the two revolutions, Cuban and Nicaraguan.

Our group was invited to have dinner with Father Cardenal. He had been the coordinator of the 1979 Literacy Campaign and was now Minister of Education. It turned out to be a fascinating, illuminating evening as Father Cardenal shared his observations on literacy, the intersection of politics and religion, and the connection between Christianity and the Nicaragua Revolution. He provided a detailed observation of the fundamental difference between the Cuban Revolution and the one he was part of in Nicaragua. "Here in Nicaragua, priests like myself, well you're absolutely in the middle of it. In Cuba you're out......Here you have a falling in love and a marriage of Christians with the revolution."

## Have a poet write a grammar book

Prior to the revolution, illiteracy in Nicaragua was 50%, with 75 to 90% in rural areas. The literacy campaign launched in 1979 resulted in the rate dropping from 50 to 12%. One third of the country's three million people were studying. This impressive campaign garnered the prestigious UNESCO Literacy Award. Part of the campaign's success, Father Cardenal observed, is because "We will not accept an education which comes from the teacher down to the student. We do not consider students as objects, but as subjects. Who are to actively participate in the education experience. They are not there just to receive knowledge."

As an English teacher, I appreciated Father Cardenal's approach to teaching grammar. He said, as Minister of Education, he knew that most students do not like learning grammar. A new approach was needed. He commissioned a poet to write a new grammar book so that the text would be far more interesting. *all quotes are from a speech by Father Cardinal, March 18, 1987, interpretation and transcription by Jeff House, a member of the delegation.

## Observations

"This is not a poor country. This is an impoverished country." stated Carlo Nunez Tellez, President of the National Assembly. Sadly, I must agree. A significant portion of the impoverished condition is likely due to the US blockade of goods, services and access to international money.

We were informed that there were three fundamental principles of the Revolution: mixed economy, political pluralism and non-alignment. Everything I saw and the candid responses to my questions supported that assertion.

The trip was superbly organized by Richard Johnston. The group quickly became cohesive. There were lots of warm, friendly times.

## Fairness results in failure

A peace process started with the Sapoá Accords in 1988 and the Contra War ended after the signing of the Tela Accord in 1989 and the demobilization of the FSLN and Contra armies. There was a second election in 1990. The Sandinistas had decided on a system of proportional representation. There were 100 seats in the Assembly. Obtain 10 per cent, you get 10 seats. There were seven political parties. The US financially backed the six opposition parties. This resulted in the election of a majority of anti-Sandinista parties and the FSLN handing over power.

## What went wrong?

Ortega and the FSLN bounced back from election defeats and won the elections of 2011, 2016, 2021. However, somewhere along the journey, it appears that Daniel Ortega and his wife Rosario Murillo, who is Vice President since 2017, have been lured by that three headed devil siren; wealth, power, prestige. Daniel Ortega's net worth is estimated to be $50 million. In 2022, Ortega cancelled nearly 200 NGOs (non governmental organizations) in what appears to be an attempt to eliminate the country's civil society. Dora Maria Tellez, who had fought along side Daniel in the 1979 successful revolution, as second in command, was jailed February 2022, for political conspiracy. She was in fact an active member of an opposition party.

Dora Tellez was later released March 2023, after 605 days in solitary confinement. She was banished from Nicaragua and now lives in the US.

I would never had guessed that Daniel Ortega would go from freedom fighter against a dictator to being one himself.

# 44

# An Act of Defiance

## Latvia — July 27 to August 4, 1991

"I would be honoured to preside at the Opening of the Latvian Parliament," was my reply to the invitation from The Popular Front of Latvia. This act of defiance against the Soviet Union would take place early August in Latvia's capital city, Riga.

Latvia was liberated from the Nazis in 1944, by the Soviet Red Army. However, the liberators didn't go home. Instead, what happened was forced collectivization of the farms and integration of the Latvian economy into that of the Soviet Union. The spirit of democracy, however, was not extinguished.

A national resistance emerged and on May 4, 1990 the Latvian Parliament passed a declaration on the renewal of independence. Struggles between Moscow and those wanting independence resulted in violent clashes in Riga, January 1991. Throughout the year great effort was made to accomplish a peaceful transition to independence. The reopening of Parliament in August was to be the culmination of the negotiations. The plan was that Pat, and I, along with a staff person who was fluent in Latvian and Russian from the

Ontario Legislature, would be on hand, as I presided at this historic re-opening of Parliament.

I knew the history of the struggle for Latvian independence. What I didn't know was what to expect during this visit. Parts of the visit were standard diplomatic events; an enjoyable dinner in Moscow with the Canadian Ambassador, Michael Bell, a delightful meeting with the Latvian Minister of Culture, an avid admirer of Oscar Peterson, and an informative meeting with Prime Minister Godmanis who detailed the economic, social and political challenges faced by Latvia.

There were, however, aspects of the stay which were surreal. The lovely villa hotel situated aside a beach on the Baltic was protected by large steel gates and armed guards. As far as I could tell, the three of us were the only guests at the hotel. Soviet troop movements were noticeable.

The organ recital at a 13$^{th}$ century Lutheran Cathedral was lovely. While we enjoyed the music, as did the audience of about 1,000, it became clear that this was also a venue for furtively passing notes to those accompanying Pat and I. Something was being organized. Abruptly we were on our way out of the Cathedral and off for a private dinner with Deputy Speaker Krastins and his wife.

Last minute complications caused the opening of Parliament to be cancelled. The increased presence of Russian troops suggested to me a reason for the cancellation. However, I could not have guessed what was about to happen.

We left Riga, had two days in Moscow, then on August 6 started our journey home. On August 18 President Mikhail Gorbachev was arrested in a coup. The formal collapse of the Soviet Empire was underway.

I was disappointed that presiding at the opening of Parliament did not happen. It would have been a powerful statement about Canada's support of parliamentary democracy for Latvia. That disappointment was offset by the remarkable experience of touring the beautiful countryside, observing how similar it is to southern

Ontario, visiting what had been collective farms, exploring the medieval section of Riga and the beautiful city parks. Discussions with the President of the University of Riga were informative and stimulating. A forestry museum, a collective fishery and a brewery all provided insight about the economic challenges faced by this small country trying to make its democratic way in the world.

The Latvians I met exuded a fervent desire for democracy and an inspiring optimism about the economic and social future of this small Baltic country. Courage and determination were clearly evident.

The staffer from the Legislative Library was an excellent interpreter and an invaluable source of detailed information. There was an incident which could have gone quite badly except for his involvement. When I recall how it all turned out, I realized later that his intervention foreshadowed a diplomatic career.

The three of us were enjoying our regular evening stroll along the beach fronting the Villa, engaged in deep discussion about the communist society, its philosophy and policies. We were oblivious to our surroundings. That is, until startled by loud shouting. Suddenly, there in front of us were three drunk, totally naked young men. One of them was gesturing frantically with a long stick. Our protector, looking the stick holder straight in the eyes, spoke calmly in Russian, while at the same time offering some cigarettes. The cigarettes were gleefully accepted and the three young men then gyrated their way along the beach. We walked on, but in the opposite direction. Apparently the three men were Russian soldiers on leave.

Latvia gained independence later that year. Our guide, interpreter, protector, under the auspices of the Ontario and Federal governments, helped to reestablish the Office of the President of Latvia. He went on to a distinguished diplomatic career, serving as the Latvian Ambassador to Greece, Spain and NATO.

# PART SEVEN

# Tales from the Trails

The following is a collection of anecdotes, real life incidents which occurred during my four terms as MPP. The story I like best is the first one, "Dill pickles anyone". I tell this story to political science students to illustrate that politics is not really a science, but an art.

## *Dill pickles anyone?*

## (The Art of Politics)

It was a lovely warm day. I was knocking on doors, as I usually did one day a week, all year round. Peering through the screen door, I could see a woman working in the kitchen. I yelled my standard greeting.

"Hi. I'm David Warner, your MPP."

"Sorry. If this is about politics, I'm busy," was the response.

"Looks like you're making something." I ventured.

"I'm preserving dill pickles and I've never done this before."

"Okay. I have a great recipe for dill pickles. I'll leave it on my card. I won't bother you any more. Good luck with the pickles."

I did as I said I would and moved on to the next house.

***

About a year later, again knocking on doors.

"Hi. I'm David Warner, your MPP."

The woman answering the door paused for a few moments, took a good look at me, then spoke.

"I remember you. You're the man with the dill pickle recipe. The dill pickles were great! I voted for you."

Although it had been a long time, I remembered her. I have never been very good at remembering names. Not a good thing for a politician. However, I have always had a knack for remembering faces and places. Often I could identify on a street which houses were politically supportive and which ones weren't. The result of two decades of routine door knocking.

I really didn't know if the woman knew which Party I represented. What I did know was that I connected with her on a personal level. Which leads me to contend that politics is more of an art than a science.

P.S. My secret to making great dill pickles is to add a pinch of cinnamon to each large jar.

## An unexpected bottle of champagne

There were a number of community associations in the riding. Several of them held an annual dinner and dance. Shortly after being elected in 1975, Pat and I were invited to Birkdale Community Association's Fall Dinner and Dance. As a gesture of support for this organization I purchased a lucky draw ticket. Everyone was very gracious in their reception of their new Provincial Member and his wife. Meeting constituents at a social occasion is ideal. Most people do not want to discuss politics and there is usually something special about meeting your MPP. There were some people I recognized from canvassing and others I knew were solid supporters.

Pat and I enjoyed a delicious dinner, then joined others on the dance floor. "Ladies and gentlemen. Time for the lucky draw. Would our newly elected Member of Provincial Parliament come forward to draw the winning ticket."

This was a new experience for me, but one I thought would be fun. The fun for me was short lived. I reached into the hat and drew out a ticket, read the name on it silently, then froze. Turning to the President of the Association I quietly said, "I pulled out my own ticket. I can't accept the prize." He looked at the ticket, burst out laughing then explained the situation to the crowd. "Although he pulled his own ticket, I think Mr. Warner should accept the prize, which is a bottle of champagne with two glasses, donated by his Conservative opponent, Brian Harrison." Laughter mingled with applause affirmed the President's suggestion.

At home as we sipped our prize bottle of champagne I observed that this bottle seemed to taste particularly sweet.

## "Nice doggy"

I love dogs. Always have. As a teenage I had a Golden Retriever named Butch, a large, super friendly playful dog. The two of us had lots of good times together. I loved dogs and they seemed to love me. Running for public office turned out to include literally running.

Every election campaign would feature at least one dog attack. Periodically, on my weekly jaunts through the Riding, I would encounter an aggressive dog. A warm, friendly "Nice Doggy" did nothing to deter deep growling, sharp barking, bared teeth and occasionally an outright attack. I asked a letter carrier one time if he could provide an explanation for this new, unhappy circumstance. His explanation was that dogs are territorial in nature. "You pick up the scent of one dog, and carry that scent with you, so that when you enter another dog's territory, that dog gets upset." I don't know if that is true, but it sounds like a reasonable explanation.

Here are two of my favourite doggy stories.

## A political dog

I have tried to perfect a welcoming knock on the door. One which beckons rather than alarms. I try for melodic, not too loud so as to sound like the police or fire department have arrive, but at a volume which could be heard just about anywhere in the house. I wait a while in case the occupant is elderly, disabled or perhaps in the furthest reaches of the house. I consider the knock on the door as an important part of the art of political canvassing.

I was standing on the front porch of house situated on a corner lot, set back about 20 metres from the curb. I had used my welcoming knock and was waiting patiently for someone to answer the door when I heard the sound of a car pulling into the driveway. Turning around I saw a family of four getting out of a car. The first one out of the car however was one very energetic dog who in a flash was bounding straight toward me, yelping loud enough to wake the dead!

As quick as a jack rabbit I hopped off the porch and ran like crazy across the lawn toward the street, the dog in hot pursuit. Suddenly, as if the dog had air brakes like a transport truck, my canine pursuer stopped at the roadside edge of the lawn. The dog kept barking. I kept running. At that moment the dog's owner must have recognized me. He shouted "It's okay. We're NDP!" I yelled back, "That's great, but your dog's a Tory!"

## Saved by a sheepskin coat

The 1981 election was conducted during a long, cold, snowy winter. A winter which carried on through mid-March. My sheepskin coat kept me warm as I trod through the snow going door-to-door with my election literature or as I prefer to call "political educational material".

I had learned over the six years of being the Member for Scarborough Ellesmere that the vast majority of my constituents were polite and considerate. Summertime I would be offered lemonade. Wintertime I would be invited to step inside to get out of the cold, warm up.

My recollection of the following event remains vivid. It was early evening, darkness had fallen. So too had the temperature. It had been another long, cold, snowy day in this campaign. My welcoming knock on the door was answered by a woman who promptly invited me to step inside, an invitation I gratefully accepted. As things unfolded I would have preferred remaining outside.

I didn't see the dog until I was fully inside the house with the door closed. As the woman said hello I saw, sitting silently on its haunches as if it was a statue, right beside the woman, was a Doberman Pinscher. I opened my mouth to launch into my political pitch. That was when the dog sprang straight for my throat. I nimbly raised my arm to protect my throat. The dog missed my throat but did latch onto my arm. I could feel its sharp teeth through my lovely, thick sheepskin coat. The dog wasn't letting go and I was not going to stop protecting myself.

The owner of this canine beast calmly reached out and grabbed the dog's collar. Seconds later the dog was sitting back where it started. What I found astonishing was that the owner said nothing. No apology, no explanation. It was as though the attack had never happened. I think the woman began asking political questions. I really don't remember. I was too busy exiting the house, shaken but glad to be outside.

## The Communists are coming!

A wide variety of housing exists in Scarborough Ellesmere; apartment buildings (both high rise and those under five stories), townhouses, single family houses (both detached and single). Generally the age of the housing increases as you go from west to east, as was the development of Scarborough. There is also a 'pioneer' portion found near Brimley Road and Lawrence Avenue. This is where the first white settlers of Scarborough lived, David and Mary Thomson. Their log home has been preserved and sits in a beautiful spacious park, a popular place for picnics. On one side of the park runs a road on which is a house, now renovated, but likely build in the early 1900's. While the house, situated on a double lot, is large it is gracious rather than pretentious. It was in front of that house that I encountered the owner who was busy gardening.

I introduced myself, commented on how beautiful was his house and attempted to hand him a piece of campaign literature. The man stood there straight faced, no smile. He looked at the literature I was moving in his direction, put his hand up signalling that he wasn't going to accept the valuable information I wanted to pass along. Carefully enunciating each word and staring hard at me as he spoke, he said, "If you people ever formed the government you would likely have another family move in with us."

I smiled, paused a moment, looked thoughtfully at the house, then back to its owner and politely said, "No. I don't think so. Your place looks big enough for six families." I think he was too startled to react. I didn't give him time for a rejoinder. With a cheery "Have a great day!", I was on my way to chat with his neighbours. I was tempted, but didn't visit him after we came to power in 1990.

## A pheasant surprise

Common sense dictates that accepting gifts from constituents or anyone else in your political world is not a good idea. Of course, a few home grown tomatoes or a bottle of wine is not going to sway you from being objective in fulfilling your MPP responsibilities.

Over the course of several years I had tried to be of assistance to a constituent who had a particularly complicated workers' compensation case. My constituent always expressed his gratitude, even in the face of a failed attempt to win his compensation appeal. I would respond by saying that I was glad to assist and would keep trying. Words of thanks were not sufficient for my constituent. He wanted to provide something tangible. This story is about one of the more unusual attempts by my constituent to say "Thank you."

Personal time for Pat and I was rare. One Saturday evening, as the two of us were getting ready to enjoy an evening out, the phone rang. As soon as the voice on the phone said "Hello," I knew who it was; my constituent with the endless workers' compensation claim.

"You like pheasant?" Having dealt directly with my constituent, over the phone and in person, over many months, I knew I had to answer his question with a question.

"Dead or alive?"

"Dead of course. I show you how to barbeque pheasant. I be there shortly." The phone line went dead. No time to reply that I was going out.

Pat was upstairs at the back of the house when my grateful constituent arrived, carrying a plastic bag. He took a pheasant out of the bag and proceeded to explain how to secure the bird to the spit for roasting on the barbeque. I thanked him and said goodbye. Checking my watch I realized I had a bit of time before we had to leave so decided to barbeque the pheasant now. Perhaps it would be a tasty late night snack when we returned home. Out to the deck I went, bird secured on the spit, ready to roast. I left the plastic bag on the kitchen counter.

Pat hadn't heard any of this brief visit by my constituent. She came downstairs, saw the plastic bag on the kitchen counter and opened it.

A shriek loud enough to rouse all our neighbours sent me rushing indoors. Pat had opened the bag to see the head of the pheasant, two shiny eyes staring at her. Oh, Oh! I should have checked the bag as soon as my constituent had left our house.

In all the commotion I neglected the bird turning on the spit. By the time I rescued the roasted pheasant, it could only be used as a door stop! On our way to the theatre I spent the time apologizing profusely. Some gifts, even the edible ones are not worth accepting.

## My first and only boxing match

Some of the details are a bit fuzzy, not just because this event took place in the 70's, but because of the outcome.

I had foolishly agreed to participate in a charity boxing match. I had never been in the ring. Not only was I not a fan of this pugilistic endeavour, I didn't know the first thing about boxing. All I knew about my opponent was that he was also an MPP.

"This is good," I thought. "Perhaps he is also someone totally unfamiliar with the sport. Two Members of Provincial Parliament in the ring for charity likely means neither of us will take the event seriously. There probably won't be any actual fighting. Therefore no chance of getting hurt."

Wrong! My opponent was David Rotenberg, Conservative Member, Wilson Heights. The two of us stepped into the ring, were greeted by the referee who thanked us for doing this charity event. We touched our boxing gloves and retreated to our respective corners.

I will never know if perhaps my daily heckling of the government motivated David Rotenberg or if he simply took this event with the same seriousness he applied to his parliamentary duties. What I did know instantly was that my ring opponent knew how to box.

No bell was needed to end round one. The bout was ended before then. The scant few minutes in the ring resulted in days of aching muscles and one very sore nose. My only consolation was that the Cabbagetown Boxing and Youth Centre garnered a few extra dollars.

I vowed that the next time any Boxing organization came looking for a volunteer fighter to help raise money I would be delighted to make a monetary donation. If I wish to donate blood I will head to the Red Cross.

## A loud, raspy, gasping cough wins the day!

Dr. Charles Godfrey, founder of People or Planes, a group protesting the proposed Pickering Airport, was elected in 1975 because of his leadership on this issue. The Davis government stopped the building of the airport. He served one term.

The following anecdote illustrates Charles Godfrey's delightful sense of humour.

In 1975 there were few smoking restrictions at Queen's Park. Every once in a while someone would move a motion to ban smoking in the Caucus Room. Always defeated. Charles, however, was not to be defeated in his quest to ban smoking, at least in the Caucus Room. One caucus meeting became a turning point in the battle for good health. Charles waited until all his caucus colleagues and staff were gathered in the room. There was a loud rap on the door. When the door was opened, Charles, wearing a white lab coat and pushing an IV pole and coughing. A loud, raspy, gasping cough. Once the laughter ceased, someone moved a motion to ban smoking in the Caucus Room. This time it passed.

Charles Godfrey, after losing in 1977 said he didn't feel too badly. After all, how many people achieve their political goal even before they take their seat in the House. Still, I knew there was so much Charles could contribute to the Caucus and the Legislature. A wider view reveals that Charles would continue to serve in ways which would help make this a better world.

## Stop thief, put the Mace down!

### March 12, 1976

It started out as a normal Question Period in the House. Questions were asked, replies received, punctuated occasionally with the usual banter across the aisle. Then...

A stranger was grabbing the Mace off the Clerk's Table and shouting, "It's illegal and undemocratic." Simultaneously, there was a lightening quick response by one of our House Attendants, Franco Carrozza. Within seconds Franco had the stranger in a one arm bear hug. Franco gently removed the mace from this unwanted visitor, and placed the mace back down on the table while still holding on to the stranger. With the Mace back where it belonged, Franco lifted the stranger off his feet and carried him out of the Chamber.

What on earth had sparked this strange event? The Mace is the authority of both the Speaker and the House, so maybe there was some political connection to the attempted theft. Mystery aside, I was glad the intruder wasn't armed.

How did the stranger get on to the floor of the Chamber? It seems that he presented himself to a Liberal staffer as a researcher for the Party and was ushered through the Opposition Lobby to the area under the press gallery reserved for opposition staff. Questions were raised by Members about lax security. It was suggested that perhaps all staff should have identity badges.

Turns out the stranger was Michael Houlton, whose political history was unusual. Michael, having lost the Liberal nomination in Mississauga in the 1972 federal election, ran as an Independent, garnering 500 votes. He next popped up as a challenger for the Leadership of the Ontario Liberals at their January 1976 convention. Of the 1,900 delegates, Michael got four votes. Dr. Stuart Smith was elected as the new Leader of the Ontario Liberals. Michael Houlton claimed that Dr. Stuart Smith's election victory was illegal and undemocratic.

Houlton, after his failed attempt to remove the Mace from Queen's Park, moved to Ottawa where he lost the Liberal nomination in the 1977 provincial election. He then started his own Party, the Canadian Alternative Canadienne Party. The CACP is no longer a registered political party.

This strange episode in the life of Queen's Park prompted an immediate upgrade in security protocols.

## The Klan pay a visit

### 1980

"Tell Mr. Warner that the Klan stopped by to say hello, was the message delivered here in person," said Lorna Prokaska, my Executive Assistant. Lorna went on to explain that I had just missed this man's visit to Queen's Park. "He didn't leave his name, just the message that the Klan says 'hello'." The experience was clearly unnerving for Lorna. I wasn't too thrilled either. My mind was racing. Would they return? Should I call Security? How dangerous were they?

Two days earlier, I had received an anonymous phone call telling me that the Ku Klux Klan were planning an official opening of an office on Gerrard Street, east end Toronto. David Duke, Grand Wizard of this white supremacist organization, would preside at the opening. I then made two phone calls; one to Canada's Border Control and one to a Press Gallery reporter. Border Control expressed their thanks for the information and would alert all border crossings. They would ensure that Duke would not enter our country. The news story helped create an "un-welcoming party" for the Klan. Local residents made sure that this Canadian chapter of the KKK was not welcome in the neighbourhood. There was a swift official response. "Both Metro Chairman Paul Godfrey and Ontario Attorney-General Roy McMurtry warned yesterday that police will carefully monitor the group's activities. McMurtry said he was concerned that the Klan appears to be establishing a beach-head in Metro."[63]

"Canadian Grand Wizard James McQuirter opened an office in Toronto's east end that quickly became a lightning rod for citizen outrage, especially since it was alleged that the KKK was recruiting in Ontario's high schools. Protests organized by the Riverdale Action Committee Against Racism prompted the Toronto KKK office to move to the other end of the city, where it was promptly met by another community group—the Parkdale Action Committee Against Racism. They were outnumbered and unwelcome, no matter where they turned."[64]

The Klan did not return to Queen's Park, nor contact me. My guess was that they had bigger problems to deal with than me.

---

63 Christie Blatchford, *Toronto Star*, 28 June, 1980

64 Christine Sismondo, *Maclean's*, August 16, 2017

I was shocked by the anonymously provided information about the Klan setting up shop in Toronto. My background likely has something to do with my naivety. I grew up in an all white, mostly Protestant community. All the kids at school and all the adults around me looked the same. I never experienced racism, subtle or otherwise. I was in high school at the time of desegregation in the United States. There was lots of news coverage, stories of violence against Blacks perpetrated by whites as well as the police. But this was in the US, couldn't possibly happen in Canada. We were immune from racism.

The reality of course is that racism, and discrimination based on colour, ethnicity, religion, sexual orientation has been a part of Canadian history from the settling and founding of our country. The Klan were here from the 1920's on. "The invasion that the *Star* worried about in 1922 didn't happen until 1924, when an official path for the Ku Klux Klan of Kanada was drawn up by two American wizards and Toronto resident James L. Cowan, who rented an office on Toronto Street near Adelaide Street, and set about recruiting. By 1926, a Barrie newspaper reported that there were gatherings of hooded men in more than a dozen Ontario towns, including Barrie, Sault-St-Marie, Exeter, London, and St. Marys."[65]

In 2023 the flames of hatred still burn brightly in various Canadian communities, including the City of Port Coquitlam. "A group calling itself "White Tri-cities Parents and Tots" posted the signs advertising a play group for mothers and children to "join other proud parents of European children as we create an atmosphere in which our kids feel like they belong."[66]

It is not my intention to explore all the avenues of intolerance and ignorance, but rather to write about my one direct contact with a hate group, the Ku Klux Klan. The episode was a reminder that intolerance, ignorance and pure hatred is out there and those

---

65 Christine Sismondo, *Maclean's*, August 16, 2017

66 *Vancouver Sun*, September 25, 2023

of us fortunate enough to be elected have a responsibility to do everything we can to turn ignorance and hatred into understanding and acceptance of our differences.

My experience with parliamentary colleagues has almost exclusively been a positive one when it comes to understanding and acceptance. Same sex marriage and sexual orientation were challenges for some Members, but overall a willingness to listen and try to understand. One disturbing exception was a Member who openly referred to Indigenous people as "drunken Indians" on numerous occasions. The same Member flung racial epithets across the floor at another Member one evening in the House. The Speaker had the offending Member withdraw his remarks. The following day, Premier Davis had the Member stand in the House and apologize for his offensive language.

One candle in the darkness is former Members using their political skills and experience to work with those in our society who are trying to bring disparate groups together to explore what they have in common, not what separates them.

## Beer in the ballpark

I have always loved baseball, as did my parents. As a youngster I would listen to New York Yankee games on the radio. Dad would take my brother Paul and I to games at the stadium, commonly referred to as the Fleet Street Flats, located at the foot of Bathurst Street. To us kids, the stadium which held just over 20,000 people seemed immense. Sometimes our seats were in the first row, right above the Leafs' team dugout or the visitors dugout. If I couldn't cheer in person, I listened to the games on radio station CKEY, both home and away.

The first Labour Day parade in Toronto was in 1872. That year it was in support of the Toronto Typographical Union's strike for a 58-hour work-week. A special feature of the 1976 parade was a contingent of NDP Members of Provincial Parliament, most of whom had been elected for the first time the previous year. The parade ended at the CNE (Canadian National Exhibition). Being Labour Day, marching in the parade got you free entrance to the CNE. Once our group of MPPs disbanded I wandered around the expansive grounds. I hadn't ventured very far when I spotted a Toronto Blue Jays kiosk. I read the pamphlet and quicker than you can say Jackie Robinson I decided to commit to season's tickets. This was too exciting an opportunity to turn down. Major league baseball in Toronto and I would be there for the first game! I was confident that I could find three friends with whom to share the tickets for 81 games and I did!

I enjoy a cold beer once in a while. It seemed quite reasonable to partner baseball outdoors in the warm weather with a cold beer. So, on April 11, 1980 I introduced a Private Member's Bill to allow the "Sale of Beer at the Canadian National Exhibition Stadium". While the Bill attracted some attention, it was never debated let alone passed. The Davis government took a cautious approach whenever pressed to make changes to Ontario's liquor laws. A guiding principle for Bill Davis was in all things, moderation. That included the consumption of alcohol. At the same time, Mr. Davis was an astute listener. He knew the province, what would be accepted and what wouldn't. In 1982 Premier Davis decided that the moment was right to allow beer in the ballpark. Of course, when Skydome opened in 1989, beer continued to be for sale.

Did my trumpeting beer in the ballpark have an effect on the government? Maybe or maybe not, but it didn't hurt. I garnered some favourable response from the general public, and it certainly was popular with quite a few members on both sides of the aisle, perhaps aiding in establishing for me better cross-party friendships.

Although I was glad to see the change in the law, such happiness was tempered after I did a bit of research. I discovered that I could have a beer in the gracious atmosphere of a four star hotel cheaper than purchasing a beer at Skydome!

I remain an avid baseball fan and a loyal Blue Jay supporter; enjoying the games, occasionally splurging to purchase the outrageously priced beer.

*The following four anecdotes are lighter moments from my term as Speaker...*

## I introduce diplomats to a Toronto Fire Brigade

It was to be a normal gracious evening with three Members and a few diplomats enjoying dinner with me in Speaker's Apartment. The evening turned out to be quite memorable mostly because of my unfortunate blunder. There is a fireplace in the living room. I asked if it was usable and got an affirmative reply. Having a log burning on a cold winter night would create an excellent atmosphere. Our diplomatic guests always arrived on time. So, light the fireplace log about 10 minutes prior to the anticipated arrival time of our guests. Soon smoke filled the room and the fire alarm sounded. I called Security to inform them that there was not a fire, so they could turn off the alarm. "Sorry, we can't do that. The fire alarms are connected to the local fire station. They will respond to the alarm."

Sure enough, a few minutes later a couple of firefighters, in full gear complete with axes, arrived at Speaker's Apartment. The group of us stood around gazing at the fireplace; the log having been doused with water was simply smouldering. Meanwhile, because the fire alarm disables the elevators, my guests were trundling up the equivalent of six floors. They arrived in time to see the firefighters exiting. Certainly a memorable evening. Definitely embarrassing.

## Which team do you favour Speaker?

A concern of every Speaker is being viewed as favouring one side of the House over the other. One two part episode underscored my concern. I had a visit from two Conservative Members. I asked them if they were concerned about something. "Yes, Speaker. We feel that you are being too favourable to the government in Question Period." There was a brief pause, then, "Why are you smiling?"

"I am smiling, because about 20 minutes earlier a government Member was here complaining that I was being too favourable to the Opposition."

One of those two Conservative Members later became Speaker. The two of us happened to meet up at an event. He saw me and came over, a big smile on his face. "I found out what you meant that day I came to your office. I went through the same experience when I was Speaker."

It is critical for the Speaker to listen carefully and thoughtfully to everything which is said in the Chamber. Yes, trying to ensure that any Member who uses inappropriate language is quickly called to order. But also, absorbing the content of what is being said so that the back and forth dialogue doesn't stray too far off topic. While Question Period continued to be an agonizing hour for me, day after day, I found it increasingly easier to be the "neutral referee". A few years later when I was visiting classrooms and was asked about what it was like to be from one political party, yet acting as a referee. I would respond, "There were times when both sides made sense and times when neither side made sense."

## "Your mother is here."

During my terms as MPP I had been in the habit of sending quick quip humourous notes across the aisle to colleagues. Once I got feeling comfortable in my role as Speaker, I resumed my note sending practice. A few notes were to a House Attendant, asking about the score in a Blue Jay game. This particular note episode happened during Question Period.

There was a government Member who routinely was quite vociferous. Never nasty and usually funny. This day, however, he was silent. I sent him a note, "Are you not feeling well? I have not heard anything from you." The return note explained his silence.

"My mother is sitting in the gallery." Of course, the following days he was back to his usual loud self. I waited a few days before sending him another note. "You might want to be not so noisy." He quickly responded with "Why?" I sent back my reply, then without diverting my attention from the House, watched his reaction as he read my note which read, "Your mother is here!" The Member whirled around in his seat, anxiously searching, for his mother in the gallery. A few seconds later, he turned toward me, smiled, then was uncharacteristically quiet for the remainder of Question Period.

## Where can I get an espresso?

"Speaker. Do you know why in the afternoon, around three o'clock, unless there is something urgent going on in the House there are no Italian Members present?"

I sat at my desk, perplexed, staring at three MPPs, immediately recognizing that they represented the three Parties. "No. I confess that I have no idea," was my response.

"Espresso coffee is not available either in the Dining Room or the cafeteria. We have to walk west on College Street some distance to find a place which serves espresso."

I didn't realize we were unable to serve espresso. I did understand that a cultural norm for Italians is a mid-afternoon espresso. "Leave it with me. I will see what I can do to remedy this terrible situation."

A visit to the Dining Room and a discussion with the Food Service Manager revealed that it would be great to be able to offer customers espresso, cappuccino and latte. Simply buying the equipment was not sufficient. We needed a water source and piping. In order to do that the floor needed to be ripped up. Total cost about $25,000. This was an important investment. We are operating a Dining Room which is open not only to Members, but their staff, the legislature's staff and the public. A good business decision to make the investment.

Espresso was also a bridge across a political divide.

# PART EIGHT

# The Joy of Teaching

*"I cannot teach anybody anything; I can only make them think."*

— Socrates

"Why not? Maybe it will be interesting." That was my reaction to the poster, inviting students to a presentation by Ontario Teachers on the university residence bulletin board. I hadn't thought much about a career after university graduation. I came away from the presentation totally enthusiastic about a teaching career. So much so, that when my second year results got me uninvited to attend third year at Carleton University in Ottawa, I decided to return to Toronto and enrol at Toronto Teachers' College. This might be fun, even exciting and rewarding. The 1960's being a time of expansion in education meant that teaching jobs were plentiful. The best part of moving back to Toronto was that I would be able to see Pat on a regular basis.

Over the next four decades I would teach a total of 25 years at seven schools plus a stint at the board office. Most of the time I taught grade seven, on occasion grades six and eight. Four of the schools were Senior schools (grade seven and eight only) which gave me the opportunity to teach the subject of my Honours degree, English. My experiences at a Junior school (grades kindergarten to six) and the K to eight as well as Audio-visual teacher consultant were primarily because of Al Mason, my first Principal who believed

I could and should seek promotion. Al was patient, understanding and wise. His guidance got me started on a path I came to treasure.

Bouncing back and forth between Queen's Park and teaching turned out to be mutually beneficial. My political experience made me a better teacher and my teaching life motivated me to establish an all-Party Literacy Committee. Returning to teaching after a defeat was possible because of the support of the Scarborough Board of Education. That support could not have been more pronounced than during my last term in office (1990-95) when the Director of Education, a strong supporter of the Progressive Conservative Party, told me in person that there would always be a teaching position for me with the Scarborough Board. A civility I will always treasure.

## Showtime — in the classroom

I was nervous when I faced my first class of grade seven students, at McCowan Road, Scarborough, 1964. By the end of the day I knew this was what I wanted to do — teach. It didn't take long for me to appreciate the challenges and the satisfaction of working with children ages 12, 13 and 14. The first year of teaching was one of continual discovery about children that age. The soccer pitch, baseball diamond, basketball and volleyball court, as well as the playground often revealed different characteristics of a student than what I had observed in the classroom. A quiet, reticent student in the classroom would often be more open and expressive when playing a sport. Mood swings are common with this age group. One day on top of the world, the following day the role reversed. Cliques would form. This small group of three or four might hang together for a couple of years, or disband in a few months. If I paid attention so that I got to know each student really well, then when interpersonal difficulties arose in the classroom I could bring several students together to "problem solve." While sometimes, because of the natural hormonal changes anger flared, there was usually a quick forgiveness.

This age group was always fun to be around. They enjoyed each others company, loved to laugh. Every day brought a new adventure. Although I considered myself an effective, even excellent teacher, I came to realize that it wouldn't be the academics which students would fondly remember. The school band, soccer team, the drama performed for the parents; these were at the heart and soul of school life.

## It was an education for me too

1964 — my rookie year

"Are you familiar with soccer?" asked Al Mason, my Principal.

"No sir."

"Well, here's the rule book. You are now the coach of the senior boys soccer team. You will get the inter-school schedule later. Good luck!"

I read the book. My announcement for tryouts netted lots of boys eager to be on the school team. I understood the rules and some basic ideas about strategy, but no real concept of what makes a good soccer player. Speed. That's what's needed. I would select the fastest, quickest boys. At the end of tryouts, I posted the list of who made the team. Those who were selected politely asked why one particular boy, Chris Bellamy, wasn't included. They claimed he was the best player. I responded that he wasn't fast enough. Decades later, when I was Speaker, I was asked to referee a charity soccer match at Birchmount Stadium in Scarborough. One team consisted entirely of referees. The other team was a group of professional hockey and soccer players. Prior to the game, a tall, athletic looking man approached me, and asked if I remembered him.

"No, can't say I do."

"I was at McCowan Road when you coached the soccer team. I'm Chris Bellamy."

"Oh! Glad to see you. What have you been doing since McCowan Road?"

"I played for a while with the Toronto Blizzard." Knowing that the Toronto Blizzard was a professional soccer team confirmed for me that in 1964 I knew very little about soccer.[67]

I apologized for not having included him on the team. Chris was gracious about the incident. We shared some stories, had a few laughs, then on to the game. I always enjoyed refereeing, although on this occasion I admit to being a bit nervous with 11 other referees on the pitch.

## I should never have been allowed to teach science

These two tales of woe are but a sampling of stories from my first few years teaching at McCowan Road Public School, 1964–69

In those days an elementary school teacher was expected to teach all subjects. Had I been given a choice I would have swallowed broken glass rather than teach Science and Music.

## An experiment to remember

The scene for this story is set in a portable classroom. The challenge for me is teaching science to my grade six class. They were a delightful group; cooperative, fun loving, hard-working. A class I enjoyed so much that I invited them to my house for an end of year party. Amazing they showed up considering the outcome of the science lesson.

"I will demonstrate the distillation of ink," I told the class as I poured some ink into a beaker of water. I had set up the equipment consisting of tubing, glass beakers, and rubber stoppers identical to the drawings in the text book. At least, I thought so. The ink and water mixture was being heated over the small portable heater. Slowly bubbles start to form in the beaker. The class seemed mesmerized by the process. I started to get anxious when there doesn't appear to be

---

67 The Toronto Blizzard were a professional soccer club based in Toronto, 1971–1984. They played in the North American Soccer League

any liquid flowing from the beaker through the rubber tubing to the other glass container. The bubbling became more vigorous. Then....a loud 'boom' and a ball of black water shot straight up, hit the ceiling and showered over three or four students. Lots of shouting, mixed in with hoots of laughter. I am momentarily stunned but quickly realized that I need to bring calm and order to this commotion.

"The thing about experiments is that they don't always work the way they should. For now, copy down the conclusion which I will write on the board. I need two volunteers to get a ladder from the caretaker, a cleaning solution and something to scrub the ink off the ceiling." There was no shortage of students eager to carry out such an important task.

While one student was up on the ladder energetically scrubbing, the other holding the ladder, I moved about the classroom, talking, asking questions related to a book the class was reading. As I passed by the ladder, out of the corner of my eye I saw small flakes of something drifting by me. Looking up I can see where the flakes are coming from — the ceiling. The ink is being removed but so too part of the ceiling. The morning is not going well.

Just prior to noon when the students would be heading home for lunch I asked the students who were the recipients of the ink water shower to stay behind. "Each of you take this note home to your parents. In the note is an apology for what happened and an offer to pay for the dry cleaning." As I provided an explanation I was thinking, "No doubt this will be expensive for me, especially on my meagre salary, but the money is nothing compared with having to explain my blunder to Al Mason (the Principal)."

Behind dark clouds there is sunshine. Every one of my science experiment victims returned after lunch with a message thanking me for informing about the mishap and there would be no need for me to cover the cost of dry cleaning. Al Mason listened to my story. Was anyone hurt? Had I informed the parents? He then smiled and suggested that next time I might read the instructions a bit more carefully.

Later I re-read the instructions. "Oh Oh. A two hole stopper required. I guess using a one hold stopper meant that the pressure built up in the beaker, no where to go and "boom".

## "It's Just Mr. Warner doing a science experiment"

The scene is my classroom on the second floor. It was a warm day so some of the windows were open for some fresh air. Directly below my classroom was John Sadler's room. He and I both arrived at McCowan Road as newly minted teachers. Both of us taught grade seven and had become good friends.

I don't recall the details about the purpose of the experiment primarily because of what happened. What I vividly recall was that the experiment involved a Bunsen burner and once again I thought I had read all the instructions thoroughly and could perform this experiment without a problem. At some point whatever was being heated by the Bunsen burner burst into a huge flame. Startled, I grabbed the closest thing at hand to put out the flames. Unfortunately what I grabbed and threw onto the fire was a large wad of paper towels. Not a good idea! My next move was brilliant. Desperately clutching the flaming wad of towels I tossed them out the window.

John Sadler was teaching a lesson when a student excitedly piped up, "Sir! There are flaming things coming down outside! John, as he told me later, calmly said to the class. "There is nothing to get excited about. It's just Mr. Warner doing a science experiment."

Footnote: At my retirement party Ernie Mee, Principal of Anson Park the last school I taught at presented me with a fire fighters hard hat. Recognition of a reputation which followed me for decades!

## A fish story

This story takes place in a primary class. I was the visiting Audio-Visual Teacher Consultant. I loved the job because it gave me an opportunity to be creative while showing teachers how they could best make use of a wide range of audio-visual equipment. On this occasion I had set up an overhead projector. First I demonstrated how the teacher could tell a story with cardboard cut-out creatures taped to sticks, move the cut-outs around on the top of the projector creating a large image on a movie screen. I then graduated to something more exciting, placing a fish bowl filled with water on the top of the projector. Into the bowl went a goldfish I had brought with me in a clear plastic bag. The goldfish would look like a whale to the six year olds sitting in front of me. I had made up a wonderful, riveting story about a whale. I love telling stories. This particular story seemed to be going well. The little ones in front of me appeared to be hanging on to every word. Then, "Teacher. Why is the whale floating upside down?" A quick glance was all that I needed to realize that the goldfish was dead. A casual hand movement to touch the glass bowl confirmed that I had managed to boil the goldfish.

The average six year old is sufficiently perceptive to figure out that a fish doesn't float upside down. The smiles, looks of quiet appreciation, joy even, vanish. Replaced by looks of shock and horror. I announced that the whale in the story lived happily ever after. He was just very tired. The teacher quickly told the students it was time for recess.

***

Teaching was never a job. I enjoyed teaching, especially those students who were struggling, emotionally or academically. When a student says "I understand," that is a special moment, a reward for applying your teaching skills.

Work hard and pour your enthusiasm into the social times which help create a cohesive staff. That was the norm for every staff I was on. When you have a staff dedicated to having excellent school sports teams, a band, drama presentations, public speaking presentations, art projects you know it can not be a nine-to-five job. We arrived early and left late. We enjoyed each others' company. The social side for us was sports night at the gym, house parties, an annual corn roast. Friday, right after school I joined the Men Teachers' Curling at Annandale Curling Club. Pat and I hosted parties at our house. A particularly joyous one was a 50's theme party; period dress, bongos, dancing, a sundae bar featuring banana splits, and a hula-hoop contest with the prize for the person who kept the hoop going the longest time being a tape of 50's hits. When you are part of a group of talented, dedicated teachers who are enthusiastic about what they are doing and whose company you enjoy it isn't work.

A few years ago I happened to meet a former student of mine. The usual opening line from a former student is, "Do you remember me?" I try to refrain from replying, "Well, you weren't six-foot, 185 pounds, with a beard when I taught you in grade seven." On this occasion, after the introductions were out of the way and a short synopsis of each other's life concluded, my former student looked straight at me. "Do you know what we liked best about you? My reply was "No. I have no idea." What he said next is for me the greatest compliment that I could possibly receive. "You never judged us." "Well," I said, "No one ever gave me the right to judge."

I appreciated the challenges I faced as a teacher and the joy when it was evident that I had helped a student overcome an academic obstacle or a personal crisis. Just as it was a privilege to be elected, it was also a privilege to teach.

> *"Education is the most powerful weapon which you can use to change the world."*
>
> — Nelson Mandela

# PART NINE

# A Quest for Justice

# Citation

*Presented to David Warner*

*"Our long-time friend in recognition and genuine appreciation for his outstanding commitment to the Armenian Community of Canada and for his ardent efforts for the recognition of the Armenian Genocide"*

Armenian National Committee of Toronto, June 11, 2002

The story of my connection with the Armenian community started in 1979 when Sarkis Assadourian, who later would be a Member of Parliament, asked me if I would co-sponsor an all-party Resolution in the House recognizing the Armenian Genocide. Not wanting to display my ignorance I replied that I would give it consideration. I headed to the library. What I read horrified me. It was a brutal history, the horrid details of which hit me hard. I was shocked. The genocide of 1915 was well documented. Turkey was responsible for the systematic killing of 1,500,000 Armenians of a population of 2,000,000. There was also the remarkable story of Armenian survival. Survivors scattered around the world, many of them coming to a very welcoming Canada.

The Ontario Legislature passed the all-party Resolution in 1980. It took another 24 years for Canada's Parliament to recognize the genocide. Finally, two years later (2006) the Stephen Harper government officially recognized the genocide.

In 1980 both Stephen Lewis and I were invited to the Armenian Community Centre in North York for the April 24 Commemoration. Stephen was the guest speaker. He had researched the topic even more thoroughly than I had. His eloquence and passion confirmed for me that I needed to be supportive in whatever way I could. I knew that whether I was elected or not, I would be committed to seeking justice for as long as I was physically able to do so.

Over the years I spoke at the April 24$^{th}$ Commemorations in Toronto, travelled with others to Ottawa for ceremonies on Parliament Hill, which were followed by a March through the streets to a public park situated adjacent to the Turkish Embassy. There I would address the crowd of 600 to 1,000, reminding everyone that truth can never die, that Turkey needs to admit its guilt, apologize and make amends.

There are some particular events which are especially significant for me. I was one of several who made presentations to the Toronto District School Board, lobbying to have the topic of genocide added to the curriculum. In 2008 the Board established a "Genocide and Crimes Against Humanity" course in high school, selecting three genocides; Armenian, Jewish Holocaust, Rwandan.

In 2012 I wrote an epic poem "Cries from 1915." Father Meghrig Parikian, a graduate of the Juilliard School of Music in New York City, who was the priest at St. Mary's Apostolic Church, North York, visioned the poem as the base for an orchestral presentation, one which would include dancers. The venue would be Roy Thomson Hall in Toronto. I was excited about having my work as the foundation for a musical presentation, telling an Armenian story which stretched back 2000 years. Working with this talented Priest was a wonderful experience. Before we could complete the project, Father Parikian was elected Prelate of Canada and had to move to Montreal. While I was happy for this talented, engaging man that his Church would be well served, I was disappointed that this creative project would not end up on stage. As it turned out, Father Parikian moved to Montreal for a year, then returned to the monastery in Antilias, Lebanon. Sadly, in Lebanon he contracted COVID, passing away in 2021.

Three years later I had the opportunity to assist in the organizing of the 100th year commemoration of the Genocide. There was a ceremony at Queen's Park, attended by about 5,000 people. Among the dignitaries were Premier Wynne and Minister of Defence, Jason Kenney. Those attending then marched through the downtown from Queen's Park to Metropolitan United Church where there was a religious service led by Cardinal Thomas Collins. It was a meaningful and memorable event.

In 2018 the Armenian Community Centre decided that it was time for me to make my first trip to Armenia. It was also the 100th anniversary of Armenian independence so there would be celebrations in Armenia. What a remarkable 10 days, touring the mountains, towns, villages, historic sites and the capital, Yerevan. We travelled to the mountainous Republic of Artsakh, population 170,000, which at the time was experiencing border skirmishes with its aggressive neighbour, Azerbaijan, population 10,000,000. War erupted in 2020, the result of which was a significant portion of Artsakh being controlled Azerbaijan.

I came away with a deeper understanding of the importance of the diaspora. While it is difficult to explain how it happens, there is a magnetic pull towards Armenia. I spoke with several visitors who acknowledged that they were not born in Armenia, had never been to Armenia and in a couple of cases didn't speak Armenian. However, they felt drawn to visit for the 100th anniversary celebrations.

The impact of the Genocide can not be understated. Yet, the desire to connect with Armenia is more than remembering the Genocide. It is the centuries of a rich cultural history, the struggles of wars, earthquakes, occupation and simply trying to survive on the land which has created an irresistible, invisible bond to Mother Armenia. The strength of the mountains is within the people.

Turkey has yet to acknowledge the truth about the Genocide. The quest for justice continues. I remain steadfastly determined to do whatever I can, for as long as I can.

> *Go ahead, destroy Armenia. See if you can do it. Send them into the desert without bread or water. Burn their homes and churches. Then see if they will not laugh, sing and pray again. For when two of them meet anywhere in the world, see if they will not create a New Armenia."*
>
> — William Saroyan

# PART TEN

# My Journey Continues

*"The political good is justice, and this is the common advantage."*

— Aristotle

I am deeply grateful for how my accidental entry to the political arena morphed from an unrelenting partisan to parliamentarian to discovering how best to make use of my political skills and experience in helping to create a stronger, better civil society.

A significant inspiration along my journey's path was Stephen Lewis. Who could not help but be inspired by this incredible leader. While I was impressed by our Provincial NDP Leader long before being elected it was when I sat in the caucus that I came to appreciate his brilliance and visionary approach to politics. He was a fierce fighter for social justice, at the same time understanding and compassionate. It was how Stephen interacted with our political opponents that helped me become a parliamentarian. Later it was his incredible work in Africa working with community-led organizations battling the HIV epidemic in countries across sub-Saharan Africa which served as a role model on using political skills to create a better civil society.

My dad wasn't alive to see the results of the life lessons he imparted to me. I believe he would be pleased with the outcome of his parental efforts. Although my dad wasn't around for my political life, my mom was able to share a very proud moment with me when my Speaker portrait was unveiled.

Unequivocally I could not have had a political career without the stalwart support of Pat. She was there through the traumatic losses, never complaining, always backing me. Pat's sensible approach to political issues helped bring my head down from the clouds. Our daughters, Barbara and Sherri, were an active part of every election, from being wheeled around in a stroller to knocking on doors when they were old enough. Barbara was the NDP Candidate in Scarborough Southwest in 2003, her twins less than a year old. I could relate emotionally to her election loss.

My Queen's Park days evoke many memorable moments, but there are two which stand above the others. Receiving the Ordre de la Pléiade from the government of France was not only a surprise but deeply appreciated. My efforts to strengthen the status of the French language at Queen's Park was being officially recognized. The most meaningful recognition is the one which is bestowed by your peers. In 2022 I was presented with the Ontario Association of Former Parliamentarians' *Distinguished Service Award,* recognizing a decade of devoted leadership of OAFP.

## An accidental author

"Your dining partners are also from Canada," said the Steward as he guided us to a table where three people were sitting. It was 2010. Pat and I, along with our grandson Sebastian, were on a Mediterranean cruise. The three of us introduced ourselves. In return, "I am Maurus. This is my wife Maria and our son Mauro Junior." It didn't take long to learn from this warm, engaging family that they lived just a 20 minute drive from our house. Every evening's dining was an opportunity to share stories of each other's activities and eventually a conversation which would change my life.

"Do you write?" asked Maria.

"I guess so. But just for myself. I have an unfinished children's story I started a long time ago."

Maria paused for a moment, then "I belong to a writers' group. Perhaps you would consider joining."

When the seven day cruise concluded, Maria and Maurus extended an invitation for Pat and I to visit them later on. That we did. It was a delightful evening. I learned that not only was Maria a poet, but a visual artist. There were some beautiful portraits she had painted hanging on the walls.

I couldn't resist Maria's invitation to join her writers' group. They were a friendly, talented group. Most of them published authors. I found the monthly gathering stimulating. We usually had a writing assignment of a page or two. At one of our meetings the assignment was to select six words at random and write a story. That was when I met Wilbur. Each month a different set of six words, resulting in a new chapter in Wilbur's life. After a few episodes our group became so enthused that they insisted I turn the episodes into a novel. Devoting the time required to write a novel would have to wait however. I was fully invested as the Editor of The Informer, spending 15 to 20 hours each and every week.

Entering 2021, trepidation aside, I felt that I needed to find the time to tell Wilbur's story. I wanted to make this a team effort. I asked two former Interns of mine, Victoria Esterhammer and Lauren Malyk to be editors and Geoff Smith, daughter Sherri's father in law, to be the illustrator. Geoff is a visual artist who at one time drew political cartoons for the Montreal Gazette. What helped attract the three of them was my declaration that all proceeds would go to Sick Kids Hospital. After the book was published my granddaughter, Jill Warner, added her expertise as a 2$^{nd}$ year Graphic Design student at York University, designing a book mark and Wilbur business cards. "Wilbur, An Adventurous Mouse — Beyond the Cornfield" was launched later that same year.

Wilbur has more stories to tell. Recently he told me about his adventure to the Land of Tranquility. So....my journey continues.

## *My Journey*

Rivulets flow, roll, run, cascade,
searching for something grander;
a brook burgeons eagerly;
a sprightly stream melds
to a meandering river;
at times turbulent,
at times tranquil,
pushing the confines of the river bank.
Reaching a lake with an unfathomable horizon,
quietly I rejoice in the glorious rising of the sun,
dreaming of a global setting of sadness and sorrow.

# Appendix

## A Caucus Colleague, a Contentious Social Issue, and Support from a Political Opponent

Evelyn Gigantes was the NDP Lead on the Justice Committee when it created the Family Law Reform Act. It was clear that she was determined to do whatever she could to create the best legislation possible. Her relentless pursuit of justice on that committee was mirrored a year later when she saw an opportunity to pursue justice for gays and lesbians.

She was supported by Phil Gillies, a Conservative MPP.

## A tribute to a courageous politician

by Phil Gillies

It was Dec. 2, 1986, the day LGBT rights came to Ontario. NDP MPP Evelyn Gigantes played a critical role in bringing that about.

Up to that point, an Ontario employer could legally refuse to hire a person because they were gay. A landlord could say "I won't rent you this apartment — I don't rent to gays." Even the government itself could rule "you are not eligible for this service because gays and lesbians are ineligible."

All this was about to change. David Peterson's Liberal government introduced "housekeeping" amendments to the Ontario Human Rights Code — to bring the Code in line with Canada's new Charter Of Rights and Freedoms. The sexual orientation equality provision was not initially included in the bill.

This is where Evelyn intervened — she introduced an amendment to the Liberal bill to include sexual orientation as a protected ground under the Code — which covered race, religion, disability and several other fields. Peterson, to his credit, decided to accept the Gigantes amendment. The now controversial legislation came to be known by supporters and foes alike as simply Bill 7.

Many clergy and organizations, such as Real Women and Campaign Life, were already putting together a tough opposition campaign.

A group of activists coalesced around Bill 7 and a campaign started — led by U of T professor David Rayside, the Reverend Brent Hawkes and others. They started contacting MPPs they thought would be supportive

The debate on Bill 7 was one of the most divisive and bitter that we've seen in the Legislature. When the vote was called, most, but not all, of the governing Liberals voted for it. All NDP members in attendance voted for it (some didn't appear for the vote). And four PC members, out of 51, voted in favour. Leader Larry Grossman, Dennis Timbrell,, Susan Fish and Phil Gillies.

And so gay rights came to Ontario in the closing days of 1986. With at least some support from all three parties.

But without a doubt — this happened in 1986 because of the courage and vision of Evelyn Gigantes.

Editor's Note: Neither bisexuals or trans people were covered in the Act. That came much later. Bill 7 only spoke to gay and lesbian rights.

## *Friendship across the aisle*

An integral part of my journey to public good was getting beyond political partisanship. Doing so allowed me to approach problem solving from a more objective angle, work collaboratively with everyone regardless of their political affiliation. The following story underscores my belief that our parliamentary democracy is best served when politicians are civil and not blinded by partisanship.

I listened intently to a well crafted speech being delivered by a government Member. I didn't really know the Member, just that he was a medical doctor. His contribution to the debate on ending extra billing by doctors was a logical, step by step argument against his government's legislation. It was the view of many, but not all, of the medical profession. Dr. Jim Henderson concluded his presentation and took his seat. I immediately sent a note across the floor, congratulating him on an excellent speech, adding that I didn't agree with his conclusion. I also commended him on having the political courage to take a stand against his government's Bill. That note was a catalyst to a friendship which lasted until Jim passed away May 2nd, 2020.

Health care issues have always been extremely important to me and the related debates emotional. Dr. Jim Henderson very clearly had a view which was opposite to mine. Yet, he exhibited an engaging parliamentary approach. Soon we discovered that the two of us could chat quite civilly about the extra billing issue, and anything else.

I was on sabbatical from 1987 to 1990. Jim was re-elected in 1987 and again in 1990. In 1992, Jim was the catalyst for my Speaker led delegations to Cuba, which in turn sparked both humanitarian and economic involvement in that Caribbean country.

Jim Henderson was a soft spoken, modest man. He really didn't fit the standard stereotype of a politician. It took some prodding and a lot of questions before I learned of Jim's remarkable achievements in Cuba. In order to be effective and efficient when rounding up $250,000. worth of medical supplies, organizing trade delegations, lecturing in Spanish at the University of Havana, acquiring and shipping 100 city buses and developing friendship alliances, command of the Spanish language was vital. Jim learned Spanish by listening to audio tapes in his car while driving to and from Queen's Park. His single handed, dedicated work earned him a private meeting with Fidel Castro, a meeting which Jim treasured, commenting that Fidel was not interested in 'small talk'. The Cuban President wanted to know Jim's observations on a wide range of global political issues.

After both of us lost in 1995 we met every few months at a Greek restaurant on Danforth Avenue in Toronto, where we could enjoy a delightful dinner, cold beer and an opportunity to solve pressing world problems. It was always a delightful time concluding with each of us heading in the opposite direction on the subway.

Parkinsons disease struck Jim and slowly, but surely, took its toll. By 2010, Jim needed to move into a retirement/long term care facility. The place had an excellent cafe where the two of us would have coffee and a fresh muffin almost every Friday. Over the next few years I learned a lot about the insidious disease which was gradually robbing my friend of his ability to walk and talk. I volunteered to make his medical appointments. Along with his personal care giver, Ena, the three of us would get to an appointment then find a place for ice cream.

When COVID struck of course I could no longer visit Jim. The virus took advantage of Jim's advanced stage of Parkinson's and on May 2, 2020, Jim passed away.

I lost a good, true friend. Someone "from across the aisle."

The following biographic snapshot is information I had to find on my own. Jim was far too modest to talk about his many achievements.

## *Biographical Snapshot*

- Jim Henderson was a psychiatrist and psychoanalyst who served as:
- Director of Psychiatry at the former Lakeshore Psychiatric Hospital (Toronto)
- Director of Psychiatric Services at Royal Victoria Hospital in Barrie
- Associate Professor, Department of Psychiatry, University of Toronto
- Psychiatrist in Chief, University of Toronto Student Health Services
- Masters degree in Public Health from Johns Hopkins University
- Diploma from American National Board of Medical Examiners
- Guest Lecturer, University of Havana, Cuba (lecturing in Spanish) where he assisted in re-introducing the practice of psychoanalysis
- Jim's specific psychiatric focus was on children, parenting, and community care. One practice was in the remote indigenous community of Bella Coola, B.C., 1000 km. north of Vancouver

Jim was a treasured friend. I miss the lively conversations and the exchange of global problem solving ideas. The two of us developed a friendship out of a political debate, one in which we held opposing views.

-0-

It was a proud moment for me when my daughter Sherri was selected to be a Page at Queen's Park. More than three decades on, Sherri reflected on her time at the Pink Palace.

## Being a Page at Queen's Park
By Sherri Warner

Being a Page was a wonderful experience.

I loved having a couple months away from school. Although I was a very good student I hated Kelsey and having time away from there made me very happy.

I loved the sense of responsibility and being treated more like an adult.

I enjoyed "having a job" and feeling like I was serving my province in some small way.

I liked having a uniform (felt very official) even though the suit was not at all flattering and was very itchy.

I loved being right in the middle of the action, getting a chance to not only be there in person for question period and hearing the debates live, but also the privilege of getting to eavesdrop a bit on conversations between members in the lounges or out in the hallways.

I loved being in the building itself every day. It's a beautiful building filled with so much history. It brought back good memories of the rare occasions when Barbara and I would go with dad to his office on the weekends. (We used to love to sit at Lorna's desk and play with her electric typewriter!) Most Ontarians never get the opportunity to darken the doors of the place, let alone explore every square inch of it.[68]

I liked meeting other kids my age who not only were really good students, but also were interested in politics!

I didn't know anyone else like that other than my own sister. Meeting other kids who were politically aware and interested in debate was a rare opportunity, even though there was only one other New Democrat, Bud Wildman's son Jody.[69] Jody stayed with us for part of the page program.

---

68 Lorna Prokaska was Dad's Executive Assistant

69 Jody Wildman, as of October 2022, is in his 7th term as Mayor of St. Joseph Island

Marco Vitafinzi played a big part in helping the students settle into their page roles and make the most out of the opportunity. He was very fun to be around and all of the pages respected him. He made our Halloween at QP very memorable by having someone take us on a tour of the building, up to the top floor which was normally off-limits. I can't remember who took us on the tour, but they told lots of ghost stories and then when we got to the top floor, Marco jumped out of a closet and scared us silly.

It was always fun to be tasked with "secret" missions by some members who liked to eat in the chamber. I can't remember who it was, but there were a handful of members who would give us cash to run down to the basement and buy them chocolate bars or candy from the little "convenience shop" kiosk. We would be warned not to get caught bringing food into the chamber and if we could pull it off successfully then we often would be allowed to keep the change.

I remember Cam Jackson being the friendliest of members towards the pages. His office was one that I delivered mail to and he always had compliments for me and engaged in conversation and on Halloween had a treat bag waiting for me when I delivered his mail.

What I did NOT like was getting lost in the building! Occasionally I had to deliver letters or packages to the Whitney building and got lost in the maze of underground tunnels and buildings connected. I remember being close to tears one day when I got really turned around and I was afraid I would get in trouble for being late to class. I loathed asking passersby for help because I was shy.

I loved travelling with dad to work each day in the car and getting to see him around Queen's Park. It was always impressive to me that EVERYONE in the building knew my dad, including the maintenance staff, dining room staff, security guards, etc. Just as it was easy to be my dad's daughter when he was teaching at Kelsey, because all the students loved him. It was very easy being David Warner's daughter at QP as so many of the members had kind words to say about him, even if they didn't agree with his politics.

I had the honour of handing out the first Liberal budget in 42 years. I handed a copy of it to Frank Miller, who had been a Conservative Treasurer. He didn't look too happy that day!

The most poignant moment of my page service was sitting on the dais while my dad delivered an incredible speech about the importance of universal healthcare and how destructive extra billing is to working-class Ontarians. If my memory serves correctly, he referenced Tommy Douglas, but the majority of his speech was about his grandfather. I don't think I had heard the full story before, or not quite in those terms, and it brought me to tears.

I had never been more proud of my dad. I wanted to leap up and clap and cheer, but of course had to remain quiet and expressionless. Inside I was bursting. It was a reminder to me that among all the game playing, competition, and theatrics, there were some members who genuinely wanted to fight the good fight to protect and enhance our social safety net. It was an honour to serve as a page and I'd do it again tomorrow if they'd let me. I'd have some problems getting up from sitting on the dais, but it would be worth it!

***

It was another proud parent moment when Barbara, my youngest daughter was selected to be a Page at Queen's Park. Years later the warm memories still flourish.

## Being a Page at Queen's Park

A letter written by Barbara Warner to her dad
December 12, 2023

When things got slow in the chamber, such as during second reading debates, you and your colleagues such as Dave Cooke would let me go get the mail from your QP offices. This was a welcome break and always neat to do.

I worked during Fall Session so there was a ghost story or two being told to the Pages.

We had a luncheon hosted by the Speaker for the Pages and any MPPs from the pages' home ridings. Although Alvin Curling was my MPP, you were also invited. We were seated around the living room of the Speakers apartment. You stood up and spoke briefly to the pages. Just as you were wrapping up, I rose and said, in my best impression of then-Speaker Hugh Edighoffer, "The Member's time has expired." This bit of nerdy legislative humour seemed to please the pages and the adults alike.

I had one particularly memorable elevator ride in late October. I was at the west wing elevators, waiting with another page. When the doors opened, it was already occupied by the Premier and an aide...but the aide was carrying a pumpkin on his shoulder, and our angle was such that it looked like David Peterson had a pumpkin-head! The pumpkin was whole, not carved, and that image has stuck with me ever since. The other page and I had to work hard to suppress our laughter and keep decorum until everyone was out of the elevator!

I also remember being glad that we girls were permitted to wear pants, and annoyed that instead of ties like the boys, we had to wear a big white lace frill. You'll see that in the photo of us which had been in your study upstairs (Sherri's old bedroom). I think it's in a double frame because I was permitted to have a photo taken with you and also with my 'real' MPP Alvin Curling.

None of us knew that, in time, both of "my" MPPs would become Mr. Speaker!

One last thing to add, but it's recent. I think it's awfully sweet and respectful that Jill, Logan and their friends call you "Mr. Speaker" (and Mom "Mrs. Speaker"). This despite you being retired for years before any of them were born.

# Acknowledgements

I did not make this journey alone.

I did not plan to enter the political arena. A friendly, yet emotional debate with a teaching colleague sparked my interest, and I was soon bitten by the "Hemiptera Politicus" bug—my political journey began. The path was sometimes bumpy, sometimes smooth, and occasionally had sharp curves. No matter the condition, I was never alone.

I had a story to tell, and I needed to appeal to a publisher. That's when Cheryl-Lee Fast entered the picture. Cheryl-Lee, a writer, producer, and actor with a flair for editing, belongs to my writers' group, even though she lives in Vancouver. She helped me prepare a package that captured the interest of Howard Aster at Mosaic Press.

All nine elections that I contested featured stalwart supporters who stuck with me through the toughest times and shared in the joy of victory.

## Gratitude to a Publisher Who is Also an Author

As soon as I met Howard Aster, I knew I was in good hands. With decades of experience in publishing and a background as a Political Science professor, Howard made it easy for me to discuss the intent of my book. Working with him has been an absolutely delightful experience.

## Thanks to the Legislative Library

For several decades, I have relied on the talented and dedicated research staff at the Legislative Library. Their assistance has been invaluable in validating my writing, including the research for this book. I am deeply indebted to this amazing team.

## Deep Gratitude to My Political Staff at Queen's Park

- **Lorna Prokaska (1975–1981):** Lorna grounded my ambitious ideas, keeping my feet firmly on the earth. Her advice was sound, logical, and often presented so subtly that I came to think it was my own.
- **Eileen Chalk (1985–1987):** Eileen, who had previously worked as a legal secretary for my late colleague Jim Renwick, was incredibly efficient and provided wise, subtle advice. When she asked, "Is this what you wish to say?" I knew she was kindly steering me clear of potential pitfalls.
- **Penny Gerrie (1985–1987):** Penny was a brilliant researcher whose expertise I shared with my caucus colleague Richard Allen.
- **Linda Mitchell (1990–1995):** Like Lorna, Linda offered sound, sensible ideas with infectious enthusiasm.
- **Irene Coleman (1990–1995):** Working part-time with Linda, Irene completed a dynamic duo whose energy together could light up Toronto.

## Heartfelt Thanks to My Amazing Constituency Staff

- **Lyn Fagel (1975–1977):** Always calm, efficient, and professional, Lyn met every challenge with a smile.
- **David Lee (1977–1981, 1985–1987):** A successful campaign manager at age 20, David was highly organized and determined to help everyone who came to the office.

- **Kaarina Luoma (1985–1987):** A successful campaign manager whose work in 1982 laid the groundwork for a win in 1985. Kaarina's skill in handling cases led her to later become Director of Mid-Toronto Community Services.
- **Hratch Aynedjian, Bruna Bertoni, and Francine Faucher (1990–1995):** This trio brought boundless energy, sparkling personalities, and dedication, with the added strength of speaking five languages collectively—English, French, Italian, Arabic, and Armenian.

## Thanks to the Talented Non-Political Staff at Queen's Park

- **Clerk of the Legislature, Claude DesRosiers:** Wise and calm, Claude convinced me to stay on my parliamentary path when I was ready to give up.
- **Executive Assistant, Gail Laws:** Gail's experience in the Speaker's Office was complemented by her deep appreciation of parliament.
- **Administrative Assistant, Judy Brathwaite:** No one was more committed to ensuring everything was done perfectly.
- **Manager of Speaker's Apartment, Gloria Richards:** Gloria, who served 14 Speakers, was as skilled at managing diplomatic events as she was in her role at Queen's Park.

## It's All About Family

Through nine elections and countless community boards, Pat, my wife of nearly 60 years, was always there—strong, resilient, and endlessly supportive. Her love has been my strength.

Sherri and Barbara have always supported me, joining in election campaigns even if they may have preferred other family activities.

Our grandchildren, Sebastian Smith and Jill Warner, contributed their talents to this book, each bringing their unique skills and creative energy to the project.

One's journey is never predictable. Mine certainly wasn't—and still isn't. Yet, the world is filled with wonderful people. Understanding the African proverb, "If you want to go quickly, go alone. If you want to go far, go together," has made my journey rich and fulfilling.